Clark County Washington

Cemetery Records

Post Military
Dead Lake (or Fallen Leaf)
Bethel Lutheran
Washougal Catholic
Sara Union
St. Mary of Guadalupe
Ridgefield
Chelatchie Prairie
Bethel Methodist
Mt. Zion (La Center)
Highland Lutheran

Volume Three

Clark County Genealogical Society

ISBN 1-892685-12-4

copies of this book may be purchased from:

Clark County Genealogical Society
P. O. Box 5249
Vancouver, WA 98668-5249
$15 plus 7.7% WA tax

Contents

NAMES & NUMBERS OF CLARK COUNTY CEMETERIES AS SHOWN ON MAP

1. Post Military Cemetery (Vol. 3)
2. St. James Cemetery (Vol. 2)
3. Old City Cemetery (Vol. 1)
4. Park Hill Cemetery
5. Evergreen Memorial Gardens
6. Fisher Cemetery (Vol. 2)
7. Knight Family Cemetery
8. Camas Cemetery
9. Dead Lake Cemetery (Vol. 3)
10. Washougal Cemetery (Vol. 4)
11. Washougal Catholic Cemetery (Vol. 3)
12. Sunnyside Memorial Cemetery
13. Fern Prairie Cemetery
14. Livingston [or Shanghai] Cemetery (Vol. 4)
15. Sifton Cemetery
16. Brush Prairie Cemetery
17. St. John's Catholic Cemetery
18. Wilson Bridge Cemetery
19. Memory Memorial Park
20. Salmon Creek Methodist Cemetery (Vol. 2)
21. St. John Lutheran Cemetery (Vol. 2)
22. Northwood Park Cemetery
23. Sara Union Cemetery (Vol. 3)
24. Elim Lutheran Cemetery (Vol. 4)

25. Bethel Lutheran Cemetery (Vol. 3)
26. Finn Hill Cemetery
27. Gravel Point Cemetery
28. Venersberg Cemetery (Vol. 4)
29. Crawford [or Kumtux] Cemetery
30. Sacred Heart [or Dublin] Cemetery (Vol. 4)
31. Lewisville Cemetery (Vol. 4)
32. Pioneer Cemetery (Vol. 2)
33. St. Mary's Catholic Cemetery (Vol. 3)
34. Bethel Methodist Cemetery (Vol. 3)
35. Ridgefield Cemetery (Vol. 3)
36. Fairchld [or Hawk] Cemetery
37. Page [or Red Rock] Cemetery
38. Gardner [or Hayes] Cemetery (Vol. 4)
39. Hurt Road Cemetery
40. Mt. Zion I.O.O.F. Cemetery (Vol. 3)
41. Highland Lutheran Cemetery (Vol. 3)
42. Mountain View Cemetery (Vol. 4)
43. Yacolt Cemetery
44. Amboy Cemetery (Vol. 4)
45. Chelatchie Prairie Cemetery (Vol. 3)
46. Columbia Tie Road Cemetery
47. Buncombe Hollow Cemetery (Vol. 4)
48. Indian Burial Grounds

49. John Pollock Gravesite

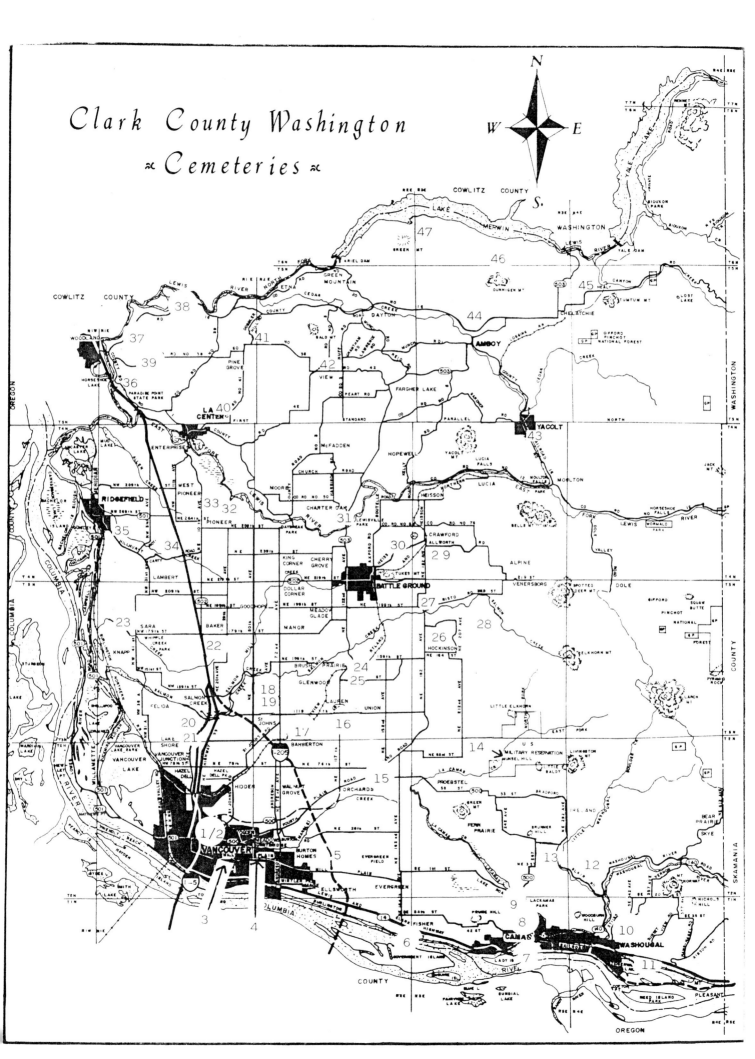

Clark County Washington ~ Cemeteries ~

ABBREVIATIONS AND NOTES

We have attempted to give the most information from the different sources available to us. In order to read the individual records, the following examples are given.

EXAMPLE:

```
[1] [2]  [3]       [4]              [5]              [6]      [7]
111/1    SMITH   John D. Smith, 1861 - 1952, In Memory Of  (John David Smith,
                         [8]        [9]                              [10]
                  12 June 1952  ** son of John Earl Smith and Rachel [Jones]

        Smith)
```

1. Lot number...111 = lot 111 in the Old Section, page xi. In some cases it was imposssible to determine lot or plot and ** was used and so noted. If letters 'A', 'N', etc. precede the lot number, burial was in Section 'A', 'N', etc.

2. Plot number

3. Surname...These are listed alphabetically.

4. Full name as it is exactly on the stone.

5. Dates exactly as are on the stone

6. Inscription as on the stone

7. ( ) = Information not on the stones but in the records. Sometimes names were given more fully or spelling or dates differed from that on the gravestone. If there are no ( ), no further information was found or they were not listed in the records.

8. Date in the records...In most cases the information from the records gives the burial date, not the death date.

9. ** = Designates information from the compilers - sometimes personal information from descendants or notes from other sources.

10. [ ] = Used at times when maiden names are known.

OTHER ABBREVIATIONS USED:

   b. = born

   d. = died

   m. = married

   WWI, WWII, Korea = World War I, World War II or Korean War

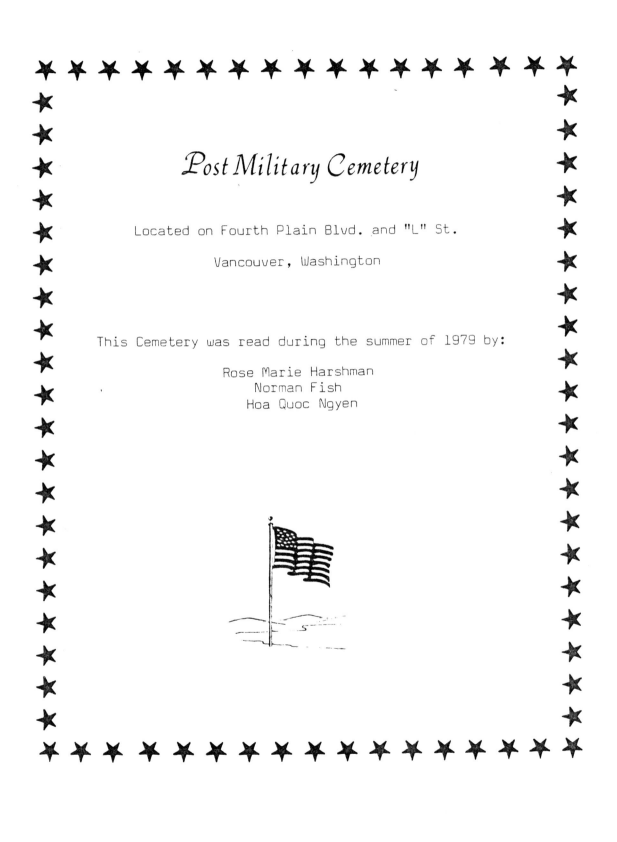

Post Military Cemetery

Located on Fourth Plain Blvd. and "L" St.

Vancouver, Washington

This Cemetery was read during the summer of 1979 by:

Rose Marie Harshman
Norman Fish
Hoa Quoc Ngyen

There are 155 graves in the Post Cemetery marked "Unknown" plus two Infants graves with names unknown.

＊

The information is given as follows for Post Cemetery:

Lot/Block	Info. from rec.	Surname	Info. as on grave marker	( ) denotes info. from Military Records

＊

Some descrepancies noted in the comparisons between gravestones and records. Some of the graves are not numbered.

＊

MILITARY CEMETERY

We are informed by Gen. Sully, that the Military Post Cemetery, at this place, has been elevated to the rank of a National Cemetery. Hereafter a yearly appropriation, will be made for the purpose of keeping it in order. It is an appropriate and beautiful place for a Cemetery, and the War Department have done a good thing by placing it under the patronage of the Government. Gen. Sully is entitled to credit for making the necessary representations to secure this benifit.
[Vancouver Independent, Sat. Jan. 1, 1876-Vol. 1 - No. 18, page 5 column 2]

＊

* 1879 R....from the records of Post Cemetery:

12 June 1879
Lt. J. W. Duncan
21st Inf. A.A.2M.
   Reported interments in the Post Cemetery, Vancouver Barracks, Washington Territory.
   Respectfully forwarded to the Chief Quartermaster, Miltary Division of the Pacific.
   It appears that the book containing the record of 302 interments in the Vancouver Post Cemetery has been lost, frequent and careful search has failed to produce it, hence this report is incomplete.
                    Signed, A. S. Wimball - Capt. & Ajd. Qr. Mr.
                    Acting Chief Quartermaster, U. S. Army

＊

1883 R...

* On a letter dated 24 Mar. 1883, 1st Lieut. John M. Ross, R.Q.M. 21st Inf., reported interments at Post Cemetery.

814   ACKLEY Mrs. Ackley (wife of Ward M. Ackley)

815   ACKLEY Ward M. Ackley, 1888 - 1927, Capt. 7 U. S. Inf., My
              Husband (interred 3 Sept. 1927)

526   ACORD Charles H. Acord, Sgt. 2 G., U. S. Inf. (interred 11
              July 1911)

477   ACORD Mrs. C. H. Acord (wife of Charles H. Acord, interred 19
              Nov. 1907)

708   ADAIR Mary Adair (no further information)

1014   ADAMS Charles H. Adams, June 17, 1933, Washington, Cook,
              Med. Corps (interred 19 June 1933)

1252   ADAMS Cranston F. Adams, Sept. 2, 1889 - June 27, 1946, Illinois
              Sgt. U. S. Army (interred 2 July 1946)

301   ADAMS Harry Adams, Only Son of Capt. J. O. and Mary Adams, 4
              Sept. 1881, aged 6 years (interred 5 Sept. 1881)

915   ADAMS Thomas E. Adams, 6 Dec. 1930, Missouri, M. Sgt., U. S.
              Army (interred 11 Dec. 1930)

855   ADKINS John Adkins, 18 Apr. 1929, Pennsylvania, Sgt. U. S. Army
              (interred 20 Apr. 1929)

    1879R AIRD John Aird, d. Jan. 25, 1866

1125   ALBERTSON Margaret P. Albertson, June 21, 1877 - Oct. 15, 1955,
              Wife of 1st Lt. T. E. Albertson (interred 15 Oct. 1955)

1125   ALBERTSON Thomas E. Albertson, Sept. 8, 1938, North Carolina,
              1st Lieut. U. S. Army (interred 10 Sept. 1938)

    1879R ALBERWORTH (____) Alberworth, d. May 24, 1865, Cpl. Co. G.,
              1 W. T. Inf.

    1883R ALBIN James E. Albin, Pvt. Co. A, 4th U. S. Art.

608   ALDRIDGE Alma Aldridge, Infant (interred 3 Oct. 1918)

1228   ALLEN Edith Behunick Allen, Former Wife of 1 Sgt. Elijah Allen
              U. S. A., Sept. 18, 1898 - Jan. 11, 1950 (interred 16 Jan.
              1950)

1227   ALLEN Elijah Allen, Mar. 15, 1878 - Apr. 15, 1945, 1st Sgt.
              U. S. Army (interred 20 Apr. 1945)

1199   ALLEN Herbert M. Allen, 1902 - 1923 (son of Brig. Gen. H. A.
              Allen, interred 7 Oct. 1923)

1199   ALLEN Hubert Allison Allen, 1872 - 1942, Brigadier General,
              U. S. Army (interred 6 May 1942)

1198   ALLEN Jessie M. Allen, July 8, 1873 - June 6, 1958 (wife of
              Brig. Gen. H. A. Allen)

570   ALLEY   Alex J. Alley, Co. C., 16 Maine Inf. (Alexander J. Alley, interred 10 Feb. 1915)

300   ALVORD   Anna C. Alvord (interred 12 Jan. 1860, daughter of Major Alvord)

---   ALVORD   Bent Alvord, Major U. S. Army, All loved who knew them

1879R   ALVORD   Clara Alvord, d. Jan. 26, 1856, Daughter of Brig. Gen'l Alvord, U. S. A.

300   ALVORD   Clarence C. Alvord (interred 26 Jan. 1856, son of Major Alvord)

315   ANCOR   Charles Ancor (Pvt., Signal Corps, U. S. A., interred 3 Oct. 1884)

1879R   ANDERSON   Canby Anderson, d. Apr. 21, 1872

311   ANDERSON   Geo. Anderson, Co. G. 21st U. S. Inf. (Pvt. George Anderson, interred 20 Aug. 1882)

159   ANDERSON   James Anderson, Died Feb. 18, 1856, Aged 27 Years, Sacred to the memory of:, Of Edinberg, Scotland

303   ANDERSON   Richard Canby Anderson, Son of H. R. & Florence Anderson, U. S. A., Born Oct. 4, 1821 - Died Aug. 3, 1822

736   ANNIS   Harry Annis, Mar. 3, 1925, Mass., Pvt 14 Inf. (interred 5 Mar. 1925)

239   APRAMBOISE   J. Apramboise, Civilian (interred 12 Sept. 1918)

1883R   ARCHER   Edward S. Archer, d. Aug. 16, 1873, Pvt. Co. B., 4th U. S. Art.

807   ARLEDGE   Alex R. Arledge, Co. C. - 6 Minnesota Inf. (Alexander Arledge, Pvt., interred 7 June 1927)

926   ARMES   Lucy Hamilton Armes, Daughter of John Bozman Kerr of Maryland. Born Wash. D.C. Feb. 9, 1851, died Vanc. Barracks July 13, 1927. Her courage became her peace (interred 15 July 1927 - mother of T. M. Knox)

965   ARNOLD   Guy W. Arnold, Oct. 7, 1931, Oregon, Tech. Sgt. 61 Serv. Sq. Air Corps (interred 10 Oct. 1931)

---   ARSHALL   Arthur J. Arshall, Corp'l 5 Indiana Art.

658   ARVIDSON   Jack E. Arvidson, Co. A., 28 U. S. Inf. (Pfc. - interred 28 Dec. 1919)

1186   AUGENBLICK   Hazel Jewell Augenblick, May 17, 1895 - Nov. 23, 1975, Wife of J. R. Augenblick, Sr., U. S. A. (interred 28 Nov. 1975)

1184   AUGENBLICK   John Herman Augenblick, Dec. 22, 1943, Son of Tech. Sgt. J. R. Augenblick, U. S. A. (interred 29 Dec. 1943)

1183   AUGENBLICK Joseph Robert Augenblick, Oct. 22, 1888 - Dec. 17,
                1967, Pennsylvania, M. Sgt. 7 Inf. Band World War I (inter-
                red 19 Dec. 1967)

659   AUGSBERGER Sebastian Augsberger, Sergt. Ord. Dept., U. S. A.
                (interred 5 Jan. 1920)

328   AUSTIN A. Austin, Died 3 Dec. 1886, Aged 53 years, 1 Lieut.
                14 U. S. Inf. (Lt. Albert Austin, interred 4 Dec. 1886)

1031   AUSTIN Ady Austin, Feb. 11, 1934, Kansas, Pvt. 7 Inf. (interred
                13 Feb. 1934)

443   BACON Infant Bacon (interred 15 June 1905, child of Col. J. M.
                Bacon)

549   BACON John M. Bacon, Apr. 17, 1844 - Mar. 1913 (interred 16
                May 1913)

465   BACON Mary D. Bacon, Sept. 15, 1870 - June 24, 1905 (interred
                25 June 1905, wife of Col. J. M. Bacon)

709   BAIRD Julia Hathaway Baird, Jan. 15, 1886 - Oct. 7, 1963, Dau-
                ghter of Brigadier General F. H. Hathaway, U. S. A. (in-
                terred 14 Oct. 1963)

426   BAIRENS Child Bairens (son of John Bairens)

377   BAIRENS Josephine Bairens (interred 22 Apr. 1896, Daughter of
                Pvt. J. Bairens)

319   BAKER Chas. Baker, Co. B., 14th U. S. Inf. (Pvt. Charles Baker,
                interred 22 Jan. 1886)

812   BAKER Clara Baker, Aug. 18, 1927 (interred 20 Aug. 1927, wife
                of Sgt. Wm. J. Baker)

1177   BAKER Edward L. Baker, Aug. 9, 1943, T. Sgt. (lot reserved)

1176   BAKER Flossie L. Baker, June 25, 1943, Wife of E. L. Baker,
                U. S. A. (interred 29 June 1943)

1011   BAKER Herbert W. Baker, Apr. 30, 1933, Oregon, Pvt. 27 Engrs.
                (interred 3 May 1933)

    1879R   BAKER J. F. L. Baker, d. Dec. 26, 1864

813   BAKER William J. Baker, Jan. 20, 1929, Washington, Sgt. 7 Inf.
                (interred 22 Jan. 1929)

728   BALES Sarah E. Bales, Sept. 8, 1926 (interred 15 Sept. 1926)

344A   BANDEL Anna Bandel, born Oct. 15, 1871 - died Dec. 16, 1893

344   BANDEL Emelie, born Nov. 20, 1840 - died May 29, 1914, Wife
                of Eugene Bandel

344   BANDEL Eugene Bandel, born July 29, 1836 - died Apr. 2, 1889

4

344A   BANDEL   Minnie Bandel, born May 5, 1878 – died Sept. 5, 1893, At Rest

194   BANKS   John Smith Banks, died Oct. 31, 1861, A Native of Dundee, Scotland

883   BARBEAU   Edward Barbeau, Dec. 10, 1929, Nevada, Pvt. 26 Engrs. (interred 22 Dec. 1929)

518   BARBEAU   Joseph Barbeau, Co. K., 21 U. S. Inf., Sgt. (interred 6 May 1910)

1879R   BARNHART   A. C. Barnhart, d. Aug. 14, 1871

336   BARTELS   Charles Bartels, Co. H., 14 U. S. Inf. (Pvt., interred 19 Nov. 1887)

790   BARTLETT   Alonzo M. Bartlett, MUS Co. B., Wisconsin Inf., May 20, 1925

790   BARTLETT   Lillian Bartlett, Feb. 27, 1857 – March 20, 1953 (wife of Alonzo Bartlett, interred 20 Mar. 1953)

---   BARTLETT   Rose Bartlett, Aug. 5, 1939

316   BARRETT   John Barrett, Born in Dublin, Ireland May 19, 1850, Died at Vancouver Barracks, W.T. Jan. 7, 1885, Sacred to the memory of:, Mus. 14th Inf., Band, Erected by his wife (interred 8 Jan. 1885)

488   BASFELDT   Carolina Basfeldt (interred 26 May 1908, Mother-in-law to Higgins)

155   BASHFORD   Julia Bashford (interred 10 Feb. 1865, Daughter of W. Bashford)

---   BASNER   Rob't P. Basner, Infant

1033   BAUERSACHS   Charles Bauersachs, Mar. 9, 1934, California, 1st Sgt. U. S. Army (interred 12 Mar. 1934)

693   BEALS   Roy Beals, Air Service, U. S. A. (Pvt., interred 13 July 1918)

1120   BEAN   Infant Child Bean, Apr. 8, 1938, Father Pvt. A. J. Bean, Jr., U. S. A. (interred 8 Apr. 1938)

702A   BEASLEY   Child Beasley, Mar. 12, 1923, Father Captain W. C. Beasley, U. S. A. (son, interred 13 Mar. 1923)

687A   BEASLEY   Jessie C. Beasley (interred 3 Feb. 1922, wife of Capt. Warren C. Beasley)

687B   BEASLEY   Ruth J. Beasley, May 24, 1886 – Mar. 23, 1967, Wife of Capt. W. C. Beasley, U. S. A. (interred 27 Mar. 1967)

687A   BEASLEY   Warren C. Beasley, Sept. 12, 1937, North Carolina, Capt. U. S. Army (interred 15 Sept. 1937)

846   BEASTON Elizabeth J. Beaston, Wife of Pvt. J. M. Beaston, U.S.A.
               (interred 17 June 1944, wife of James M. Beaston)

---   BEASTON   James W. Beaston, Co. B. 1 Regt., Oregon Inf., Sp. Am.
               War

555   BEASTON Jas. M. Beaston, G.G.B. 1 Oregon Inf. (Pvt., interred
               13 Nov. 1913)

1274   BEAVER Chester E. Beaver, Dec. 1, 1916 – Jan. 2, 1978, M. Sgt.
               U. S. Army, World War II – Korea (interred 5 Jan. 1978)

649   BECK Humphrey T. Beck, Aug. 6, 1940, Oregon, 2 Lt., U. S. Army
               (interred 8 Aug. 1940)

756   BECK Paul Beck, Mar. 25, 1926, Sgt. 1 Inf. (interred 27 Mar.
               1926)

1166   BECK Ruth W. Beck, Wife of 2 Lieut. H. T. Beck, U. S. A., July
               24, 1942 (interred 28 July 1942)

45   BECKER Charles Becker, Born 1804 – In The Kingdom Of Hanover,
               Germany, Died Mar. 17, 1868, 'I have fought a good fight,
               I have finished my course, I have kept the faith', 2nd Tim.
               Chap. IV v. 7

921   BEERS Daisy May Beers, 1884 – 1967, Husband Capt. Theo. L. Beers
               (interred 14 Mar. 1967)

922   BEERS Capt. Theo. L. Beers, 1880 – 1937, Q. M. Corps (wife
               Daisy May Beers, interred 9 Dec. 1937)

469   BEERS T. L. Beers, Jr., Child (interred 9 Dec. 1906)

517   BELLAMY Alb't Bellamy, Child (Albert Bellamy, interred 3 Feb.
               1910, infant son of S. G. M. Albert C. Bellamy)

771   BENNETT Charles H. Bennett, 1846 – 1927 (Pvt., shares lot with
               Marion Bennett)

771   BENNETT Marion Bennett, 1851 – 1932 (shares lot with Charles
               H. Bennett)

1883R   BENSON John Benson, Pvt. Co. F., 21st U. S. Inf.

1010   BERG Olav Berg, died Apr. 25, 1933, Pvt. 166 Depot Brig., Alaska
               (interred 3 May 1933)

347   BERGIN Christopher Bergin, Com. Sgt., U. S. A.

785   BERNHARD Sgt. A. Bernhard, 1867 – 1936 (interred 29 July 1936)

786   BERNHARD Nellie D. Bernhard, 1875 – 1935 (interred Mar. 21,
               1935)

944   BERNSTEIN Emmett R. Bernstein, Apr. 17, 1931 (interred 21 Apr.
               1931)

605   BERTLESON   C. F. Bertleson, U. S. Army   (interred 27 Aug. 1918)

582   BESNA   Robert P. Besna   (interred 12 Jan. 1916, son of Pvt.
                    Besna)

345   BETZING   Child Betzing   (interred 4 Oct. 1889)

840   BIGGS   Leo H. Biggs, Jan. 1, 1929, Ohio, Pvt. 112 Engrs.   (in-
                    terred 7 Jan. 1929)

166   BILES   Charles Esmond Biles, Only child of J. D. & Rachel H.
                    Biles, Born at Vancouver, W. T. Nov. 10, 1852 - Died at
                    Portland, Oregon Feb. 27, 1872, Blessed are the pure in
                    heart, for they shall see God. Shelter and safe from
                    sorrow. (interred 28 Feb. 1872)

156   BILICKE   Emma Bilicke, Born in New York Nov. 28, 1857 - Died
                    Sept. 29, 1864, In memory of:, Dau. of C. & ___ Bilicke,
                    Rube Sanft (interred 30 Sept. 1864)

458   BILLUPS   Ellen M. Billups, Child (interred 16 June 1906, infant
                    daughter of Sgt. Billups)

     1879R   BIRD   Henry Bird (no other information)

667   BIRDSALL   John S. Birdsall, 1st Sgt., U. S. Army (interred 23
                    Aug. 1920 - shares lot with Rebecca Birdsall)

667A   BIRDSALL   Rebecca Birdsall, Dec. 18, 1928 (interred 20 Dec. 1928,
                    wife of John S. Birdsall)

86   BISHOP   Chas. Bishop, Band, 1st U. S. Cav. (interred 14 Dec.
                    1866)

703   BISHOP   Ralph E. Bishop, Mar. 8, 1923, Oregon, Fireman 3 Cl.
                    U. S. Navy

985   BISSNER   Harry A. Bissner, Apr. 13, 1932, Oregon, Sgt. 328 Aero
                    Sq. (interred 15 Apr. 1932)

681A   BLACK   Minnie Free Black, Nov. 21, 1937, Wife of Pvt. 1 Cl. Will
                    Black, U. S. A. (former wife of Sgt. Frederick E. Free)

470   BLANKE   Frances K. Blanke, Infant (interred 7 Feb. 1907, daugh-
                    ter of Pvt. Carl C. Blanke)

868   BLATTER   Conrad W. Blatter, July 18, 1929, Oregon, Pvt., Infantry
                    (interred 22 Jan. 1929)

     1883R   BLOOM   Louis Bloom, Pvt. Co. A, 4th U. S. Art.

887   BLOUNT   Tillie Blount, 1867 - 1930 (interred 12 June 1930, Ma-
                    tilda Blount)

780   BLYSTONE   Lorine Blystone, Co. D., Washington Inf., Sp. Am. War
                    (Pvt., interred 10 Feb. 1927)

893   BOARDMAN   Geo. Boardman, Wisconsin (Pvt., interred 9 Aug. 1930)

1879R   BOHUND William Bohund, Citizen, d. Mar. 15, 1852

617   BOLT Eric P. Bolt, 1891 - 1918, Y. M. C. A., At Rest (in-
                   terred Nov. 12, 1918)

1157   BOUDER Thomas L. Bouder, M.D., Nov. 23, 1941, 1 Sgt. U. S.
                   Army (interred 26 Nov. 1941)

676   BOVCE Clinton M. Bovce, Co. F., 18 U. S. Inf. (Pvt., interred
                   1 Apr. 1921)

1231   BOWEN Margaret K. Bowen, Sept. 26, 1872 - May 21, 1962, Wife of
                   1st Lt. Taylor Bowen (interred 24 May 1962)

711   BOWEN Margaret M. Bowen, Nov. 9, 1923 (interred 10 Nov. 1923,
                   wife of Col. Bowen)

1230   BOWEN Taylor Bowen, Sept. 16, 1880 - Jan. 29, 1946, Indiana,
                   1 Lieut. U. S. Army (interred 2 Feb. 1946)

949   BOYD Edna May Boyd, Wife of Pvt. 1 Cl. R. L. Boyd, July 4, 1931
                   (interred 7 June 1931 **there is a definite discepancy in
                   the death and burial dates here!)

1112   BOYD Otto R. Boyd, Oct. 8, 1937, Oregon, Pvt. 7 Inf. (interred
                   12 Oct. 1937)

950   BOYD Robert L. Boyd, May 28, 1931, West Virginia, Pvt., 7 Inf.
                   (interred 2 June 1931)

669A   BOYER Margaret M. Boyer, Dec. 17, 1925 (interred 20 Dec. 1925,
                   wife of Sgt. Wm. Boyer)

669   BOYER William Boyer, 1840 - 1920, Co. F, 15th Iowa Inf. (in-
                   terred 24 Oct. 1920, Sgt.)

789   BRACKETT Bettie Brackett, 1863 - 1941, Mother (interred 23
                   May 1941, wife of George H. Brackett)

789   BRACKETT George H. Brackett, 1842 - 1925, Father (interred
                   29 Jan. 1925)

406   BRADY Howard Brady (interred 17 NOv. 1901)

381   BRADY Lucie J. Brady (interred 3 Aug. 1897, daughter of Pvt.
                   John Brady)

581   BRADY Margaret Brady, died July 13, 1915, aged 56 yrs. (inter-
                   red 15 July 1915, wife of MIchael Brady)

428   BRADY Michael Brady, died Jan. 12, 1904, aged 46 yrs., Pray for
                   the soul of:, Rest In Peace (Sgt., interred 11 ____ 1904)

507   BRALEY Edw'd R. Braley, Infant (Edward R. Braley, son of Pvt.
                   Charles E. Braley, interred 17 June 1909)

1234   BRANCH Wilburn Gentry Branch, Sr., Mar. 23, 1912 - July 13,
                   1947, North Carolina, Capt. U. S. Army, World War II (in-
                   terred 17 July 1947)

1235   BRANCH   Mrs. W. G. Branch, Sr., Wife (lot reserved)

1233   BRANCH   Wilburn G. Branch, Jr., May 21, 1945, Son of Capt. W. G.
                Branch, U.S.A. (interred 25 May 1945)

    1879R   BRANDT   H. A. Brandt, d. Nov. 16, 1857

---   BRANT   J. F. Wolf Brant, U. S. Army (no other information)

468   BREITER   Corp'l Anthony Breiter, Co. M, 14 U. S. Inf. (inter-
                red 8 Oct. 1906)

841   BREMMER   Charles Bremmer, Wisconsin (Pvt., interred 12 Jan.
                1929)

    1879R   BRICKE   Lloyd Bricke, July 8, 1860

586½   BRIERLY   Phillip G. Brierly (interred 18 Oct. 1918, infant son
                of Pvt. Brierly)

685   BRISBOIS   Wm. M. Brisbois, U. S. Navy (Seaman, interred 23
                Jan. 1922)

---   BRYAN   Travis T. Bryan, Dec. 7, 1935, Arkansas, Sgt. 7 Inf.

320   BROWN   Dan'l Brown, Co. E., 1st U. S. Art. (Pvt., Daniel Brown,
                interred 30 Jan. 1886)

1235   BROWN   Floyd Wellington Brown, Sept. 8, 1906 - May 9, 1970,
                Washington, Colonel U. S. Army, World War II (interred 12
                May 1970)

    1879R   BROWN   F. M. Brown, Sept. 8, 1864

    1883R   BROWN   John J. Brown, Oregon Militia

    1879R   BROWN   Rebecca W. Brown, July 2, 1864

1256   BROWN   Wm. Brown, May 12, 197_, Wife (lot reserved, date year
                unreadable)

792   BRYAN   Travis T. Bryan (interred 9 Dec. 1925)

520   BUCK   Sergt. Aug. Buck, Co. D, 14 U. S. Inf. (August Buck, Pvt.
                interred 27 June 1910)

71   BUCHANAN   Mich'l Buchanan, Apr. 9, 1859, Co. G, 3rd U. S. Art.
                (Pvt., interred 10 Apr. 1859, Michael)

    1879R   BUCKLEY   J. H. Buckley, Aug. 2, 1865

365   BULLIAN   P. A. Bullian, Co. G, 14 U. S. Inf. (Phillip A. Bullian,
                Pvt., interred 15 May 1893)

888   BUNKER   Helen Bunker, July 5, 1930 (interred 9 July 1930, wife
                of Cpl. Henry Bunker)

891   BUNKER Henry K. Bunker, Corp., Nebraska (interred 24 Mar. 1937)

1087   BURBIEN Biambick Burbien, Sept. 28, 1945 (Pvt., interred 2 Oct.
              1945)

61   BURKE F. Burke, Nov. 7, 1860, Co. C, 3rd U. S. Art. (Pvt., in-
              terred 8 Nov. 1860)

553   BURGES Alb't Burges, U. S. A. (Albert Burges, Cook, interred
              5 July 1913)

501   BURLEW Grant Burlew, Co. L, 3 U. S. Art. (interred 5 Feb. 1909)

554   BURLEIN Jacob Burlein, Corpl., U. S. A. (Cpl., interred 20
              Sept. 1913)

---   BURT Catherine Burt, Oct. 25, 1930 (interred 28 Oct. 1930,
              wife of PFC. Isom Burt)

902   BURT Isom Burt, PFC, Oct. 1930 (lot reserved)

1168   BURRUCKER George Rupert Burrucker, Nov. 7, 1942, Indiana, M.
              Sgt. U. S. Army (interred 11 Nov. 1942)

1085   BURTNETT James R. Burtnett, Aug. 22, 1935, Washington, Pvt. 7
              Inf. (interred 26 Aug. 1935)

330   BUSH George Bush, died Feb. 1, 1887, aged 38 yrs., Erected by
              his wife Nellie Bush (1 Sgt., interred 2 Feb. 1887)

1018   BUSSE Arthur G. Busse, Nov. 6, 1933 (interred 10 Nov. 1933)

1096   BUSSEY Thomas E. Bussey, Nov. 29, 1936, 1 Lieut., Sn. Corps, Ohio
              (interred 2 Dec. 1936)

778   BYBEE Grace Ethel Bybee, Feb. 1, 1927 (interred 5 Feb. 1927,
              wife of MSG Warren W. Bybee)

779   BYBEE Warren W. Bybee, Dec. 20, 1904 - Aug. 5, 1971, MSG, U. S.
              Army, World War II, Missouri (interred 11 Aug. 1971)

535   CALLAGHAN George A Callaghan (Pvt., interred 23 June 1912)

879   CAMPBELL Chester A. Campbell, Mar. 17, 1887 - Feb. 20, 1930,
              Pvt. Co. G, 44th Inf., enlisted 29 May 1917, discharged 21
              June 1919 (interred 22 June 1930)

529   CAMPBELL [2 children] Campbell (interred 8 Nov. 1911, 2 still
              born sons of 1 Lt. S. Campbell)

1175   CAMPBELL Homer Charles Campbell, Son of Holmer Campbell, U.S.A.,
              May 26, 1943 (interred 29 May 1943)

877   CANNISON Samuel P. Cannison, U. S. Vol. Cav. (interred 13 Feb.
              1930)

---   CANROW Bettsey M. Canrow, Child, Apr. 3, 1929

73   CARLIN   Corporal Charles Carlin, July 11, 1877, In Memory Of,
             Company I, 21 Inf., Killed in action at Clearwater, I. T.

663A   CARLISLE   Kate E. Carlisle, Jan. 15, 1885 - Oct. 28, 1957, Wife
             of 1st Sgt. R. E. Carlisle, U. S. A.

663   CARLISLE   Roger E. Carlisle, 1st Sgt. Co. G, 32 U. S. Inf. (in-
             terred 7 Mar. 1920)

---   CARMACK   Alfred Carmack, Jan. 26, 1882 - Jan. 24, 1944, Texas,
             Sgt. U. S. Army, World War I

1879R   CARR   Bernard F. Carr, Oct. 4, 1865

1079   CARROLL   Charles A. Carroll, July 29, 1935, Missouri, Tech.
             Sgt., U. S. Army (interred 1 Aug. 1935)

306   CARROLL   Sergeant Michael Carroll, A native of Tipperary, Ire-
             land, died at Vancouver Bks, W. T. Apr. 6, 1880 aged 38 yrs.
             May he rest in peace. Comp. K, 21st Inft. Erected by mem-
             bers of his company

1081   CARROLL   Miles H. Carroll, Jan. 16, 1884 - Jan. 16, 1963, T. Sgt.
             QMC, World War I, Missouri (interred 21 Jan. 1963)

1879R   CARTER   Wm. F. Carter, June 11, 1858

875   CARSON   John Carson, Dec. 15, 1929 (Pvt., interred 18 Dec. 1929)

453   CHALLAR   John H. Challar (interred 13 Feb. 1906, son of W. W.
             Challar)

433   CHAMBERS   Dorothy M. Chambers, Child (interred 7 Nov. 1904,
             child of T. H. Chambers)

706   CHAPPELLE   William E. Chappelle, June 11, 1923, Washington,
             Bosn. Mate 1 Cl., U. S. Navy (interred 23 June 1923)

293   CHARLES   Mr. John Charles, Jun_r, Sacred to the memory of, Who
             unfortunately lost his life by the accidental discharge of
             a gun in the hand of his companion and fellow traveler on
             the 21 of October 1849 in the 22 year of his age. Much to
             the discovery regretted by his friends and connections. In
             the midst of life we are in death. (interred 22 Oct. 1849)

1153   CHASE   Robert D. Chase, Sept. 27, 1941, Minnesota, 2 Lieut.,
             U. S. Army (interred 29 Sept. 1941)

825   CHASE   Leland L. Chase, 1869 - 1928

559   CHESKIN   Harry Cheskin, Hosp. Corps, U. S. Army (PFC, interred
             28 Apr. 1914)

391   CHILDS   Mary Bridget Childs, Died May 6, 1899, aged 57 yrs., In
             memory of, Rest in Peace (wife of Gernart Gunrity)

---   CHRISTIE   D. T. Christie, U. S. Army (Douglas T. Christie,
             Pvt., interred 29 Sept. 1910)

880   CHRISTIE   Robert F. Christie, Mar. 5, 1930, New York, Sgt. 14
                  U. S. Inf. (interred 8 Mar. 1930)

---   CLAGHORN   Anna Claghorn, died Jan. 10, 1860, aged 10 Yrs. 2 Mos.

---   CLAGHORN   Clarence Claghorn, died Jan. 26, 1856, aged 4 yrs. &
                  5 mos.

1006   CLAPSADDLE   Budd L. Clapsaddle, U. S. Inf. (interred 19 Mar.
                  1933)

1007   CLAPSADDLE   Emma Clapsaddle, wife of Pvt. B. L. Clapsaddle, U.S.A.
                  Dec. 2, 1945 (interred 12 Dec. 1945)

312   CLARK   Pat'k Clark, Co. H, 21st U. S. Inf. (Pvt Patrick Clark,
                  interred 29 July 1882)

73   CLARKE   Private Charles Clarke, Company I, 21 Inf., Killed in
                  action at Clearwater, I.T. July 11, 1877

671   CLIFTON   Isaac W. Clifton, Co. D, 1 Michigan, E & M (interred
                  14 Nov. 1920)

629   CLINTON   Chas. L. Clinton, U. S. Army (Pvt. Charles L. Clinton
                  interred 21 Dec. 1918)

324   COCHLAN   Dan'l Cochlan, Co. A, 9 U. S. Inf. (Daniel Coghlan, Pvt.
                  interred 24 Mar. 1859)

932   COLLINS   Rebecca J. Collins, Mar. 12, 1931 (interred 14 Mar.
                  1931)

486   COLLINS   1st Sgt. S. M. Collins, U. S. A. (Stephen M. Collins,
                  interred 18 Mar. 1908)

73   COMPTON   Alson Compton (Killed in action at Clearwater, I.T.
                  11 July 1877, Company I, 21st Inf.)

    1879R   CONNELL   John Connell, Co. B, 14 U. S. Inf.

493   CONRAD   George H. Conrad, Clerk, QMD (civ. cl., interred 17 Nov.
                  1908)

1169   COOPER   Lloyd Walter Cooper, Dec. 28, 1942, Washington, Seaman,
                  2 Cl. U. S. N. R. (interred 5 Jan. 1942)

1164   COOPER   George N. Cooper, Apr. 5, 1942, Oregon, Sgt. 58 QM Regt.
                  (interred 9 Apr. 1945)

1117   COPE   Anna L. Cope, May 13, 1934 (interred 16 May 1934, wife of
                  Capt. Jessie D. Cope)

1116   COPE   Cpt. Jessie D. Cope, May 16, 1934 (lot reserved)

787   CORLEW   Donald Corlew, May 20, 1931, Oregon, Pvt. 7th Inf. (in-
                  terred 22 May 1931)

1151   COUSLEY Robert G. Cousley, 1878 - 1941, Major Inf. (interred
                  2 Aug. 1941)

598   COWAN Archie E. Cowan (Pvt., interred 1 Mar. 1918)

987   COX John J. Cox, Nov. 19, 1932, Washington, Corp. 361 Inf. 91
                  Div. (interred 22 Nov. 1932)

704   COX William W. Cox, Sept. 24, 1923, Pennsylvania, Sgt. 2, U.S.
                  Inf.

      1879R   CRAFT Eliza Craft, Feb. 21, 1856

705   CRANE Ulysses E. Crane, Co. F, 19 New York Cav. (interred 21
                  May 1923)

---   CRANNIS John W. Crannis, Co. K. I.G., New York Inf.

---   CRANVILLE Henry G. Cranville, Sept. 16, 1922, California, Q.M.
                  Sgt. U. S. Army

      1879R   CRAWFORD Mary Crawford, Aug. 22, 1868

721   CRECOR Abdalin Crecor, Illinois, Mess Sgt., U. S. Army (inter-
                  red 5 May 1919)

1288   CREGO Alan J. Crego (DEP., interred 13 Apr. 1979, Son of
                  SFC Larry H. Joyce)

969   CRISCOLA Myra Violet Criscola, Sept. 30, 1905 - Oct. 17, 1975,
                  Wife of 1 S.G. - D.A. Criscola [Don] U. S. M. C. (interred
                  21 Oct. 1975)

684   CRONK Geo. Cronk, Corpl. Co. B. 14 U. S. Inf. (interred 27 Dec.
                  1921)

738   CRONK Corp'l Henry G. W. Cronk, Co. E. 120 Indiana Inf. (inter-
                  red 1 May 1925)

739   CRONK Mary Cronk, Apr. 4, 1926 (interred 7 Apr. 1926)

      1883R   CROOKS Jeremiah H. Crooks, Citizen, Feb. 1, 1873

304   CROOKS William C. Crooks, Co. D, 21 U. S. Inf. (Pvt., interred
                  22 Mar. 1877)

1078   CROSBY William Crosby, 1851 - 1935 (Cook, interred 8 July 1835)

637   CROWHURST Sgt. Seth J. Crowhurst, Co. E, 12 Iowa Inf. (inter-
                  red 25 Apr. 1919)

1002   CRUMLY Angelinne L. Crumly, wife of Pvt. J. Crumly, Jan. 11, 1933

309   CUMMINGS Matthew Cummings, Co. G, 21st U. S. Inf, Apr. 8, 1881
                  (Pvt., interred 9 Apr. 1881)

---   CUMMONS Elva Cummons, Feb. 21, 1897 - Sept. 1, 1915, Dau. of
                  N. M. & C. D. Cummons, Only Gone Before

764   CUPITT Florence Isabelle Cupitt, Oct. 10, 1885 - Jan. 29, 1970
       (wife of MSG Hatton Cupitt)

764   CUPITT Hatton Cupitt, Apr. 8, 1874 - Nov. 22, 1957, Washington,
       1st Sgt. Co. K, 7 Inf. Sp. Am. War, - World War I

---   CURRY Adah Curry, Born Jan. 9, 1884 - Died Feb. 11, 1904

424   CURRY Edward Curry (interred 11 Feb. 1904)

---   CURRY John Curry, Born Jan. 9, 1884 - Died Feb. 11, 1904

1879R CURTIN Wm. Curtin, Jan. 4, 1860

1879R CUSTIN Hannah Custin, Jan. 20, 1872

799   CUSTROM Annie Custrom, Apr. 9, 1927 (wife of Sgt. Samuel
       Custrom)

798   CUSTROM Samuel Custrom, Oct. 18, 1871 - Dec. 8, 1946, Washing-
       ton, Band Sgt., U. S. Army (interred 12 Dec. 1946)

1159   CZARNY Walter Czarny, Jan. 4, 1942, Illinois, Pvt. 1Cl. Q. M.
       Corps (interred 13 Jan. 1942)

1123   DANESZERWSKI Kasemar Daneszerwski, July 10, 1938, Michigan,
       Pvt. 7 Inf. (interred 19 July 1938)

348   DANKE James Danke, Co. C, 14th U. S. Inf. (interred 5 Mar.
       1890)

656   DANNER Harvey A. Danner, Corp'l Q. M. Corps, U. S. A. (inter-
       red 10 Dec. 1919)

494   DARCY Josie L. Darcy (interred 25 Oct. 1908, wife of Sgt. F. F.
       Darcy)

462   DAUB Sgt. Jno. Daub, Co. A, 22 U. S. Inf. (John H. Daub, in-
       terred 25 July 1906)

1879R DAVIDSON Jane Davidson, May 31, 1862

2   DAVIS Capt. Alf'd Davis, 15th Illinois Inf. (interred 1 Apr.
       1869, Alfred Davis)

956   DAVIS Charles S. Davis, July 25, 1931, Tennessee, Sgt. 7 Inf.
       (interred 27 July 1931)

957   DAVIS Mrs. Charles S. Davis, Wife, Jly 27, 1931

968   DAVIS Oscar E. Davis, Oct. 25, 1931, Delaware, Pvt. 59 Inf.
       (interred 28 Oct. 1931)

630   DAWSON Olive Dawson (interred 2 Jan. 1919, wife of Sgt. John
       Dawson)

416   DAY Dorthy L. Day (interred 22 Aug. 1902, daughter of Pvt.
       D. L. Day)

367   DAY Filve L. Day (interred 15 Mar. 1894, infant son of D. L. Day)

788   DeLOTAL John DeLotal, July 17, 1880 - Mar. 25, 1945, Ohio, 1 Sgt. U. S. Army, P. H. (interred 28 Mar. 1945)

788   DeLOTAL Margaret DeLotal (wife of John DeLotal, cremated, shares lot)

1043   DENTLER Clarence E. Dentler, Apr. 9, 1859 - Apr. 2, 1955, Oregon, Col. U. S. Army, S.A.W. & W.W. (interred 6 Apr. 1955)

1044   DENTLER Delia G. Dentler, Aug. 25, 1873 - Aug. 2, 1951, Wife of Col. C. E. Dentler, U. S. A. (interred 7 Aug. 1951)

1045   DENTLER Robert G. Dentler, Mar. 20, 1932, Son of Col. C. E. Dentler (interred 23 Mar. 1932)

839   DENNISON Charles W. Dennison, Jan. 1, 1929, Michigan, Pvt. 2 Field Art. (interred 5 Jan. 1929)

457   DENSEVICH J. J. Densevich, Co. H, 14 U. S. Inf. (interred 6 May 1906, Joseph J. Densevich)

1256   DICKSON Jack Preston Dickson, Apr. 10, 1914 - Jan. 21, 1979, Cpt. U. S. A., World War II (interred 24 Jan. 1979)

695   DILLABAUGH John E. Dillabaugh (interred 1 Aug. 1922, son of Pfc. W. E. Dillabaugh)

251   DILLON Chas. Upton Dillon, Died Sept. 29, 1856, aged 3 yrs. 10 days, Son of J. T. & S. Dillon (interred 30 Sept. 1856)

08   DIOGUARDI Vincenzo Dioguardi, Dec. 22, 1945, Italy, Sgt. Italian Army, World War II

540   DOBROVICH M. Dobrovich, Co. B, 21 U. S. Inf. (Michael Dobrovich, Pvt., interred 13 Sept. 1912)

---   DOGAN Pat'k Dogan, 8 Batt'y Field Art.

231   DOHERTY Lizzie Doherty, Baby Daughter of J. & S. A. Doherty, Went home Sept. 19, 1865 aged 5 mos. 28 days, Not decl____ but gone before. (interred 20 Sept. 1865)

1883R   DONAHUE [____] Donahue, Pvt. Co. G., 1st U. S. Cav.

382   DONLEY Corp'l Thos. Donley, Comp. B, 14th U. S. Inf. (interred 30 Sept. 1897)

802   DONNELLY Arthur Donnelly, May 12, 1927, Massachusetts, 1st Sgt. U. S. Army (interred 14 May 1927)

992   DONOVAN Louise Donovan, May 29, 1932, Wife of Color Sgt. P. Donovan, U. S. A. (interred 1 June 1932)

371   DOOLY Wm. Dooly, Co. H, 14 U. S. Inf. (William Dooly, interred 25 June 1895)

1152 DONOVAN Patrick Donovan, July 24, 1941, Washington, Color Sgt. U. S. Army (interred 28 July 1941)

--- DOTTEN G. H. Dotten, Co. G, 14 U. S. Inf.

1879R DOUGHERTY Lydia Dougherty, Sept. 19, 1865

455 DOUGLAS Joseph Simonton Douglas, Son of John and Margaret Douglas, Born in Fairfield Co., S. C. Feb. 8, 1879, died Army Post Hospital, Vancouver, Wash. May 23, 1905. Member of Co. M. 19th Reg. of Inf. I will arise and go to my father's house (Pvt., interred 24 May 1905)

1146 DOW Edwin Dow, May 21, 1941, Illinois, Pvt. 7 Inf. (interred 21 June 1941)

754 DOWNING. Mary T. Downing, 1844 - 1926 (interred 20 Jan. 1926)

755 DOWNING Robert W. Downing, 1838 - 1926 (Cpl., interred 18 Mar. 1926)

73 DOYLE Corporal James Doyle, July 11, 1877, Company I, 21 Inf. Killed in action at Clearwater, I. T.

572 DRECKSLER John H. Drecksler, Co. A, 13 Missouri Inf. (Pvt., interred 11 Feb. 1915)

686 DREW Frank Ephraim Drew, Co. E. 7th Maine Inf. (Pvt., interred 1 Feb. 1922)

1879R DUGAN Joseph Dugan, Nov. 25, 1866

1879R DUGAN Nancy F. Dugan, Sept. 5, 1872

418 DUGGAN Patrick Duggan (Pvt., interred 3 June 1903)

1210 DUNBAR Robert E. Dunbar, Mar. 23, 1884 - Sept. 22, 1944, Minnesota, 1st Sgt. U. S. Army (interred 26 Sept. 1944)

827 DURANT Eunice M. Durant, Dec. 9, 1937 (wife of 1 Sgt. P. A. Durant)

826 DURANT Pliny Durant, Apr. 12, 1928, U. S. Soldier (interred 15 Apr. 1928)

472 DURBIN Chester D. Durbin (interred 12 Aug. 1907, son of J. D. Durbin)

680 DURBIN John D. Durbin, Dec. 12, 1862 - Aug. 11, 1921, Oregon, Cpl. Band Co. 28 Inf., Sp. Am. War (interred 14 Aug. 1921)

1879R DURBIN J. L. Durbin, Nov. 6, 1875

531 DURBIN Mary Ellen Durbin, Aug. 19, 1908 - Dec. 25, 1911, Dau. of J. D. & E. E. Durbin, Innocence, Gone to the Angels (interred 27 Dec. 1911)

1879R   DURLING [___] Durling, Jan. 11, 1872

1127   DUSENBERY William R. Dusenbery, Sept. 22, 1938, Oregon, Pvt.
             1 Cl., 7 Inf. (interred 24 Sept. 1938)

476   DWYER Corp'l Jno. Dwyer, Co. G, 14 U. S. Inf. (John Dwyer, in-
             terred 5 Nov. 1907)

1027   DYE Frank Dye, May 17, 1932, Son of Pvt. H. E. Patterson

1025   DYE Frank Dye, Feb. 28, 1859 - Apr. 1, 1945, Tennessee, Comsy.
             Sgt. U. S. Army (interred 4 Apr. 1945)

1026   DYE Jean Dye, Nov. 8, 1939, Wife of Comsy. Sgt. Frank Dye,
             U. S. A. (interred 11 Nov. 1939)

96   DYE Margaret Dye, Daughter of F. & J. Dye, born at Fort Craw-
             ford, Colorado. Died at Vancouver, W. T. Sept. 30, 1888,
             aged 6 yrs. 8 mos. 16 ds. She is not dead, this child of
             our affection, but gone into that school, there she no
             longer needs our poor protection and Christ Himself doth
             rule

834   DYSART William J. Dysart, Oct. 15, 1928 (1 Sgt., interred 19
             Oct. 1928)

1167   EAKINS Herman Eakins, Aug. 10, 1942, California, Staff Sgt. 7
             Inf. (interred 15 Aug. 1942)

;879R   EBERT Eunice Ebert, Aug. 15, 1862

719   ECK Franz H. W. Eck, Chief MUS, U. S. Army (interred 26 Oct.
             1938)

716   ECK Frieda Maurine Eck, Mar. 21, 1900 - Jan. 31, 1974, Wife of
             CMUS F. H. W. Eck, U. S. A. (interred 4 Feb. 1974)

724   ECK Mareta Eck, July 25, 1859 - Sept. 28, 1923 (Marietta Eck,
             Wife of Franz H. W. Eck, interred 29 Sept. 1923)

723   ECK Rose Eck, Dec. 9, 1931, Wife of Ore. MUS - F. H. W. Eck
             (interred 11 Dec. 1931)

379   EDSON Henry Edson, Corpl., Co. F, 14th U. S. Inf. (interred
             24 July 1896)

889   EDWARDS George T. Edwards, Nov. 19, 1862 - Mar. 25, 1953, Wash-
             ington, Sgt. U. S. Army, S. A. W. & W. W. I (interred 27
             Mar. 1953)

890   EDWARDS Sara A. Edwards, 1858 - 1930 (interred 17 June 1930)

1883R   EGGLING Christ Eggling, Oct. 12, 1874, Pvt. Co. B, 1st U. S.
             Cav.

464   EISENHOWER W. H. Eisenhower, Co. D., 14 U. S. Inf. (Pvt., in-
             terred 26 Aug. 1906)

885   ELEY Gwendolyn Eley, May 28, 1930 (interred 30 May 1930,
                     daughter of Mr. Howard Eley)

878   ELISBARASCHWILI Elisbar Elisbaraschwili, Aug. 6, 1945 (Pvt.,
                     interred 10 Aug. 1945)

1265   ELKINS David Cecil Elkins, Sr., May 27, 1940 - Apr. 4, 1979,
                     C W 2, U. S. Army, Vietnam (interred 10 Apr. 1979)

516   ELLERMAN, Sgt. Maj. Fred'k Ellerman, 21 U. S. Inf. (Frederick
                     Ellerman, interred 20 Jan. 1910)

404   ELLINGSVOLD Corp'l J. L. Ellingsvold, Co. K, 7th U. S. Inf.
                     (Cpl. John Ellingsvold, interred 14 Sept. 1901)

1015   ENDICOTT Infant Endicott, son of Pvt. L. B. Endicott (inter-
                     red 26 June 1933)

     1879R   ERNEST Caroline Ernest, Feb. 2, 1868

     1879R   ESKRIDGE J. B. Eskridge, Jan. 7, 1866

186   ESKRIDGE E. R. Eskridge, Civilian (interred 8 Jan. 1886)

169   ESMOND Charles Esmond (no further information)

678   EVANS Hannah H. Evans (interred 17 May 1921, wife)

574   EVANS Mary Kennon Evans, I. H. S., Born Mar. 21, 1824 - Died
                     May 14, 1915 (interred 18 May 1915, mother of General
                     Robert K. Evans)

     1883R   EVERITT Henry Everitt, Oct. 13, 1873, Pvt. Co. G, 12th U. S. Inf.

1095   .   EVERSOLE Joseph Eversole, Nov. 29, 1936, Washington, 1 Sgt.
                     U. S. A.

730   EWART John Ewart, Aug. 16, 1924, New York, 1st Sgt. 1 Inf. (in-
                     terred 18 Aug. 1924)

805   FARRELL Fannie Farrell, 1886 - 1927, Wife of John Farrell, Our
                     Loved One (interred 28 May 1927)

806   FARRELL John Farrell, May 18, 1939, Washington, Cook U. S.
                     Army (Sgt., interred 22 May 1939)

1239   FARQUHARSON Gordon Farquharson, Dec. 11, 1907 - July 2, 1945,
                     Washington, Tec. 4 Q. M. Corps

428A   FAUBLE Betty Jane Fauble, Died Nov. 17, 1917, Aged 14 mos.,
                     Grand daughter of Michael Brady (interred 20 Nov. 1917)

836   FAUST Joseph J. FAust, Nov. 8, 1928, Pennsylvania, 1st Sgt.
                     U. S. Army (interred 16 Nov. 1928)

425   FELINAS Infant Felinas (interred 11 Feb. 1904, daughter of
                     1 Sgt. Felinas)

463   FELLER Nicholas Feller, Co. I, 14 U. S. Inf. (Pvt., interred
             28 July 1906)

1205   FEMLING Herbert Hugh Femling, Jan. 2, 1920 - Aug. 27, 1944,
             Washington, Seaman 1 Cl., U. S. N. R. (interred 31 Aug.
             1944)

417   FENNER Raymond Henry Fenner, Feb. 24, 1903 - Apr. 9, 1903,
             Son of R. H. & C. E. Fenner, God Son of the Class of 1900,
             U.S.M.A. (interred 10 Apr. 1903)

1024   FERRIER Mardlisa Ferrier, Feb. 19, 1933, Wife of T. Ferrier
             (interred 21 Feb. 1933)

1023   FERRIER Thomas H. Ferrier, Minnesota (Pvt., interred 22 Nov.
             1931)

828   FICHT Dwight Bernhardt Ficht, Apr. 15, 1928, Washington, Fire-
             man 3 Cl., U. S. Navy (interred 22 Apr. 1928)

594   FICKLIN Waverly Ficklin, Mess Sgt. Co. I, 21 U. S. Inf. (in-
             terred 12 Dec. 1917)

1092   FINCH Louis Finch, Sept. 27, 1898 - Mar. 24, 1946, 1 Sgt. U. S
             Army, Kentucky (interred 29 Mar. 1946)

1091   FINCH Infant Daughter of Louis Finch, U. S. A., May 7, 1939
             (interred 9 May 1939)

---   FINNERAN Thos. Finneran, Co. K, 21 U. S. Inf.

478   FIPPS F. A. Fipps, 33 Co. Coast. Art. (Fred A. Fipps, Cpl.,
             interred 26 Nov. 1907)

571   FIRMERAN Thomas Firmeran (Pvt., interred 11 Feb. 1915)

423   FISCHER Alex Robinson Fischer, Infant Son (interred 17 Dec.
             1903, son of 1 Sgt. Fischer)

509   FISCHER Elizabeth J. Fischer (interred 4 Aug. 1909, wife of
             Jacob F. Fischer)

943   FITZGERALD John H. Fitzgerald, Apr. 4, 1931, Missouri, Sgt. 4,
             U. S. Cav. (interred 9 Apr. 1931)

506   FITZPATRICK Mary E. Fitzpatrick, Infant (interred 2 June 1909,
             daughter of Sgt. M. Fitzpatrick)

329   FITZPATRICK P. Fitzpatrick (Patrick Fitzpatrick, Rct., inter-
             red 17 Oct. 1886, Mil. Convict)

955   FLEET Clinton C. Fleet, Virginia, Bn. Sgt. Major, 19 U. S. Inf.
             July 7, 1931 (interred 9 July 1931)

1072   FLETCHER Howard F. Fletcher, Jan. 29, 1936, Washington, Sgt.,
             7 Inf. (interred 4 Feb. 1936)

1879R   FLETCHER Rhoda Fletcher, Nov. 5, 1865

1879R   FLETCHER Wm. S. Fletcher, Dec. 10, 1868

982   FLOYD Anna A. Floyd, 1872 - 1923 (interred 28 Feb. 1923)

1883R   FLYNN Michael Flynn, Pvt. Co. E. 12th U. S. Inf.

528   FODDER George Fodder, Co. L, 1st U. S. Inf. (Pvt., interred
               31 Oct. 1911)

1107   FOERSTER Lt. Col. Lewis Foerster, 1868 - 1936, Wife Melanie
               (interred 26 Dec. 1936)

1108   FOERSTER Melanie Foerster, 1879 - 1962, Husband Lt. Col. Lewis
               Foerster (interred 10 Feb. 1962)

310   FOLLY Wm. Folly, Co. G., 2nd U. S. Inf. (Pvt. William Folly,
               interred 25 June 1882)

69   FOLZ Louis Folz, Co. D, 3rd U. S. Art., died Feb. 8, 1859
               (Faltz, Pvt., interred 9 Feb. 1859)

734   FORBORG Charles H. Gorborg, Feb. 2, 1925, Maryland, Sgt. 14
               Inf. (interred 3 Feb. 1925)

185   FOREST Wm. Forest, Died Oct. 20, 1865, aged 26 yrs., In Memory
               Of, Born in Killeagh Parish, County Cork, Ireland

670   FORSYTH Robert T. Forsyth, 1894 - 1920 (Cpl., interred 5 Nov.
               1920)

751   FOSTER Edgar Foster, Co. E, 44 Iowa Inf. (Pvt., interred 30
               Sept. 1925)

600   FOSTER Geo. W. Foster, Sig. Corps, U. S. A. (George W. Foster
               Pvt., interred 1 Apr. 1918)

931   FOX James Fox, Massachusetts (Pvt., interred 16 Feb. 1931)

444   FOX Robert Fox, Hosp. Corps, U. S. A. (Pvt., interred 16 June
               1905)

674   FRADENBERG Alonzo Fradenberg, New York (Cpl., interred 19 Apr.
               1931)

524   FRANCIS Harry Francis (Pvt., interred 15 Dec. 1910)

674   FRADENBERG Minnie W. Fradenberg (interred 23 Jan. 1921, wife
               of Cpl. Alonzo Frandenburg)

1879R   FRANCIS Simeon Francis, Maj. [Ret.] U. S. A., died Oct. 25, 1872

681   FREE Fred'k E. Free, Sergt. Co. D, 14 U. S. Inf. (Frederick E.
               Free, Sgt., interred 25 Sept. 1921)

870/619A   FREEMAN Infant Freeman (interred 10 Jan. 1919, daughter of
               1 Lt. Walter Freeman)

870   FRENCH Arthur D. French, Aug. 9, 1929, Washington, Pvt. 146
           Field Art. (interred 12 Aug. 1929)

622   FRENCH Claude A. French, Nov. 27, 1918, Oregon, Pvt. 83 Aero
           Sqdn. (interred 28 Nov. 1918)

290   FRIERSON John Frierson, Apr. 14, 1940, Tennessee, Sgt. U. S.
           Army

715   FRIERSON Ellen Frierson (reserved plot - 16 Apr. 1940, wife of
           John Frierson)

592   FURLEY John W. Furley, Employee, U. S. Army, Aug. 30, 1917
           (Civ. Clk.)

505   FURLONG Jos. D. Furlong, Co. B, 1 U. S. Engrs. (Pfc., Joseph
           D. Furlong, interred 22 Apr. 1909)

746   GAGE William Gage, July 13, 1858 - Sept. 7, 1959, South Carolina,
           Drum Major, 24 Regt. Inf. Band (interred 11 Sept. 1959)

1048   GALLICKER Charles M. Galliker, Nov. 15, 1932, Washington, Pvt.
           7 Inf. (interred 18 Nov. 1932)

854   GRANROW Bettsey M. Ganrow (interred 5 Apr. 1929, daughter of
           Pvt. Ganrow)

84   GARD Jos. Spay Gard, 4th U. S. Inf.

313   GARD W. S. Gard, Co. G, 21 U. S. Inf. (Winfried J. Gard, Pvt.,
           interred 29 May 1883)

1012   GATES Eldridge Gates, May 2, 1933, Civilian (father-in-law of
           Cpl. T. Gates)

   1879R GEARY Dominick Geary, Jan. 31, 1872, Co. E, 23rd U. S. Inf.

720   GEISER Albert Geiser, Jan. 19, 1924, Cook 19 Inf.

323   GENROLL Thos. M. Genroll, Co. A, 9 U. S. Inf.

1154   GEOHEGAN Nicholas J. Geohegan, Oct. 12, 1941, Washington, 1
           Lieut. U. S. Army (interred 15 Oct. 1941)

353   GERONINE Tyrggve J. Geronine, Co. F. 14 U. S. Inf.

722   GEROM Peter Gerom, 1857 - 1924, Corp. Hosp. Corps, Born in
           Germany (interred 22 Feb. 1924)

---   GHEINEMANN John Gheinemann, July 11, 1877, Musician, Company I,
           21 Inf., Killed in action at Clearwater, I. T.

350   GIBBON John T. Gibbon (interred 14 May 1890, Pvt.)

   1879R GIBBONS Emanuel Gibbons, died Sept. 17, 1865

232   GIBBONS Nathaniel Gibbons, Infant Son of N. & M. G. Gibbons,
           died Sept. 17, 1868, aged 11 mos. 29 dys. An Angel With God
           (interred 18 Sept. 1868)

411   GIBBONS Warren Gibbons, Co. D, 17 U. S. Inf. (Pvt., interred
                    9 Feb. 1903)

611   GIBSON Wm. E. Gibson, 17 U. S. Field Art. (Pvt., interred 19
                    Oct. 1918)

      1883R   GIEB Fred M. Gieb, Pvt. Co. E, 12th U. S. Inf.

397   GILDERSLEEVE E. W. Gildersleeve, Co. G., 14th U. S. Inf. (Pvt.
                    Emmett W. Gildersleeve)

57   GILMORE J. H. Gilmore, Oregon Volunteers, U. S. Soldier

---   GENTY George W. Genty, Son, May 16, 1928

---   GIBLIN John T. Giblin, Died May 13, 1890 aged 30 yrs. 7 mos.,
                    In memory of, Co. C, 14 Inf., Born at Cork, Ireland (erected
                    by members of Co. C.)

1225   GJERBERG Bruce V. Gjerberg, Dec. 5, 1922 - Mar. 2, 1945, Wis-
                    consin, Cpl. Trans. Corps. (interred 6 Mar. 1945)

1071   GODFREY Bertha Godfrey, Aug. 10, 1935, Wife of Sgt. Thomas
                    Godfrey, U. S. A. (interred 13 Aug. 1935)

---   GOODENOW Lyman Goodenow, Co. H, 21st U. S. Inf.

314   GOODWIN Lyman Goodwin (Pvt. interred 1 July 1884)

54   GOULD Theodore Gould, Nov. 26, 1863, aged 23 yrs. Sacred to the
                    memory of, Who was a member of B Squadron, 1 Oregon Cav.
                    Born in the state of Wisconsin, Died at Ft. Vancouver, W.T.
                    (Pvt., records gives death date as 1865)

---   GOWAN Archie E. Gowan, U. S. Army

---   GRADY Howard Grady (no further information)

422½   CRAEFEN Anna W. Graefen, May 26, 1931, Wife of Clerk. C. E.
                    Graefen (interred 30 May 1931)

422   GRAEFEN Charles E. Graefen, 27 Wisconsin Inf. (interred 6 Dec.
                    1903)

362   GRAEFF Adolph Graeff, May 15, 1940, Wisconsin, Bn. Q. M. Sgt.
                    U. S. Army (interred 17 May 1940)

616   GRAF Dan Graf, U. S. Army (Pvt., interred 9 Nov. 1918)

679   GRANNIS John W. Grannis, Co. K, Lieut., 116 New York Inf. (2
                    Lt., interred 5 Aug. 1921)

666   GRANT Wm. Grant, Co. I, 15 U. S. Inf. (Cook, interred 27 Jan.
                    1920)

696   GRANVILLE Henry G. Granville, Sept. 16, 1922, California, Q. M.
                    Sgt., U. S. Army (interred 19 Sept. 1922)

238   GRATE   W. F. Grate, Civilian   (interred 12 July 1858)

783   GRAVES .Ada A Graves, Mar. 21, 1934, Daughter of Ord. Sgt.
                            A. G. Potter, U. S. A.   (interred 24 Mar. 1934)

1217   GRAVE   Owen Silas Grave, Dec. 9, 1905 - NOv. 5, 1944, Oregon,
                            Carpenter Mate, 3 Cl., U. S. N. R.   (interred 12 Nov. 1944)

        1883R   GREEBERG Jethro Greeberg, Pvt. Co. A, 1st Oregon Vols., Nov. 29
                            1865)

295   GREEN   C. Green (son of Major Green)

544   GREEN   John Green, lost Sgt. Co. B., 14 U. S. Inf. (interred
                            26 Dec. 1912)

1202   GREEN .Tressa W. Green, Aug. 2, 1899 - Feb. 21, 1946, Wife of
                            Tech. Sgt. G. M. Green, U. S. A. (interred 25 Feb. 1946)

845   GREY   Samuel J. Grey, 845, Maine (Pvt., interred 6 Jan. 1929)

304   GROOKS   W. G. Grooks, Co. D., 21st U. S. Inf.

56   GUINTY   Bernard Guinty, Sept. 14, 1870, Co. D. 23rd U. S. Inf.
                            (Pvt., interred 11 Oct. 1870)

829   GUINTY   George W. Guinty, May 16, 1928, Son (interred 18 May
                            1928, son of Pvt. Bernard Guinty)

        1883R   GULLAGHER   Daniel Gallagher, Dec. 12, 1872, Pvt. Co. B, 1st U.S.
                            Cav.

537   HAHN   Sarah .P. Hahn (interred 29 July 1912, wife of Sgt. N.
                            Hahn)

        1883R   HALLECK   Stephen J. Halleck, Apr. 2, 1866, Pvt. Co. I, 1st Ore-
                            gon Vols.

389   HALTERS   F. S. J. Halters, Born Jan. 2, 1880 - Died July 2,
                            1898, Co. B., 4th U. S. Inf.

1160   HAMMONDS   Ethelbert D. Hammonds, Feb. 5, 1942, Kentucky, 1 Sgt.,
                            U. S. Army (interred 7 Feb. 1942)

467   HAMMOND   W. A. Hammond, 17 Batty., Field Art. (William A.
                            Hammond, Pvt., interred 21 Sept. 1906)

---   HANCOCK   Frank J. Hancock, Aug. 5, 1923, U. S. Soldier

539   HANCOCK   J. F. Hancock (Pvt., interred 19 Aug. 1923)

717   HANCOCK   Millie Hancock, Jan. 1, 1924 (interred 2 Jan. 1924,
                            wife of Frank J. Hancock)

        1883R   HAND   Charles Hand, Citizen

---   HANN   Nichol Hann, May 17, 1922, Regt. Com. Sgt. U. S. Army

690   HARDESTY Gertrude E. Hardesty (interred 20 Apr. 1922, wife of
              Pfc. John M. Hardesty)

354   HARNER John H. Harner, Co. G., 14th U. S. Inf. (Pvt., interred
              12 Feb. 1891)

861   HARP George H. Harp, Illinois (Pvt., interred 29 May 1929)

1225   HARRELSON Gideon Harrelson, Alabama, Staff Sgt. U. S. Army,
              Apr. 22, 1874 - Apr. 6, 1945 (interred 14 Apr. 1945)

    1883R   HARRIS James Harris, Pvt. Co. B., 1st U. S. Cav., died Nov. 29,
              1872

384   HASKINS Silas Haskins, Co. B., INCP. T. Batt'n, Washington Inf.
              (Pvt., interred 18 Aug. 1898)

708   HATHAWAY Alice Webster Hathaway, 1846 - 1923, Wife of Forrest
              Henry Hathaway (interred 26 June 1923)

707   HATHAWAY Brigadier General Forrest Henry Hathaway, 1844 - 1912,
              U. S. Army (interred 7 Aug. 1912)

707B   HATHAWAY Paul Hathaway, Sept. 30, 1887 - Apr. 26, 1974, Maj.,
              U. S. Army (interred 15 May 1974, son of B. G. Forrest H.
              Hathaway)

1062   HAWORTH Jean Haworth, May 26, 1934, Daughter of Pvt. 1 Cl. L. S.
              Haworth, U. S. A.

1020   HAYES Lillian Moriarity Hayes, 1903 - 1923, At Rest (interred
              15 Aug. 1923, daughter of Sgt. Moriarity)

366   HAYWOOD Chas. Haywood, Co. A, 14 U. S. Inf. (Charles Haywood,
              Pvt., interred 18 Jan. 1894)

935   HAZARD Bryce D. Hazard, Feb. 19, 1931 (son of Clay W. Hazard,
              interred 23 Feb. 1931)

475   HAZE P. J. Haze, 1st Sgt., U. S. A. (Peter J. Haze, interred
              31 Oct. 1907)

856   HEADLEY George Headley, Apr. 28, 1929, Washington, Pvt. 314
              French Mortar Battn. (interred 1 May 1929)

    1879R   HEALY Daniel Healy, d. Nov. 12, 1866

749   HECK Frank A. Heck, 1897 - 1928 (interred 19 Nov. 1928)

1118   HECKEL Daisy H. Heckel, Jan. 29, 1938, Wife of 1 Sgt. L. E.
              Heckel, U. S. A. (interred 31 Jan. 1938)

1119   HECKEL Lawrence E. Heckel, Aug. 29, 1881 - Jan. 3, 1948, West
              Virginia, 1 Sgt., U. S. Army, World War I (interred 6 Jan.
              1948)

745   HEFTY Fred'k Hefty, Co. G., 3 Wisconsin Inf. (Pvt.)

776   HEGEMAN Lieut. Co. Harry A. Hegeman, 1874 - 1927 (L T C - in-
              terred 14 Feb. 1927)

777   HEGEMAN Isabel M. Hegeman, 1878 - 1943, Wife of Lieut. Co. Harry
              A. Hegeman (interred 13 Jan. 1943)

321   HEIDINGER Frank Heidinger, Co. A., 14th U. S. Inf. (Pvt., in-
              terred 3 Apr. 1886)

75   HEIDICK Chas. Heidick, Band, 21st U. S. Inf. (Pvt. Charles
              Heidick, interred 7 Sept. 1877)

73   HEINEMANN John C. Heinemann (Company I, 21 Inf., killed in action
              at Clearwater, I. T. 11 July 1877)

551   HEINRICHS Ord. Sgt. Louis Heinrichs, U. S. A. (interred 11 June
              1913)

268   HEITLER Kate Heitler, Born Apr. 24, 1872 - Died Sept. 29, 1872,
              Daughter of R. H. & S. E. Heitler (interred 30 Sept. 1872)

415   HEMMINGER Adolph Hemminger, Died Apr. 2, 1903 age 53 years, In
              Memory Of, Dum Taget Clamat, Here rests a woodman of the world
              (interred 3 Apr. 1903)

533   HEMSLEY Sarah A. Hemsley (interred 14 Mar. 1912, Mother-in-law
              to G. W. Sturley)

593   HENDERSON A. J. Henderson, Co. F, 4 U. S. Engrs. (Andrew J.
              Henderson, Pvt., interred 10 Nov. 1917)

552   HENDERSON Chas. Henderson, Corpl., Co. A., 21 U. S. Inf. (in-
              terred 12 June 1913)

951   HENDRIX William G. Hendrix, Dec. 5, 1866 - May 23, 1957, 1st
              Sgt., 1 Regt. Inf., Sp. Am. War (interred 27 May 1957)

538   HENRICHSEN Oscar Henrichsen, Sergt. Band, 14 U. S. Inf. (inter-
              red 2 Aug. 1912)

587   HENRICI Wm. J. Henrici, Co. F., 14 U. S. Inf. (William J. Hen-
              rici, Pvt., interred 22 June 1917)

1053   HERRING Guy W. Herring, Nov. 14, 1932, Illinois, Corp. 7 Inf.
              (interred 17 Nov. 1932)

429   HERTENSTEIN W. J. Hertenstein, Co. B. 28 U. S. Inf. (Pvt., in-
              terred 22 June 1904)

430   HESSELSCHWARDT Fredrick Hesselschwardt, Born Aug. 4, 1904 - Died
              Aug. 10, 1904, Only Sleeping (infant son of Pvt. Hessel-
              schonedt, interred 11 Aug. 1904)

534   HILBRETH Frank Hilbreth, Hosp. Corps, U. S. A. (Pvt., interred
              17 Mar. 1912)

650   HILL James Madison Hill, Apr. 23, 1845 - Sept. 17, 1919, Com.
              Sgt., U. S. Army (interred 23 Sept. 1919)

652   HILL   Mary J. Hill, 1849 - Mar. 9, 1926, Wife of Comsy. Sgt. J.
           Hill (interred 12 Mar. 1926)

651   HILL   William Joseph Hill, May 28, 1876 - Nov. 28, 1907 (interred
           2 Dec. 1907, son of Sgt. James M. Hill)

1050   HISLOP   Alexander Hislop, Wisconsin (Pvt., interred 14 Feb. 1933)

1049   HISLOP   Mary E. Hislop, June 10, 1937, Wife of Pvt. Alex Hislop
           (interred 12 June 1937)

1879R   HOAG   D. S. Hoag, d. May 7, 1868

460   HOBBS   J. W. Hobbs, Co. H 14, U. S. Inf. (Pvt. James W. Hobbs,
           interred 24 July 1906)

1879R   HODGES   E. A. Hodges, d. Nov. 10, 1865

1879R   HODGES   H. D. Hodges, d. July 24, 1868

1879R   HOGUE   Joseph Hogue, June 16, 1862

653   HOLDEN   Vivian Holden, Infant (interred 17 Oct. 1919)

523   HOLLOWAY   Jno. L. Holloway, Co. B, 2 U. S. Field Art. (John L.
           Holloway, interred 14 Dec. 1910)

691   HOLT   Samuel Holt, May 2, 1922, Oregon, Sergt., U. S. Army (in-
           terred 3 May 1922)

1016   HOLTSCLAW   Michael William Holtsclaw, Jr., Nov. 20, 1976 - Mar.
           5, 1977, Son of CWO2, M. A. Holtsclaw, Sr., U. S. A. (inter-
           red 9 Mar. 1977)

596   HOMAN   Chas. A. Homan, Corp'l Co. F, 35 New Jersey Inf. (interred
           1 May 1918)

596½   HOMAN   Ona Homan, Sept. 16, 1933, Wife of Cpl. C. A. Homan, U. S. A.

975   HOPPE   Alfred L. Hoppe, Dec. 30, 1931, New York, Sgt. U. S. Army
           (interred 31 Dec. 1931)

976   HOPPE   Louise C. Hoppe, Oct. 26, 1871 - Aug. 27, 1952, Wife of
           A. L. Hoppe, U. S. A. (interred 2 Sept. 1952)

1276   HOOPER   Lester Guy Hooper, 1st Lt., U. S. Coast Guard, WWII, Aug.
           13, 1906 - Oct. 17, 1978 (interred 20 Oct. 1978)

800   HOOVER   Willis P. Hoover, Washington, Pvt. 19, Spruce Sqdn., Air
           Service, May 4, 1927 (interred 17 May 1927)

354   HORNER   J. H. Horner, Co. G., 14 U. S. Inf.

1030   HOTTELL   Infant Hottell (interred 12 Feb. 1934, father-Pvt. John
           Hottell, U. S. A., died 10 Feb. 1934)

978   HOUGHTALING   George L. Houghtaling, Jan. 28, 1941, Minnesota,
           Master Sgt., U. S. Army (interred 31 Jan. 1941)

896   HOWARD   Emma Olive Howard, Apr. 28, 1939, Wife of Cpl. Henry
               Howard, U. S. A. (interred 29 April 1939)

897   HOWARD   Henry Howard, Sept. 7, 1950, Corp. 5 Inf. (interred 9
               Sept. 1930)

1181   HOWE   Charles S. Howe, Aug. 25, 1943, Illinois, Sgt. Major, U. S.
               Army (interred 29 Aug. 1943)

---   HOWE   Louisa Howe, Apr. 30, 1867 - July 14, 1954, Wife of Sgt.
               Maj. C. S. Howe, U. S. A. (interred 19 July 1954)

682   HUBERS   John Hubers, May 27, 1853 - Oct. 20, 1921 (1 Sgt., inter-
               red 22 Oct. 1921)

1165   HUGHES   Emery Hughes, May 15, 1942, Montana, Tech. Sgt., U. S. A.
               (interred 19 May 1942)

76   HUGHES   F. G. Hughes, Co. D., 21st U. S. Inf. (Pvt. Francis G.
               Hughes, interred 3 Jan. 1878)

1066/1067   HUGHEY   1 Sgt. Joseph Hughey and Mrs. Hughey - lots reserved

900   HUGUENIN   Marguerite Randin Huguenin, Jan. 23, 1872 - Oct. 17,
               1956, Wife of Sgt. P. A. Huguenin, U. S. A. (interred 19 Oct.
               1956)

901   HUGUENIN   Paul A. Huguenin, Apr. 25, 1934, New York, Sgt. U. S.
               Army (interred 27 Apr. 1934)

245   HUNT   Ellen Hunt (died 18 Oct. 1857)

1242   HURLEY   Michael J. Hurley, Oct. 2, 1877 - July 5, 1945, Mass.,
               2 Lt., U. S. Army (interred 9 July 1945)

---   HUTELL   Infant Son Hutell, Father-Pvt. J. Hutell, U. S. A., 10
               Feb. 1934

564   JACKSON   Sherman Jackson, Co. D, U. S. Inf. (Pvt., interred 16
               July 1914)

769   JAMES   Eliza. James, 1884 - 1972 (Elizabeth James, wife of Sgt.
               Oliver W. James, interred 2 Sept. 1972, shares lot with Oli-
               ver)

769   JAMES   Oliver M. James, 1878 - 1926, Co. E, 14th Inf. (interred
               6 July 1926, shares lot with wife, Elizabeth)

609   JAMISON   Wm. Jamison, Lieut. Q. M. Corps, U. S. A. (1 Lt. William
               Jamison, interred 15 Oct. 1918)

454   JAMISON   W. S. Jamison, 18 Batty. Field Arty. (Cpl. William S.
               Jamison, interred 23 April 1906)

297   JANES   Carita Belknap Janes, Died Apr. 18, 1871, Aged 9 Mos. 18
               Ds., Dau. of H. W. & L. E. Janes, U. S. A. (interred 19 Apr.
               1871)

1278   JENSEN Reita Jane Jensen, Jan. 16, 1935 - Nov. 12, 1978. Wife
                of Col. R. W. Jensen, U. S. A. (interred 16 Nov. 1978)

725   JEPSON Mrs. Neil H. Jepson, Apr. 24, 1924 (interred 25 Apr.
                1924)

634   JOHNSON Albin T. Johnson, Air Service, U. S. A. (Pvt., interred
                14 Jan. 1919)

882   JOHNSON Clarence C. Johnson, July 25, 1896 - June 10, 1968, Ore-
                gon, 2d Lieutenant, U. S. Army Ret., WW I & II (interred
                13 June 1968, father Sgt. R. C. Johnson)

163   JOHNSON Edward A. Johnson, Died Apr. 29, 1865, aged 1 yr. 5 mos.
                Son of J. L. & N. J. Johnson (interred 30 Apr. 1865)

164   JOHNSON John L. Johnson, Died Feb. 6, 1865, aged 33 yrs. (in-
                terred 7 Feb. 1865)

882   JOHNSON Raymond C. Johnson (Sgt., interred 18 May 1931)

    1879R   JONES Carita B. Jones, died Apr. 15, 1871 (this is probably the
                same as Carita Belknap Janes)

525   JONES Ed D. Jones, Co. A, 2 U. S. Field Art. (Pvt., interred
                8 Jan. 1911)

578   JONES Elva Jones (interred 16 Sept. 1915)

04   JONES Eric Ray Jones, June 29, 1972 - June 18, 1973, Son of Sgt.
                M. R. Jones, U. S. A.

1063   JONES Harry C. Jones, July 11, 1934, Master Sgt., U. S. Army,
                Illinois (interred 13 July 1934)

473   JONES John W. Jones (Civ. Eng. interred 10 Sept. 1907)

---   JONES J. W. Jones (employee A. C. Dept. - probably the same as
                above)

1019   JONES Kyle H. Jones, Jan. 28, 1941, Washington, Pvt. 1 Cl. Inf.
                (interred 30 Jan. 1941)

628   JORDAN Jas. Jordan, Corp'l, Air Service, U. S. A. (Cpt. James
                Jordan, interred 24 Dec. 1918)

---   KAHARDT Adolf Charles Kahardt, Aug. 25, 1838 - Aug. 14, 1871,
                Born in Friedersdorf, Germany

1098   KARASIEWICZ John B. Karasiewicz, May 6, 1937, Oregon, Master Sgt.
                U. S. Army (interred 9 May 1937)

1099   KARASIEWICZ Rebecca Karasiewicz, Nov. 7, 1940, Wife of Master
                Sgt. J. B. Karasiewicz, U. S. A. (interred 9 Nov. 1940)

912   KATES   Cpl. Kates, 1936 (lot reserved)

913   KATES Fanny Kates, 1874 - 1930 (wife of Cpl. Kates, interred 29
               Oct. 1930)

627   KAUFFMAN Ray C. Kauffman, S. A. T. C., U. S. A. (Pvt., interred
               21 Dec. 1918)

647   KEENAN Chas. Keenan, U. S. Army

1194   KEITH Neil C. Keith, Apr. 24, 1918 - Mar. 27, 1944, Montana,
               Pvt., U. S. Army (interred 28 Mar. 1944)

742   KELLY Carolina Kelly, Feb. 4, 1942, Wife of 1 Sgt. Patrick Kelly,
               U. S. A. (interred 6 Feb. 1942)

5A   KELLY Eleanor B. Kelly, 1859 - 1944, Daughter of Maj. Wm. Kelly

383   KELLY James Kelly, Infant (interred 20 Mar. 1898, son of S. G.
               M. Kelly)

1248   KELLY James A. Kelly, Jan. 29, 1901 - Nov. 28, 1945, Wisconsin,
               Cpl. Trans. Corps, WWII (interred 5 Dec. 1945)

---   KELLY James Kelly, Born at Greggsville, Illinois June 21, 1860 -
               Died at Dyen, Alaska Mar. 19, 1898, I. H. S., Pray for the
               Soul of, Sgt. Major, 14 U. S. Inf., R. I. P.

8   KELLY Mary A. Louise Kelly, Born at Gabrator Dec. 13, 1821 - Died
               at Portland, Oregon Dec. 25, 1872, Wife of Wm. Kelly (in-
               terred 26 Dec. 1872)

741   KELLY Patrick Kelly, July 5, 1925, Pennsylvania, Q. M. Sgt., U. S.
               Army (interred 8 July 1925)

5   KELLY William Kelly, Born at Hillsey, England June 23, 188? -
               Died at Denver City, Col. Dec. 28, 1871, Maj., 8th U. S. Cav-
               alry (interred 29 Dec. 1871)

9   KELLY Winnie Kelly, Born July 20, 1861 - Died May 22, 1862, In-
               fant daughter of W. & M. A. L. Kelly (interred 23 May 1862)

357   KEMPER G. F. Kemper, Co. D, 14 U. S. Inf. (George F. Kemper,
               Pvt., interred 20 Aug. 1891)

545   KENDALL Henry Fletcher Kendall, Born in Paris, France June 1855 -
               Died Portland, Oregon Jan. 1913, Major 12th Cavalry, U. S. A.
               Retired, Son of Geo. Wilkins and Adeline DeValcourt Kendall
               (interred 18 Jan. 1913)

     1879R   KENGHTON Henry M. Kenghton, d. June 17, 1862

203   KENNEY Josephine Kenney, July 27, 1869 (interred 28 July 1869)

466   KENNINGTON Ellen Kennington (interred 3 Nov. 1906, wife of Cpt.
               J. Kennington)

877   KENNISON Sam'l P. Kennison, U. S. V. Cav.

     1879R   KIATHS Albert Kiaths, May 24, 1865, Cpl. Co. E., 1 W. T. Inf.

1077   KID Minnie A. Kid, Jan. 9, 1838, Wife of Sgt. W. P. Kid, U. S. A.
            (interred 12 Jan. 1938)

1075   KIDD Ida Nora Kidd, Apr. 18, 1935 (interred 22 Apr. 1935, mother
            of 1 Sgt. Wallace Kidd)

286   KIDD Thos. Kidd, May 16, 1859

1076   KIDD Wallace P. Kidd, Apr. 8, 1890 - Apr. 26, 1948, 1 Sgt. U. S.
            Army, WWII, Washington (interred 27 Apr. 1948)

512   KIMBERLING Mark Kimberling, Infant (interred 4 Sept. 1909)

    1879R   KISER Mary Ann Kiser, d. July 25, 1862

851   KISSANE Thomas J. Kissane, Mar. 9, 1929 (interred 12 Mar. 1929,
            father of Lt. Thomas L. Kissane)

675   KITTLE Geo. B. Kittle (George B. Kittle, interred 24 Feb. 1921,
            father-in-law of F. B. Reynolds)

599   KITTLESON Norman Kittleson, Co. I, 21 Inf. Sp. Am. War (Pvt.,
            interred 26 Mar. 1918)

998   KLEIN Alvin C. Klein, Oct. 19, 1932, Ohio, Pvt. 308 Engrs., 83
            Div. (interred 25 Oct. 1932)

331   KLEINER William A. Kleiner, Co. D, 14 U. S. Inf. (Cpl., interred
            15 June 1887)

930   KNOX Edith A. Knox, Jan. 16, 1887 - June 17, 1974, Wife of Col.
            T. M. Knox, U. S. A.

927   KNOX Edith Patricia Knox, Born in Kentucky Aug. 26, 1906 - Died
            at Vancouver, Wa Apr. 15, 1928, Love, Courage, Peace (inter-
            red 19 Apr. 1928, daughter of Col. T. M. Knox)

929   KNOX Thomas M. Knox, May 13, 1880 - Apr. 6, 1963, Col. Q. M. C.,
            WW I, Oregon (interred 20 May 1963)

872   KOCH Elizabeth Koch, Mar. 22, 1937, Wife of Sgt. Michael Koch,
            U. S. A. (interred 25 Mar. 1937)

871   KOCH Michael Koch, Sept. 28, 1929, Texas, 1st Sgt., U. S. Army
            (interred 30 Sept. 1929)

643   KOZLER Anthony Kozler, Co. A., 19 U. S. Inf. (Cook - interred
            28 Apr. 1919)

    1879R   KRAFT Mary Kraft, d Aug. 13, 1857

909   KREYSER August Kreyser, 1847 - 1929, Reg. Q. M. Sgt. Ret. (in-
            terred 14 Nov. 1929)

908   KREYSER Frances Kreyser, 1853 - 1935, Wife of August Kreyser
            (interred 27 Nov. 1935)

1042   KREYSER Gus Kreyser, Oct. 13, 1939, Washington, M. Sgt. U. S.
                   Army (interred 17 Oct. 1939)

541   KREYSER Josephine L. Kreyser (Sgt., interred 30 Sept. 1918)

374   KUBIAK Albert Kubiak, Born at Rokorr, Prussia - Died at Vancouver
                   Bks., Co. F, 14 Inf., Erected by Co. F, 14 Infantry (Pvt.,
                   interred 9 Dec. 1895)

590   LAFFEAR David Laffear, Co. B,, 4 Minnesota Inf., Sp. Am. War
                   (interred 8 Aug. 1918)

   1879R   LAFRAMBERNE Z. Laframberne, d. Sept. 4, 1858

---   LAIPPLE Anna Laipple, 1888 - 1964

862   LAIPPLE Anna M. Laipple, 1873 - 1945 (interred 2 Oct. 1945, wife
                   of Sgt. John J. Laipple)

864   LAIPPLE Charles F. Laipple, 1891 - 1929, A. E. F., Corp'l 256th
                   Medical Corps (interred 24 Nov. 1929)

863   LAIPPLE John J. Laipple, 1853 - 1929 (Sgt., interred 2 June
                   1929)

---   LAIPPLE John J. Laipple, 1890 - 1966

521   LAMB Archie F. Lamb, Co. E, 1 U. S. Art. (Pvt., interred 8 Sept.
                   1910)

916   LAMB Ellen A. Lamb, Mar. 4, 1856 - Dec. 19, 1949, Wife of Sgt.
                   A. F. Lamb, U. S. A. (interred 22 Dec. 1949)

405   LANSING Eug.' Lansing, Co. F, 7 U. S. Inf. (Eugene Lansing, Pvt.
                   interred 4 Nov. 1901)

452   LAPSLEY Dorothy M. Lapsley, Child (interred 28 Dec. 1905, dau-
                   ghter of J. M. Lapsley)

971   LAPSLEY Joseph M. Lapsley, 1865 - 1931, Father (interred 2 Nov.
                   1931)

1141   LARSEN Edward Larsen, Jan. 10, 1941, Minnesota, Master Sgt., U. S.
                   Army (interred 14 Jan. 1941)

1035   LARSEN Minnie Larsen, June 27, 1939, Wife of Peter Larsen, U. S.
                   A. (interred 1 July 1939)

1267   LARSEN Peter Larsen, May 25, 1877 - Aug. 26, 1949, Washington,
                   1st Lieutenant, U. S. Army, WW I

1142   LARSEN Phyllis Drew Larsen, Aug. 7, 1894 - Sept. 10, 1965, Wife
                   of M. Sgt. Edward Larsen (interred 14 Sept. 1965)

1192   LARSON Howard Gustave Larson, Nov. 9, 1921 - Feb. 12, 1944, Wash-
                   ington, Coxswain, U. S. Navy (interred 19 Feb. 1944)

1883R   LARSON Waldmer Larson, Dec. 7, 1873, Pvt., Co. E, 21st U. S. Inf.

1883R   LAVILLE _____Laville, Pvt. Co. G., 1st U. S. Cav.

837   LAWS Clement M. Laws, Born Apr. 2, 1861, Died Dec. 6, 1928,
               Faithful in Enlisted and Civilian Service from 1881 - 1922,
               A friend of man (interred 9 Dec. 1928)

838   LAWS Rosa K. Laws, Dec. 17, 1870 - May 7, 1965 (wife of Sgt.
               Clement M. Laws)

399   LAWS Thomas J. Laws, Born July 31, 1869 - Killed in battle at
               Imus, P. I. June 13, 1899, With life and name unstrained, the
               good man dies (Sgt., interred 8 Jan. 1900)

556   LAWSON Mary Lawson (interred 11 Jan. 1914, domestic of Cpt.
               Sweeney)

1879R   LEARY Joseph Leary, d. Apr. 14, 1856

1883R   LEBENTHAL Louis Lebenthal, July 28, 1869, Pvt. Co. K, 23rd U. S.
               Inf.

369   LEE (Child) Lee (interred 24 Nov. 1894, daughter of H. L. Lee)

773   LEE Henry L. Lee, Mar. 3, 1927, Oregon, Warrant Officer, U. S.
               Army (interred Mar. 5, 1927)

589   LEFLORE Chas. Leflore, 21 Inf., U. S. A. (interred 7 Aug. 1917)

733   LEHMAN Fred Lehman, Dec. 25, 1924, California, Sgt. 7 Inf. (in-
               terred 29 Dec. 1924)

1249   LEIBFRIED Charles J. Leibfried, Sept. 10, 1893 - Aug. 12, 1955,
               Washington, 2D Lt., U. S. Army, WW I

1251   LEIBFRIED Charles L. Leibfried, Mar. 28, 1946, Washington, Cpl.
               11 Air Depot G. P. 1919 (son of Charles J. Liefried, inter-
               red 7 Apr. 1946)

1250   LEIBFRIED Marvel Leibfried, 1955, Wife of Chas. J. Leibfried
               (lot reserved)

940   LEITZEN Lillian L. Leitzen, 1879 - 1931 (wife of Cpl. Mathew
               Leitzen, interred 7 Apr. 1931)

941   LEITZEN Mathew Leitzen, 1876 - 1952 (Cpl., interred 11 Aug.
               1952)

1140   LeMAY Cecelia Mary LeMay, Dec. 25, 1943, Wife of 1 Sgt. F. E.
               LeMay, U. S. A. (interred 28 Dec. 1943)

1139   LeMAY Frank E. LeMay, Jan. 1, 1941, Maine, 1 Sgt. U. S. Army
               (interred 10 Jan. 1941)

1280   LEMON Holmes Willis Lemon, Sr., Oct. 3, 1923 - Dec. 28, 1978,
               CWO2, U. S. Army, WW II & Korea (interred 2 Jan. 1979)

32

POST CEMETERY

318   LENYHAM Cornelius Lenyham, Co. A, 14th U. S. Inf. (Pvt.,
           interred 24 Dec. 1885)

793   LEONBERGER Bessie M. Leonberger

793   LEONBERGER William Leonberger, W. O., U. S. Army, WWI, 6 Nov.
           1881 - 15 Dec. 1925 (interred 17 Dec. 1925)

01   LEONHARDT Friedrick Leonhardt, 17 Apr. 1945, Pvt. 1 Cl., German
           (POW - German)

583   LERIS Gus M. Leris, Co. E, 21 U. S. Inf. (Pvt., interred
           29 Nov. 1916)

1150   LESH Elmer Ray Lesh, 30 July 1941, California, U. S. Navy
           (Mch. Mate 1st Class, interred 2 Aug. 1941)

1059   LESLIE Lucy A. Leslie, 18 Mar. 1934, Wife of Staff Sgt. W. R.
           Leslie, Q.M.C. (interred 21 Mar. 1934)

1058   LESLIE William Raymond Leslie, 18 Sept. 1882 - 24 Mar. 1955,
           Washington, M. Sgt., U. S. Army, WWI (interred 28 Mar. 1955)

560   LEVINGSTON John Levingston, Co. B, 6 East Tennessee Inf.
           (Pvt., interred 1 June 1914)

396   LEWIS Henry Lewis, Sgt., 14th U. S. Inf. (interred 8 Jan.
           1900)

271   LEWIS Kate Lewis, Died 5 Jan. 1859, Aged 1 yr. 5 mos., Daughter
           of E. H. & L. Lewis (interred 6 Jan. 1859)

42   LIPP Michael Lipp, Died 12 Dec. 1870, Aged 38 yrs., Born in
           Germany (Pvt., Ord. Dept.)

1070   LIVINGSTON Hugh Livingston, 12 July 1935, Son of 2nd Lt. R. W.
           Sellers, U.S.A.)

592A   LOFTON Russell Lofton, Infant (interred 16 Nov. 1917, son of
           Cpl. Lofton)

698   LOOMIS James A. Loomis, 4 Dec. 1922, Ohio, 1st Sgt., U. S.
           Army (interred 6 Dec. 1922)

317   LORENZO Jacob Lorenzo, Co. H, 14th U. S. Inf. (Pvt., interred
           21 Mar. 1885)

1069   LORMER Edward Lormer, 24 Jan. 1935, Washington, Sgt., U. S.
           Army (interred 27 Jan. 1935)

       LORYEA Infant Loryea

576   LORYEA Lellia Loryea, Infant (interred 22 Oct. 1918, Grand-
           daughter of Loryea)

667   LOUDEN Mary J. Louden (interred 4 Dec. 1920)

532   LOUIS   John G. Louis, Sergt., Co. I, 4 U. S. Cav. (interred
                    10 Mar. 1912)

1240   LUCAS   Ralph L. Lucas, 27 Apr. 1914 - 3 July 1945, Oregon,
                    Pvt., 7 Inf. (interred 7 July 1945)

832   LUCH   Henry Luch, 24 July 1928, Pvt., 14 Inf., Oregon (inter-
                    red 26 July 1928)

824   LUDDERS   Ferdinand Ludders, 28 Nov. 1927, Sgt., 21 U. S. Inf.
                    (interred 1 Dec. 1927)

842   LUDEMAN   Albert Ludeman, 23 Jan. 1941, Washington, 1 Lt., U. S.
                    Army (interred 27 Jan. 1941)

844   LUDEMAN   Ella Ludeman, 10 July 1943, Wife of Master Sgt. Albert
                    Ludeman, U. S. A. (interred 19 July 1943)

843   LUDEMAN   Luella Jean Ludeman, 30 Jan. 1929, Child (interred
                    2 Feb. 1929, Daughter of M. Sgt. Albert Ludeman)

305   LUNDY   E. J. Lundy, Co. D., 21st U. S. Inf. (Elvas J. Lundy,
                    Pvt., interred 13 Mar. 1878)

803   LUSTER   Archie C. Luster, Co. M., 2 U. S. V. Engrs., Sp. Am.
                    War (Pvt., interred 24 May 1927)

804   LUSTER   Ellen E. Luster, 31 Aug. 1879 - 11 Oct. 1957, Wife of
                    1 Cl. Pvt. A. C. Luster, U. S. A. (interred 15 Oct. 1957)

   1879R   McARDLE   William McArdle, died 3 Sept. 1865

387   McCABE   Michael McCabe, Ord. Sgt., U. S. A. Retired (Sgt.,
                    interred 6 Oct. 1898)

821   McCAFFREY   William McCaffrey, 22 Sept. 1927, Pvt., 4 Engrs.,
                    4 Div., Mass. (interred 5 Oct. 1927)

390   McCAMMON   Alfred E. McCammon, Born 30 Aug. 1892 - Died 30
                    Apr. 1899, Son of W. W. & E. M. McCammon (interred 2 May
                    1899)

668   McCAMMON   Eda Marie McCammon (interred 22 Oct. 1920, Wife of
                    M. Wm. McCammon)

412   McCAMMON   W. W. McCammon, Major Retired, U. S. Army (William
                    W. McCammon, interred 28 Mar. 1903)

579   McCARTHY   Corp'l Edw'd McCarthy, Co. H, 14 U. S. Inf. (Cpl.
                    Edward McCarty, interred 23 Oct. 1915)

1039   McCARTHY   Florence P. McCarthy, 26 Sept. 1886 - 4 Nov. 1969,
                    Wife of Maj. Louis L. McCarthy)

352   McCARTHY   George McCarthy, Died 4 July 1890, Aged 26 yrs. 6
                    mos., Born in Chattanoga, Tenn. (Pvt.)

1039   McCARTHY   Louis L. McCarthy, 1883 - 1931, Major   (interred 11
                        Aug. 1931)

       1879R   McCARTY   Eliza McCarty,   died 11 Jan. 1872

       1879R   McCARTY   J. B. McCarty, died 9 June 1864

1013   McCLEARY   Roy A. McCleary, 29 Apr. 1933, Oregon, Pvt., 7 Inf.
                        (interred 5 May 1933)

830   McCOLLUM   Adam McCollum, 26 May 1928, Pvt., 14 Inf. (interred
                        30 May 1928)

536   McCORMICK   Thos. McCormick, Co. G, 21 U. S. Inf. (Thomas
                        McCormick, Cook, interred 23 June 1912)

259   McCOUNE   Henry McCoune (interred 29 Oct. 1860, Civilian)

338   McCOY   Katherine L. McCoy (interred 18 Feb. 1888, wife of
                        Lt. McCoy)

70   McCUE   Jno. McCue, Died 9 Feb. 1859, Co. B, 3rd U. S. Art.
                        (John McCue, Pvt., interred 10 Feb. 1859)

325   McDOUGAL   F. B. McDougal, 1 Lieut., 2nd California Inf. (in-
                        terred 15 Mar. 1862)

323   McDURALL   Thomas H. McDurall (Pvt., interred 13 Mar. 1858)

819   McENANY   Amy V. McEnany, 1868 - 1940, Mother (interred 16
                        April 1940, wife of Pvt. William McEnany)

819   McENANY   William H. McEnany, 1856 - 1927, Father (interred
                        21 Sept. 1927)

387   McGAGE   Mich McGage, Ord. Sgt., U. S. A. Retired

402   McGEE   Corp'l J. J. McGee, Co. G., 14 U. S. Inf. (John J.
                        McGee)

       1879R   McGUIRE   Jas. McGuire, died 7 Dec. 1861

274   McGUIRE   J. J. McGuire, Civilian, died 17 Jan. 1864 (James J.
                        McGuire, interred 18 Jan. 1864)

546   McINTYRE   John P. McIntyre, Co. G., 21 U. S. Inf. (Pvt., in-
                        terred 24 Jan. 1913)

       1883R   McKAY   David McKay, Child

356   McKINNEY   T. J. McKinney, Hosp. Corps, U. S. A. (Thomas J.
                        McKinney, Pvt., interred 17 July 1891)

       1879R   McMANUS   O. McManus

876   McMILLAN   David McMillan, 16 Dec. 1929, New York, Seaman, U. S.
                        Navy (interred 19 Dec. 1929)

479   McPHERSON   Alex McPherson (Sgt., interred 8 Oct. 1919)

1208   McRAE   Anna Ellen McRae, 5 July 1892 - 5 Sept. 1973, Wife of
                    MSG. R. W. McRae, U. S. A. (interred 7 Sept. 1973)

1207   McRAE   Robert W. McRae, 1 Jan. 1892 - 17 Sept. 1944, Oregon,
                    Master Sgt., U. S. Army (interred 20 Sept. 1944)

1036   McROBERTS   Harold B. McRoberts, 5 Jan. 1940, Washington, Sgt.
                    Inf. (interred 8 Jan. 1940)

503   McSPARREN   Margaret McSparren, 23 Feb. 1909 (interred 26 Feb.
                    1909, wife of J. McSparren)

    1879R   MAHLON   W. F. Mahlon, died 22 Aug. 1864, Capt., 1st Oregon Inf.

966   MAITLAND   John W. Maitland, New York (Pvt., interred 17 Oct.
                    1931)

    1879R   MAJSOVITCH   Margaretta Majsovitch, died 13 June 1873

1054   MAKALOUS   Joseph Makalous, 7 Dec. 1932, Kansas, 1st Sgt.,
                    U. S. Army (interred 14 Dec. 1932)

1156   ·   MAKLEY   Fred A. Makley, 1 Nov. 1941, Washington, 1 Sgt., Coast
                    Arty. Corps (interred 12 Nov. 1941)

1187   MALLOY   Francis Malloy, died 30 Jan. 1944 (interred 31 Jan.
                    1944)

1005   MANEELY   William J. Maneely, 7 Mar. 1933, Washington, Pvt.,
                    321, Inf. 81 Div. (interred 9 Mar. 1933)

    1879R   MARKING   Louisa S. Marking, died 25 July 1864

626A   MARLEY   Infant Marley (interred 18 May 1919, daughter of Sgt.
                    Marley)

1122   MARSHALL   Rodney Paul Marshall, 28 June 1938, Son of Pvt. L. P.
                    Marshall, U. S. A. (infant son, interred 29 June 1938)

    1879R   MARTIN   Charles Martin, died 11 Oct. 1865, Pvt., Co. K, 1st
                    Oregon Inf.

576A   MARTIN   Delbert A. Martin, Infant (interred 21 June 1915, son
                    of Earl C. Martin)

874   MARTIN   Earle Clifford Martin, 27 Aug. 1885 - 3 Apr. 1957, Wash-
                    ington, Pvt., 4 Reg't Field Arty. (interred 8 Apr. 1957)

984   MARTIN   Edwin J. Martin, 7 Apr. 1932, Washington, Pvt., Horse-
                    shoer, 16 Inf. 1 Div. (interred 9 Apr. 1932)

662A   MARTIN   Elda K. Martin, 19 Aug. 1923, Washington, 1st Sgt.,
                    U. S. Marine Corps

644   MARTIN   Everett E. Martin, Corpl., Marine Corps (interred 21
                    June 1919)

150   MARTIN Louisa S. Martin (interred 25 July 1864, wife of G. W.
                Martin)

873   MARTIN Nellie L. Martin, Wife of Pvt. E. C. Martin, U. S. A.,
                14 Nov. 1921 (interred 16 Nov. 1921)

1148   MASLACH Albert Maslach, 19 June 1941, California, M. Sgt., 19
                Air Base Group (interred 21 June 1941)

4   MASON William F. Mason, Capt., 1st W. T. Infantry U. S. Vol.,
                Born in Kentucky, Died at Ft. Vancouver, W. T., 22 Aug.
                1864, Aged 36 Yrs. Erected to his memory by the officers
                of his regiment. (interred 23 Aug. 1864)

997   MATNEY Jimmy W. Matney, 28 Feb. 1951, Oregon, Fireman 2 Cl.,
                U. S. Navy

561   MAXWELL Lieut. Geo. W. Maxwell, Co. B, 1 Oregon Rangers, Indian
                War (2 Lt., interred 2 June 1914, George W. Maxwell)

568   MAY Esther May (wife of Pvt. Thomas May, interred 26 Dec. 1918)

1213   MAY Hortense May, 15 Oct. 1862 - 18 Sept. 1949 (mother of
                1 Sgt. R. E. Dunbar, interred 22 Sept. 1949)

568   MAY Thos. May, Co H, 7 Illinois Inf. (Pvt. Thomas May, inter-
                red 2 Nov. 1914)

363   MAYER Henry E. Mayer (interred 20 Feb. 1893, son of F. Mayer)

358   MAYER J. J. Mayer, Civilian (Joseph J. Mayer, interred 1 Oct.
                1891)

---   MAYNARD Nan Maynard, 14 Oct. 1877 - 16 Nov. 1973, Granddaughter
                of Maj. William Kelly

229   MAZZANOVICH A. Mazzanovich, Child

230   MAZZANOVICH Margareta Mazzanovich, Born in Austria 18 July
                1837 - Died 13 June 1873, Wife of Lorenzo Mazzanovich
                (interred 14 June 1873)

434   MEISEL Joseph Meisel, Sgt. 1st Cl., Hosp. Corp., U. S. A.
                (interred 14 Dec. 1904)

1883R   MENHIMUET (____) Menhimuet, Child, died 9 May 1878

264   MEYERS Adeline Meyers, 24 Sept. 1931 (interred 28 Sept. 1931)

672   MEYERS Jas. H. Meyers, Co. K, 148 Pennsylvania Inf. (James H.
                Meyers, interred 24 Nov. 1920)

1879R   MILLER Frederick Miller, died 15 Dec. 1860

1879R   MILLER Frederick Miller, died 27 May 1862

1879R   MILLER John Miller, died 4 Oct. 1860

623   MILLER   Louis W. Miller, Mortar Trans. Corps., U. S. A.   (Cpl.,
                        interred 4 Dec. 1918)

904   MILLER   Marion Miller, 30 Sept. 1931

866   MILLER   Ralph A. Miller, 9 July 1929, Washington, Pvt. 1 Cl.,
                        Finance Dept.   (interred 21 July 1929)

      1879R   MILLER   Rhoda Miller, died 6 Nov. 1868

726   MILLER   Verle Douglas Miller, 29 July 1914 - 15 May 1977, Col.,
                        U. S. Army, WWII   (interred 25 May 1977)

977   MINKLER   John W. Minkler, Iowa   (Pvt., interred 7 Jan. 1932)

436   MODEEN   Chester B. Modeen, Co. A, 4 U. S. Field Art.   (interred
                        11 June 1909)

1060   MOLINA   John A. Molina, Jr., 23 Aug. 1974, Son of Sp. 4 J. A.
                        Molina, Sr., U. S. A.   (interred 26 Aug. 1974

      1879R   MONCHEN   Lee Monchen, died 13 May 1867

449   MONTGOMERY   J. W. Montgomery, Chf. M. U. S. N., 14 U. S. Inf.
                        (interred 17 Aug. 1905, John Montgomery)

1126   MOODY   Herschel A. Moody, 7 Inf., died Sept. 1, 1938   (PFC, in-
                        terred 23 Sept. 1938)

      1883R   MOONEY   Lawrence Mooney, Cpl., Co. A, 4th U. S. Art.

744   MOORE   Annie C. Moore, 1 Feb. 1939   (interred 4 Feb. 1939,
                        mother of MSG James A. Moore)

      1879R   MOORE   Edward Moore, Co. K, 4th U. S. Inf., died Jan. 31, 1860

510   MOORE   Frank M. Moore, Clerk, A. G. Dept.   (interred 15 Aug.
                        1909)

      1883R   MOORE   Harry De Witt Moore, 9 May 1878, Lt., Co. F, 21st U. S.
                        Inf.

743   MOORE   Joseph G. Moore, Co. G, 28 Illinois Inf.   (Pvt., inter-
                        red 12 Aug. 1925)

1266   MOORE   Robert Dewey Moore, SFC, U. S. Army, WWII, 2 May 1918 -
                        23 Feb. 1978   (interred 28 Feb. 1978, retired)

550   MOORE   Valentine Moore, Inf.   (interred 5 June 1913, Stillborn
                        son of J. N. Moore)

---   MOPHERSON   Alex Mopherson, U. S. Army

240   MORAN   Eliza Moran   (interred 17 May 1860)

1037   MORGAN   Amos Morgan, 30 Jan. 1940, 1 Sgt., U. S. Army   (interred
                        2 Feb. 1940)

1021   MORIARITY Emilia Moriarity, 1865 - 1932, Mother, At Rest
            (interred 21 Feb. 1932, wife of Pvt. Eugene Moriarity)

380   MORRIS   C. C. Morris, Band, 14 U. S. Inf. (Charles C. Morris,
            Pvt., interred 24 July 1896)

---   MORRIS   William T. Morris, Died in P. I. 14 May 1901, aged
            48 yrs. 4 mos. 14 ds.

409   MORRIS   W. T. Morris, PR. MUS'N, 16 U. S. Inf. (interred
            14 May 1901)

1171   MORRISON   John Spencer Morrison, 11 Mar. 1943, Son of Tech.
            Sgt. S. G. Morrison, U. S. A. (interred 23 Mar. 1943)

1170   MORRISON   Spencer Gibson Morrison, 17 Mar. 1943, California,
            2 Lieut. U. S. Army (interred 23 Mar. 1943)

1172   MORRISON (Lot reserved for Mrs. Spencer G. Morrison)

530   MORSE   Fred D. Morse, Chief MUS'N, 14 U. S. Inf. (interred
            14 Nov. 1911)

341   MORTON   Arthur C. Morton, Died 3 Jan. 1888, Aged 32 yrs.,
            Sergt., Co. A, 14 Inf., In Memory Of

1103   MORTON   Caro Emelia Morton, 18 Sept. 1937, Daughter of Sgt.
            George Morton, U. S. A. (interred 20 Sept. 1937)

697   MOSER   Albert Moser, 8 Oct. 1922, Louisiana, Corp'l., 7 Inf.
            (interred 10 Oct. 1922)

858   MOSIER   John Hector Mosier, 8 May 1929, Oregon, Fireman 3 Cl.,
            U. S. Navy (interred 11 May 1929)

632   MOUSER   Earold D. Mouser, Air Service U. S. A. (Pvt., interred
            5 Jan. 1919)

184   MOWDER   S. A. Mowder, Born 19 Dec. 1832 - Deid 13 May 1867, In
            Memory Of, Here by the king of terror reign, Fire links
            composed the chain, One link is broken but soon in Heaven,
            God shall join each link again. (interred 14 May 1867)

1883R   MOYAR Nancy Moyar, Laundry, B 1, U. S. Cav.

766   MSCHICHOWSKI Boleslaus Mschichowski, 1 Sept. 1889 - 20 Apr.
            1975, 1 SG, U. S. Army (interred 2 May 1975)

1879R   MUHOLLAND   James B. Muholland (no further info.)

1883R   MUNSON   Dr. W. C. Munson, Citizen

515   MURPHY   Michael J. Murphey, Sgt. Co. A, 14th U. S. Inf. (in-
            terred 27 Dec. 1909)

615   NAPIER   Wm. J. Napier, U. S. Army (Pvt., interred 1918)

355   NELLY   Edw'd Don Nelly, Co. G., 14 U. S. Inf.

----   NELSEL   1st G.L. Sgt. Jos. Nelsel, Hosp. Corps, U. S. A.

368   NELSON   (Child) Nelson   (interred 26 Aug. 1894, infant son of Pvt.
                 J. W. Nelson)

----   NELSON   John Nelson, U. S. A., 1849 - 1925

----   NELSON   Josephine Nelson, 1852 - 1930, Wife of John Nelson

740   NICHOLS   Theodore Nichols, Co. C, 36 Wisconsin Inf.   (interred
                 2 July 1925)

108   NOBLE   Catherine Noble, Died 6 May 1852, Aged 19 Yrs. 7 Mos. 13
                 Dys., I. H. S., Wife of John F. Noble   (interred 7 May 1852)

569   NOLLE   Felix Nolle, Co. A, 1 Colorado Inf.   (interred 29 Jan. 1915)

624   NORTHERN   Howard L. Northern, 5 Dec. 1918   (interred 6 Dec. 1918)

   1879R   NYE   George W. Nye, Citizen, died 1 June 1853

   1879R   NYE   John W. Nye, died 12 Feb. 1866

55   OBERLANDER Jno. Oberlander, Co. D, 23rd U. S. Inf.   (John Ober-
                 lander, Pvt., interred 28 Dec. 1875)

   1883R   O'BRIEN   Richard O'Brien, Died 5 ___ 1879, Pvt., Co. L, 1st U. S.
                 Cav.

----   O'CALLAGHAN   Geo. A. O'Callaghan, 2 U. S. Inf.

   1879R   O'CONNELL   John O'Connell, Died 5 Dec. 1867, Sergt., Co. I, 1st
                 U. S. Cav.

660   O'DELL   Sam'l B. O'Dell, Co. C, 44 U. S. Inf.   (interred 7 Jan. 1920)

993   OFTEN   Infant Often, 23 July 1937, Son of Pvt. C. V. Often   (interred
                 25 July 1937)

519   O'GORMAN   Wm. O'Gorman, Co. D, 14 U. S. Inf.   (interred 27 May 1910)

859   O'HARA   John O'Hara, Ohio   (Pvt., interred 19 May 1929)

446   O'HARA   Pat'k O'Hara, Co. E, 19 U. S. Inf.   (Pvt., interred 30 July
                 1905)

1219   OHLEMEYER   William Charles Ohlemeyer, 5 Nov. 1923 - 14 Nov. 1944,
                 Washington, Ensign U. S. N. R.   (interred 22 Nov. 1944)

   1879R   O'KAN   Kate O'Kan, died 23 Aug. 1864

   1879R   O'KAN   Mary O'Kan, died 28 Sept. 1864

----   OLAVBERG   Alaska Olavberg, 25 Apr. 1933, Pvt., 166 Depot Brig.

67   O'LEARY Mich'l O'Leary, Co. A, 3rd U. S. Art. (Pvt., died 8 Feb.
              1859, interred 9 Feb. 1859)

1009   OLSON Axel Olson, 10 Apr. 1933, Pvt. 4, U. S. Inf. (interred 12
              Apr. 1933)

1008   OLSON Martin Olson, 29 Mar. 1933, North Dakota, Pvt., Motor Trans.
              Corps (interred 2 Apr. 1933)

74   OLIVER Elizabeth Oliver, Died 22 Oct. 1879 Aged 49 Years, Wife
              of James Oliver, My Wife

307   OLIVER James Oliver, Ord'n Dept., U. S. A. (Sgt., interred 5
              Sept. 1880)

441   ONAHUNDRA Margaret Onahundra, died 4 June 1905, aged 52 Yrs. (In-
              terred 5 June 1905, wife of Sgt. S. S. Onahundra. This stone
              spelling is OMOHUNDRO while husband's stone is spelled ONAHUNDRA)

439   ONAHUNDRA Samuel S. Onahundra, 23 Apr. 1860 - 7 May 1905, Maryland,
              Color Sgt., 19 Inf (interred 8 May 1905)

646   O'REAR Mallisa R. O'Rear (interred 4 Apr. 1921, wife of Wallace
              H. O'Rear)

---   O'REAR Wallace H. O'Rear, Co. G, 11 Indiana Inf. (interred 16 July
              1919)

747   ORTSEIFER Theodore M. Ortseifer, 14 Sept. 1925, Pvt., 1 Inf. (in-
              terred 17 Sept. 1925)

58   O'SHEA Thomas O'Shea, Died Ft. Vancouver, W. T. 15 Apr. 1869, Co. D,
              23 U. S. Inf., 1 Sgt.

435   OUTEN Charles H. Outen, Co. G, 14th U. S. Inf. (Pvt., interred
              15 Jan. 1905)

1883R   PACKARD McKenzie Packard, died 15 Dec. 1863, Pvt. Co. C, 1st Ore.
              Vols.

1226   PAGE Robert Ernest Page, 13 Feb. 1923 - 19 Jan. 1946, Washington,
              Motor Mach. Mate 2 Cl., WWII (interred 24 Jan. 1946)

762   PALMER George W. Palmer, 1888 - 1926 (Sgt., interred 20 Mar. 1926)

933   PANCOAST William F. Pancoast, 13 Mar. 1951, Washington, Pvt. 14
              U. S. Inf. (interred 18 Mar. 1951)

654   PARSHALL Arthur J. Parshall (Cpl., interred 18 Nov. 1919)

1879R   PATCHER Michael Patcher died 12 Feb. 1869

1023   PATTERSON Edah Patterson (interred 19 May 1932, wife of Frank
              Patterson)

1027   PATTERSON Frank Patterson (interred 19 May 1932, Son of Pvt.
              Harold Patterson)

962   PAUL   Bertha Augusta Paul, 12 Aug. 1878 - 21 Dec. 1956, Wife of
        Major William Paul, U. S. A. (interred 26 Dec. 1956)

963   PAUL   William Paul, 6 Aug. 1879 - 21 July 1953, Washington, Major
        Q M, Res. - S.A.W. & W.W.I. (interred 24 July 1953)

1128   PAYNE   Elizabeth M. Payne, 13 Mar. 1959 (wife of 1 Sgt. Edward
        Payne)

979   PEARSON   Andrew Pearson, Illinois (Pvt., interred 2 Feb. 1932)

400   PERDUE   Charles Perdue, Co. D, 6th U. S. Inf.

794   PERDUE   Charles W. Perdue (Pvt., interred 15 July 1926)

419   PETERSEN   Emilie E. Petersen (interred 11 Aug. 1903, Daughter of
        Chris Peterson)

752   PETERSEN   James Petersen, 1870 - 1925, Father (1 Sgt., interred
        3 Nov. 1925)

753   PETERSEN   Sophie Petersen, 1875 - 1958, Mother (interred 4 Dec.
        1958, wife of 1 Sgt. James Peterson)

1065   PETTERSON   Johan E. Petterson, 7 Nov. 1934, New Jersey, Pvt. 7 Inf.,
        (interred 13 Nov. 1934)

448   PFISTERER   H. Pfisterer, Co. D, 14 U. S. Inf. (Herman Pfisterer,
        Pvt., interred 8 Aug. 1905, Medal of Honor winner - see story
        following this section)

822   PFUNDT   Maj. Franz Pfundt, 1870 - 1927, 2 Inf., Co. B, 2nd U. S.
        Inf., Tech. Sgt. QMC (interred 8 Nov. 1927)

655   PHILLIPS   Andrew Phillips, 31 Aug. 1912   - 5 Nov. 1974, SFC, U. S.
        Army (interred 11 Nov. 1974)

388   PHILLIPS   (Child) Phillips (interred 18 Dec. 1898)

895   PHILLIPS   Isaac Phillips, 1854 - 19__, Sgt., Co. B, 1st Batt. Eng.
        (lot reserved 3 Sept. 1930)

894   PHILLIPS   Mary F. Phillips, 1858 - 1930 (interred 3 Sept. 1930,
        wife of Sgt. Isaac Phillips)

483   PIERCY   J. T. Piercy, Co. A, 4 Field Art. (James T. Piercy, Pvt.,
        interred 13 Feb. 1908)

1086   PIERSON   Daniel A. Pierson, 5 May 1944 (interred 8 May 1944)

1084   PIERSON   Maude Pierson, 16 Mar. 1886 - 18 June 1975 (interred 20
        June 1975)

06   PLANKER   Jakob Planker, 3 Aug. 1945, Cpl., German (P.O.W., German)

597   POLEY   Monte B. Poley, 31 May 1931, Oregon, Sgt., Coast Art. Corps

781   POLLARD   Andrew Merrill Pollard, 5 July 1907 - 3 Sept. 1975, LTC,
            U. S. Army

1155   POLLOCK   LeRoy L. Pollock, 21 Oct. 1941, Washington, Pvt., 11 Field
            Arty. (interred 29 Oct. 1941)

1131   POMERENE   Rose Bartlett Pomerene (died 5 Aug. 1959, interred 8 Aug.
            1959, wife of Maj. J. D. Pomerene)

784   POTTER   Allen G. Potter, 9 Nov. 1925, New York, Ord. Sgt., U. S.
            Army (interred 11 Nov. 1925)

---   POTTER   Eliza Potter

718   POWELL   Frank D. Powell, 11 Jan. 1924, Pennsylvania, Pvt., QM Corps
            (interred 14 Jan. 1924)

810   POWELL   James Powell, Jr., 12 May 1927 (interred 14 May 1927)

1254   POWERS   Robert William Powers, 26 Oct. 1907 - 5 Mar. 1971, SFC.
            H H C, 2 BG 47 Inf., WW II, Korea (interred 11 Mar. 1971)

1061   PRICE   Jacob W. Price, 5 May 1934, Pennsylvania, Tech. Sgt., U. S.
            Army (interred 9 May 1934)

580   PRUTZMAN   Jacob D. Prutzman, Co. D, 150 Pennsylvania Inf. (interred
            23 Nov. 1915)

693   PRUTZMAN   Malilba Prutzman (interred 21 May 1922, wife of Jacob D.
            Prutzman)

612   PULLMAN   Jesse A. Pullman, 3 Recruit Co., U. S. A. (interred 18
            Nov. 1919)

1879R   PULSKY   Annie Pulsky, died June 1873

1093   PURCELL   Bruce Purcell, 5 Dec. 1944, Indiana, Captain 13 Engineer
            Co., WW I (interred 7 Dec. 1944)

1093   PURCELL   Selma S. Purcell, 14 July 1889 - 10 June 1972 (interred
            23 June 1972, wife of Capt. Bruce Purcell)

522   QUEEN   Violet M. Queen, Child (interred 19 Sept. 1910)

1879R   QUINN   W. A. Quinn, died 29 July 1868

228   QUINN   W. A. Quinn (William A. Quinn, interred 30 Jan. 1868)

665   RACIOOT   Gladys Racioot (interred 26 May 1920, Step-daughter of
            Sgt. Kibbler)

125   RADARDT   Chas. Radardt, Ord'n Dept. U. S. A.

602   RADONSKI   August Radonski, 27 June 1918, Washington, Pvt., 407
            Aero Cons. Sq., WW I

492   RADTKA   Chas. Radtka, Hosp. Corps, U. S. A.   (Charles Radtka, PFC,
            interred 7 Oct. 1908)

83   RAHARDT   Adolph C. Rahardt   (interred 14 Aug. 1871)

136   RAHARDT   Chas. Rahardt, Ord. Dept., U. S. A.   (PFC, died 14 Aug. 1871,
            interred 15 Aug. 1871)

1109   RASPPERY   Karl Rasppery   (interred 3 June 1977, no stone)

---   RAWLEY   Louisa P. Rawley, 31 May 1930

---   REARDON   Edmond A. Reardon, 1887 - 19__

---   REARDON   Edmond A. Reardon, Jr., 1930 - ____

1041   REARDON   Lillian R. Reardon, 1902 - 1932   (interred 4 Mar. 1932, wife
            of MSG Edward A. Reardon)

732   REED   Thomas H. Reed, 14 Nov. 1924, New Jersey, Pvt., 10 Inf.   (in-
            terred 17 Nov. 1924)

694   REEVES   Riley A. Reeves, Co. B, 48 Indiana Inf.   (Pvt., interred 17
            June 1922)

694A   REEVES   Sarah L. Reeves, 2 Nov. 1944, Wife of Pvt. R. A. Reeves, U. S.
            A.   (interred 5 Nov. 1944, wife of Pvt. Riley A. Reeves)

---   REIMBACH   J. W. Reimbach, Civilian

688   REMICK   Harriet A. Remick   (interred 5 Feb. 1922, wife of Franklin
            Remick)

727   RENART   Michael J. Renart, 23 Oct. 1925, New York, Pvt., 21 Inf.
            (interred 24 Oct. 1925)

923   REVENEW   Ida M. Revenew, 12 Feb. 1931, Wife of W. H. Revenew   (in-
            terred 13 Feb. 1931)

456   REVENEW   Infant Revenew   (interred 4 May 1906, Daughter of Pvt.
            William Revenew)

496   REVENEW   Mary D. Revenew, Infant   (interred 18 Sept. 1909, Dau-
            ghter of W. II. Revenew)

1182A   REXROAD   Esther Jean Rexroad, 4 Nov. 1896 - 28 July 1965, Wife of
            S 1 L. L. Rexroad, U. S. N. R.   (interred 30 July 1965, wife
            of Seaman Lawrence L. Rexroad)

1180   REXROAD   Lawrence Lee Rexroad, 23 Aug. 1943, Washington, Seaman 1 Cl.,
            U. S. N. R.   (interred 24 Aug. 1943)

797   REYNOLDS   Charles Reynolds, 12 Sept. 1931, Pennsylvania, 1st Sgt.,
            U. S. Army

796   REYNOLDS   Isabelle Reynolds, 20 Feb. 1927   (wife of 1 Sgt. Charles
            Reynolds)

    1883R   RHODES Anna Rhodes, Citizen

308   RICE Charles Rice (Pvt., interred 17 Sept. 1880)

308   RICE G. W. Rice, Band 21st U. S. Inf.

514   RICE Gertrude L. Rice, 1875 - 1909 (interred 18 Sept. 1909)

591   RICE Infant Rice (interred 27 Aug. 1917, Still-born, father - M. Rice)

---   RICE Nannie K. Rice, died 7 Apr. 1890

774   RICE Nannie Maynard Rice, 1877 - 1973 (Granddaughter of Major Wm. Kelly, interred 19 Nov. 1973)

447   RICHARDS Barbara Richards, Child (interred 14 Aug. 1905, daughter of R. L. Richards)

925   RICHARDS Hayden James Richards, 11 Mar. 1931, Washington, Pvt. 1 Cl., 30 Inf. (interred 14 Mar. 1931)

1004   RICHARDS Lee H. Richards, 1 Mar. 1933, Montana, Cook, 28 Inf., 1 Div. (interred 6 Mar. 1933)

421   'RICHARDSON Sentiticia Richardson (interred 4 Dec. 1903, wife of 1 Sgt. Richardson)

613   RICKMAN Timothy Rickman, Co. B, 14 U. S. Inf. (Pvt., interred 24 Oct. 1918)

335   RILEY Sylvester Riley, Sacred to the Memory Of, Co. G. 14 Inf., Born at New Orleans, La., Died 29 Sept. 1887, Erected by Members of Co. G. (Pvt., interred 30 Sept. 1887)

242   RINEBACK Joseph W. Rineback (interred 29 Apr. 1859)

   1883R   ROBERTS Geo. W. Roberts, Citizen, died 9 Feb. 1873

1179   ROBERTS Ira Roberts, 24 Aug. 1943 (lot reserved)

999   ROBERTS John Roberts, 15 Dec. 1882 - 27 Feb. 1973, M. Sgt., WW I (interred 3 Mar. 1973)

1178   ROBERTS Mae Roberts, 29 July 1943, Wife of Staff Sgt. Ira Roberts, U. S. A. (interred 9 Aug. 1943)

994   ROBERTS Ollie Mae Roberts, 1 Apr. 1900 - 29 Dec. 1975, Wife of M. Sgt. John Roberts, U. S. A. (interred 5 Jan. 1976)

1003   ROBERTS Virginia L. Roberts, 31 Feb. 1933, Daughter of Sgt. J. Roberts, U. S. A.

342   ROBERTSON Charles & Cady Robertson, Two Brothers, Sons of G. & E. Robertson, Died 28 Aug. 1888 - Died 24 May 1889

   1879R   ROBINSON Henry Robinson, Pvt. Co. F, 21st U. S. Inf., Died 7 June 1873

1135   ROBSON Gladys Robson, 25 Feb. 1904 – 23 Jan. 1979, Wife of S. S. G.
        Ira Roberts, U. S. A. (spelling on both names is correct as
        given)

1134   ROBSON Charles Robson, 15 Oct. 1940, Missouri, 1 Sgt., U. S. Army
        (interred 19 Oct. 1940)

1017   ROCKEY Infant Son Rockey, 26 Sept. 1933, Father Pvt. 1 Cl. M. J.
        Rockey, U. S. A. (interred 27 Sept. 1933)

1133   ROCKEY Michael John Rockey, 24 July 1895 – 17 Feb. 1977, SSG, U. S.
        Army (interred 25 Feb. 1977)

1111   ROGERS Abert F. Rogers, 28 Sept. 1937, Arkansas, Corp. 13 Cav. (in-
        terred 5 Oct. 1937)

1163   ROGERSON Catherine Viola Rogerson, 19 Jan. 1884 – 2 Aug. 1964, Wife
        of 1st Sgt. Thomas Rogerson, U. S. A. (interred _____1964)

1162   ROGERSON Thomas Rogerson, 12 Mar. 1942, Washington, 1 Sgt. Ord.
        Dept. (interred 17 Mar. 1942)

543   ROLFE Geo. Rolfe, 1st Sgt. Co. C, 19 U. S. Inf. (George Rolfe, in-
        terred 3 Dec. 1912)

44   ROLLA Indian Boy (interred 11 Aug. 1860)

1282   ROMINE Howard W. Romine, 6 July 1930 – 18 Jan. 1979, C. S. M., U. S.
        Army, Korea, Beloved Husband & Father (interred 22 Jan. 1979)

1879R   ROONEY L. Rooney, Co. H, 4th U. S. Inf., Killed in the Indian War

1068   ROSS Caroline B. Ross (interred 19 Sept. 1963, wife of PFC Charles
        Ross)

1068   ROSS Charles O. Ross, 29 June 1890 – 13 Nov. 1934, California, PFC
        Air Corps, WW I (interred 19 Nov. 1934)

249   ROSS Daniel Ross, In Memory Of, Died July 1861, Aged 35 Yrs. (in-
        terred 13 July 1861)

302   ROSS Edward C. Ross, Only Son of G. V. & Lieut. John M. Ross, 21 Inf.,
        Drowned at Fort Townsend, W. T., 25 Sept. 1873, Aged 6 Years.

1129   ROTH Charles J. Roth, 22 Feb. 1940, Kansas, Chief M U S, U. S. Army
        (interred 24 Feb. 1940)

1130   ROTH Mary Roth, 29 June 1869 – 20 Jan. 1951, Wife of Chief M U S,
        C. J. Roth, U. S. A. (interred 23 Jan. 1951)

1106   ROWLEY Beulah L. Rowley, 23 July 1937 (interred 26 July 1937,
        Mother-in-law of Sgt. Anderson)

886   ROWLEY Louisa P. Rowley (interred 4 June 1930)

626   RUSSELL Gilbert O. Russell, 4 June 1940, Oregon, Sgt. 15 Inf. (in-
        terred 6 June 1940)

1121   RUSSELL Thurlow J. Russell, 25 Apr. 1938, Washington, Pvt., Q.M.
            Corps (interred 25 Apr. 1938)

485   RYAN Pat'k Ryan, 1st Sgt., U. S. A. (interred 2 Mar. 1908, Patrick
            Ryan)

735   SAFRANEK John Safranek, 1841 - 1925, Band Master 12th Minnesota
            Vols., 1898, Chief Misician 34th U. S. Inf. 1899, Honorably Dis-
            charged 1900. Member of Wash. Lodge #4 F + AM, Vancouver, Wa.
            (interred 12 Feb. 1925)

960   SALMELA Aili Irene Salmela, 11 Oct. 1904 - 19 June 1964, Wife of
            Pvt. C. L. Salmela, U. S. A. (interred 22 June 1964)

959   SALMELA Charles L. Salmela, 1 Jan. 1894 - 16 Dec. 1966, Oregon,
            P H, Pvt., Co. H, 357 Inf., WW I (interred 20 Dec. 1966)

972   SALMON Louis Salmon, 1873 - 1931, 1st Sgt. U. S. Army (interred
            9 Nov. 1931)

973   SALMON Sallie Salmon, 20 Sept. 1917, Wife of Louis Salmon, U. S. A.

1073   SALMON Sallie Salmon (interred 4 Oct. 1947, Wife of M.S.G. Thomas
            Salmon, died 30 Sept. 1947)

1074   SALMON Thomas Salmon, 22 May 1936, Kentucky, Master Sgt., U. S. Army

577   SALVAGIN Anthony Salvagin (interred 27 June 1915)

585   SANGREEN Sergt. August Sangreen, Co. A, 1 U. S. Inf. (interred 18
            May 1918)

633   SARATIDES Gust Saratides, Air Service, U. S. A. (Pvt., interred
            10 Jan. 1919)

386   SAULS A. R. Sauls, U. S. Sig. Corps (Archie Sauls, PFC, interred
            29 Aug. 1898)

87 1879R   SAUDERS J. W. Sauders, Co. I, 21st U. S. Inf. (John W. Sauders,
            interred 8 Oct. 1872....stone and records spell Sauders as shown,
            but record 1879R gives this...John W. Saunders died 7 Oct. 1872)

1215   SAWYER Cecil Claude Sawyer, 16 Aug. 1897 - 20 Oct. 1944, Washington,
            Pvt., Chauffeur 656 Aero. Sq. (interred 22 Oct. 1944)

1149   SAYLES Clarence L. Sayles, 21 June 1941, Oregon, Pvt. 1 Cl., 162
            Inf. (interred 1 July 1941)

375   SCALDENBRAND Joseph Scaldenbrand, Co. E, 14 U. S. Inf. (Pvt., in-
            terred 13 Dec. 1895)

983   SCALLY Ann Scally, Mother of Capt. John S. Scally (interred 2 Apr.
            1932)

795   SCHERMERHORN George E. Schermerhorn, 8 Aug. 1926, New York, Sgt.,
            U. S. Army (interred 19 Aug. 1926)

---   SCHIER Alfred H. Schier, 3 June 1877 - 20 Dec. 1941, Illinois, M.
        Sgt., H & S Co., WW I

490   SCHLOSSER Sgt. Frank Schlosser, Band, 1 U. S. Inf. (interred 9 Sept.
        1908)

648   SCHNEIDER Anna Schneider (interred 19 Aug. 1919, wife)

857   SCHOENLEBER Frank J. Schoenleber, 3 May 1929, Missouri, Sgt. 7
        Field Art. (interred 7 May 1929)

946   SCHONBERG Eugene Schonberg, 21 Mar. 1936, New York, Capt. U. S.
        Army   (interred 24 Mar. 1936)

945   SCHONBERG Mrs. Eugene Schonberg (lot reserved 1 Apr. 1936)

664   SCHROEDER Theodore Schroeder, 1st Sgt., Co. A, 32 U. S. Inf. (in-
        terred 7 Dec. 1920)

701   SCHWERTNER George J. Schwertner, 8 Apr. 1894 - 10 Feb. 1923, Bakery
        Co. 325 AEF (Ch. MUS, interred 14 Feb. 1923)

---   SCHWILL Elisbar Elisbara Schwill, 6 Aug. 1945

1190   SCRIPTURE Harold P. Scripture, 2 May 1906 - 6 Feb. 1944, Washington,
        1 Lt. Corps of Mil. Police (interred 11 Feb. 1944)

513   SEAL Sgt. Labana D. Seal, Co. B, 14 U. S. Inf. (interred 9 Sept.
        1909)

1883R   SEELING Herman Seeling, Sgt., Co. A, 4th U. S. Art.

588   SEIB Anna M. Seib, 1874 - 1917, Wife of Christ F. Seib, Regt'l
        Supply Sergt. 21st Inf.

588   SEIB Frederick H. Seib, S. S. G. (interred 12 May 1971)

351   SEIFRIZ Anton Seifriz, Co. C, 14 U. S. Inf. (Pvt., interred 27 May
        1890)

461   SEIGLER C. H. Seigler, Band 19 U. S. Inf. (Pvt., interred 25 July
        1906)

1070   SELLERS Hugh Livingston Sellers, Infant, 12 July 1935 (son of 2 Lt.
        R. W. Sellers, U. S. A.)

451   SERGEANT 1st Sgt. B. O. Sergeant, Co. G, 19 U. S. Inf. (Bert. O.
        Sergeant, interred 20 July 1905)

1034   SEXTON Felix H. Sexton, 23 July 1938, California, Pvt. 1 Cl. 15 Inf.
        (interred 28 July 1938)

1189   SHACKELFORD Bishop K. Shackelford, 29 Aug. 1879 - 31 Jan. 1944,
        Kentucky, Captain U. S. Army

1188   SHACKELFORD Edna Cronk Shackelford, 4 Feb. 1887 - 11 May 1973,
        Washington, Wife of Capt. B. K. Shackelford, U. S. A. (interred
        16 May 1973)

849   SHAW   Harry Keith Shaw, 9 May 1931   (interred 11 May 1931, infant son of Sgt. Shaw)

640   SHAW   Thos. M. Shaw, Co. E, 4 U. S. Cav.   (Pvt. Thomas Shaw, interred 17 Mar. 1919)

639   SHAW   William M. Shaw, 16 Dec. 1930, Washington, Pvt., 21 Inf.   (interred 19 Dec. 1930)

1879R   SHAY   Joseph Shay, died 18 June 1859, Leader-Band, 4 U. S. Inf

1879R   SHEFFIELD   L. A. Sheffield, died 22 July 1858

291   SHEFFIELD   Phebe Sheffield   (interred 23 July 1858, Daughter)

607   SHELTON   Jas. Shelton, 37 Co., 10 Batt'n., 166 Depot Brig.   (James E. Shelton, Pvt., interred 25 Sept. 1918)

378   SHERINGER   Peter Sheringer, U. S. A., Retired   (Pvt.)

1158   SHIER   Alfred H. Shier, 3 June 1877 - 20 Dec. 1941, Illinois, H & S Co., 2nd Engineers, WW I   (MSG, interred 23 Dec. 1941)

1158   SHIER   Ella A. Shier, 28 Dec. 1895 - 23 June 1960   (wife of MSG Alfred H. Shier, interred 24 June 1960)

677   SHINABARGER   Hugh P. Shinabarger, Co. A, 37 U. S. Inf.   (interred 29 May 1921)

1879R   SHORE   Esther Shore, died 27 June 1862

596   SHOVER   William F. Shover, 15 Dec. 1917, M. Engr. (J.G.), 4 Engrs., U. S. A.

385   SHULTZ   Mary I. Shultz   (interred 23 Aug. 1898)

1879R   SIAHLM   John Siahlm   (no further information)

635   SIDEAN   Oscar A. Sidean, Air Service, U. S. A.   (Pvt., interred 10 Jan. 1919)

562   SIEBER   Q. M. Sgt. Joh Sieber, U. S. Army   (interred 3 June 1914)

1879R   SIGELKEN   Otto Sigelken, died 28 July 1860, Lieut. Co. C, 3 U. S. Art.   (Also spelled SEGELKY)

1143   SILLITO   Louis A. Sillito, 17 May 1941, Minnesota, Master Sgt., U. S. Army   (interred 31 May 1941)

157   SILVER   Stephen W. Silver, Who departed this life 21 June 1852 aged 27 yrs., Sacred to the memory of, Of North Bend, Hamilton Co., Ohio   (interred 22 June 1852)

1104   SINKOWSKI   Stanley Sinkowski, 16 July 1937, Master Sgt., U. S. Army   (interred 21 July 1937)

1132   SIRES   Elsa A. Sires, 16 Mar. 1940, Wife of Major E. B. Sires, U. S. A.   (interred 23 Mar. 1940)

1032   SKINNNER Charles W. Skinner, 10 Feb. 1934, California, 1st Sgt.,
        U. S. Army (interred 16 Feb. 1932**there is a discrepency be-
        tween the dates on the stone and the records)

905   SLEYS Anna P. Sleys, 1876 - 1930

907   SLEYS Charles Sleys, 25 Sept. 1940, New York, 1 Sgt., U. S. Army
        (interred 28 Sept. 1940)

905   SLEYS Phoebe A . Sleys (interred 11 Feb. 1930, wife of 1 Sgt.
        Charles Sleys)

906   SLEYS Rose Sleys, Wife of 1st Sgt. Charles Sleys, U. S. A. 4 Jan.
        1940 (interred 6 Jan. 1940)

  1883R SMITH ____Smith, Pvt. Co. G, 1st U. S. Cav.

349   SMITH Batthias Smith, Co. C., 14 U. S. Inf. (interred 31 Mar. 1890)

563   SMITH Charles E. Smith, 13 July 1876 - 16 June 1914, Texas, Pvt.,
        C. A. C.

---   SMITH Chas. E. Smith, 93 Co., U. S. C. A. Corps (**probably the
        same as the Charles Smith, above)

618   SMITH Earl M. Smith, U. S. Army (Pvt., interred 13 Nov. 1918)

343   SMITH F. C. Smith, Co. E, 1st U. S. Art. (Frederick C. Smith, Pvt.,
        interred 21 Dec. 1888)

280   SMITH Ida Smith (died 27 May, interred 28 May 1865)

914   SMITH Infant Smith, 6 Nov. 1930 (interred 7 Nov. 1930, son of Pvt.
        E. E. Smith)

974   SMITH Infant Smith, 19 Dec. 1931 (interred 21 Dec. 1931, son of
        Carl E. Smith)

563A   SMITH Mary Jemima Smith, 4 Mar. 1940, Wife of C. E. Smith, U. S. A.
        (wife of Charles Smith)

---   SMITH Matilda Smith (**no further information)

566   SMITH Oliver J. Smith, Co. E, 21 U. S. Inf. (Pvt., interred 30 Sept.
        1914)

325   SMITH Thos. Smith, Co. A, 9 U. S. Inf. (interred 17 Mar. 1859, Thomas
        Smith)

980   SMITH William J. Smith, 7 Feb. 1932, Oregon, Sgt., Q M Corps (in-
        terred 11 Feb. 1932)

981   SMITH (Lot reserved for Mrs. Wm. J. Smith, 11 Feb. 1932)

1203   SNIDER Jack R. Snider, 18 Aug. 1921 - 15 July 1944, Oregon, Cpl.,
        Q M Corps (interred 21 July 1944)

782   SNOW Eugene Snow, 9 Nov. 1908 - 29 Aug. 1975, S.S.G., U. S. Army,
        WW II (interred 2 Sept. 1975)

1090   SOBOLEWSKI Elizabeth Sobolewski, 26 Apr. 1928, Daughter of Corp.
                 F. Sobolewski, U. S. A.

398   SODEN Cpl. Guy B. Soden, Killed in Battle of Manila, P. I., 5 Feb.
                 1899, aged 23 yrs. 6 mo. 11 dys. In Memory Of, Erected by his
                 comrades in Co. E 14 Inft.

527   SOEBY Jens P. Soeby, Band, 5 U. S. Inf (Pvt., interred 16 July
                 1911)

k964   Solcany Thelma Solcany, 7 Aug. 1934, Wife of Sgt. W. J. Solcany,
                 U. S. A. (interred 10 Aug. 1934)

731   SOLDOS George Soldos, 1905 - 1976, M Sgt. U. S. Army, WW II & Korea
                 (interred 12 Aug. 1976, Wife - Annie L. Soldos)

---   SPARREN Margaret Sparren, 23 Feb. 1909, Wife of 1st Sgt. J. M. C.
                 Sparren, U. S. A.

84   1879R   SPAY Joseph Spay, Band, 4th U. S. Inf. (interred 19 June 1859,
                 died 18 June 1859)

     1879R   SPAY William Spay, Pvt., Co. E, 1st Oregon Inf.

910   .SPEAR Herbert C. Spear, 1871 - 1936, Cpt., U. S. A. Ret'd (interred
                 7 May 1936)

911   SPEAR Minnie B. Spear, 1872 - 1963, Wife of Cpt. Herbert G. Spear
                 (interred 12 Aug. 1963)

482   SPENCER Fred'k Spencer, Co. E, 14 U. S. Inf., Mus'n (Frederick
                 Spencer, interred 26 Jan. 1908)

     1879R   SPINNY L. Spinny, died ca. 1855-1856

898   SPIVEY Carrie Spivey, 28 Sept. 1930 (wife of 1 Sgt. Wm. Spivey, in-
                 terred 30 Sept. 1930)

899   SPIVEY William Spivey, 2 Sept. 1937, North Carolina, 1 Sgt., 14 Inf.
                 (interred 5 Sept. 1937)

1144   SPURLING Beulah Dorothy Spurling, 21 May 1886 - 2 Oct. 1956, Wife
                 of M. Sgt. G. T.Spurling, U. S. A. (interred 4 Oct. 1956)

1145   SPURLING George T. Spurling, 4 June 1941, California, M. Sgt.,
                 U. S. Army (interred 7 June 1941)

---   SQUIRES Asa Squires, Co. H., 18 Michigan Inf.

557   SQUIRES Asa Squires, Pvt. (interred 11 Feb. 1914 **no doubt the
                 same as the above Asa Squires)

504   SQUIRES Isabelle Squires (interred 10 Mar. 1909)

353   SGURDIVINE Tryggve Sgurdivine (Pvt., interred 15 Dec. 1890 **this
                 name out of order)

440B   STAFFORD Julia M. Ehl Stafford, 30 July 1890 - 20 Dec. 1918, BASE
               (interred 23 Dec. 1918)

6   STARRING William S. Starrring, Died 18 Feb. 1889, aged 48 yrs., In
               Memory Of, Capt., Ordnances Dept., U. S. Army, Genial Duffie,
               Semper Fidelis

   1883R   ST. CLAIR Julius St. Clair, Cpl., Co. E, 12 U. S. Inf.

631   STEELANT C. Steelant, U. S. Army (Pvt. Constant Steelant, interred
               21 Dec. 1918)

614   STEELMAN Thos. C. Steelman, U. S. Army (Pvt., interred 27 Oct. 1918)

1051   STEFFEN Infant Child Steffen, 16 Sept. 1932, Stillborn son of Pvt.
               L. L. Steffen, U. S. A.

625   STEGEMAN Chas. Stegeman, 14 U. S. Inf. (interred 18 Dec. 1918)

455   STEVENS W. J. Stevens, 18 Batty., Field Arty. (William J. Stevens,
               Pvt., 26 Apr. 1906)

683   STEWART Chas. L. Stewart, Co. F, Minnesota Inf. (CHarles L. Stewart,
               interred 29 May 1921)

376   STEWART Infant Stewart (interred 4 May 1896, son of O'Kiel H.
               Stewart)

361   STEWART Child Stewart (interred 4 Oct. 1892, infant son of O'Kiel
               H. Stewart)

760   STEWART John N. Stewart, 1849 - 1930 (Civ. Ck., interred 9 Aug.
               1935)

761   STEWART Josephine Stewart, 1852 - 1930 (interred 24 Nov. 1930, wife
               of John N. Stewart)

508   STEWART O'Kiel H. Stewart (Civ. Clk., interred 17 June 1909, **see
               STUART, O'Kiel H.)

759   STEWART Ralph Stewart, 15 Nov. 1930, Staff Sgt., Q M Corps.

   1879R   STEWART Thomas Stewart, Pvt., Co. E, 2nd Bat., Ore. Inf. died 3 June
               1866

558   STIVERS Jos. B. Stivers, Co. E, 18 U. S. Inf. (Joseph B. Stivers,
               Cook, interred 27 Mar. 1914)

848   STOCKFORD Henry S. Stockford, 28 Feb. 1929, Pvt., 31 Inf. (interred
               2 Mar. 1929)

847   STOCKFORD Sarah J. Stockford, 27 Oct. 1931, Wife of H. S. Stockford
               (interred 29 Oct. 1931)

702   STOCKSTILL Infant Stockstill, 16 May 1923, Child of Cpl. Stockstill,
               U. S. Army

438   STONE K. C. Stone, Child (Kenneth C. Stone, son of Pvt. Fred C.
               Stone, interred 23 Feb. 1903)

831   STONE Seth H. Stone, Indiana (interred 6 July 1928)

442   STOTTS Rob't Stotts, Co. H, 14 U. S. Inf. (Robert Stotts, Pvt.,
               interred 9 June 1905)

502   STRATON Ezra M. Straton, 11 A. L. A. (interred 11 Feb. 1909)

    1879R STRAUGHTEN E. E. Straughten, 4 Sept. 1871

990   STRONG Charlotte Strong, 26 Dec. 1932, Wife of Corp. J. C. Strong,
               U. S. A. (interred 29 Dec. 1932)

989   STRONG James C. Strong, 20 May 1932, Washington, Corp., 4 U. S. Art.
               (interred 24 May 1932)

508   STUART Elise E. Stuart, 1866 - 1936, Mother (wife of O'Kill H.
               Stuart, interred 17 Nov. 1936 **see O'Keil Stewart)

508   STUART O'Kill H. Stuart, 1861 - 1909, Clerk, A. G. Dept., Father
               (interred 17 June 1909 **see also O'Kiel H. Stewart. Records
               show different spelling of name than tombstone)

332   STURGEON Infant Sturgeon (interred 16 Nov. 1886)

700   STURGESS Frank R. Sturgess, 4 Feb. 1923, Fireman 1 Cl., U. S. Navy
               (interred 7 Feb. 1923)

340   STURGSON (Child) Sturgson (interred 26 June 1888, daughter of Pvt.
               J. C. Sturgson)

60   SUCELKIL Otto Sucelkil, Co. C, 3rd U. S. Art. (Pvt. Sinelkil is
               shown in records as spelling for this name. interred 29 July
               18__)

661   SULLIVAN Ella M. Sullivan (interred 20 Feb. 1920)

491   SULLIVAN Florence Sullivan (interred 13 Sept. 1908, wife of
               Pvt. A. Sullivan)

500   SULLIVAN John Sullivan, 3 Jan. 1909, Drum Maj., 15 Cav. Band

584   SULLIVAN Sergt. Jos. G. Sullivan, Med. Dept., U. S. Army (Sgt.
               Joseph Sullivan, interred 29 Nov. 1916)

495   SULLIVAN Sgt. Michael Sullivan, Co. A, 1st U. S. Inf. (interred
               27 Oct. 1908)

    1883R SUMMERS Geo. A. Summers, Horse Steward, U. S. A., died 10 Dec. 1866

673   SUTHERLAND Ellen Sutherland, 1857 - 1936, Mother (interred 11 Jan.
               1936, wife of Sgt. George Sutherland)

394   SUTHERLAND George Sutherland, Died 25 Aug. 1899 aged 52 yrs. 2 ms.,
               A precious one from us is gone, A voice we loved is stilled, A
               place is vacant in our home, Which never can be filled. In Mem-
               ory Of (interred 25 Aug. 1899, Sgt.)

673   SUTHERLAND Infant Sutherland (interred 12 Jan. 1921, daughter of
        Sgt. George Sutherland)

333   SUTHERLAND Nellie M. Sutherland, Died 5 June 1887 aged 5 years,
        Daughter of Geo. & Ellen Sutherland, In Memory Of (interred 6
        June 1887)

808   SUTTON Harry Sutton, 18 June 1927, 1st Sgt., U. S. Army (interred
        27 June 1927)

437   SWARTZ Fanny G. Swartz, Child (interred 14 Feb. 1905, daughter of
        Ira M. Swartz)

437A   SWARTZ Harry M. Swartz, Employee, U. S. A. (Ch. Eng., interred 16
        Nov. 1918)

437B   SWARTZ Ira M. Swartz, Co. E, 1 Mich. Cav. (Pvt., interred 17 May
        1927)

699   SZABLINK MIke Szablink, 5 Dec. 1922, Connecticut, 7 Inf. (interred
        7 Dec. 1922, PFC)

360   SZLEZAS Jakemas Szlezas, Co. F, 14 U. S. Inf. (Pvt., interred 10
        July 1907)

810   TALIAFERRO Bertha H. Taliaferro, 1893 - 1927, Wife of PFC William
        C. Taliaferro (interred 5 July 1927)

809   TALIAFERRO William C. Taliaferro, 1896 - 1927, In Loving Memory Of,
        Co. K, 7 Inf., U. S. A. (PFC, interred 5 July 1927)

407   TAYLOR Mrs. A. W. Taylor (wife of A. W. Taylor, interred 19 Nov.
        1901)

750   TAYLOR Andrew W. Taylor, 27 June 1931, Oregon, Pvt., 31 Inf. (in-
        terred 3 July 1931)

327   TAYLOR Frank Eveleigh Taylor, Born 28 May 1843 - Died 25 Nov. 1886,
        Capt. First Regt. Art. and Brevet Major U. S. Army, In Memory Of,
        And this too shall pass away.

811   TAYLOR Infant Taylor, 16 Aug. 1927 (interred 18 Aug. 1927, son of
        Pvt. Robert C. Taylor)

547   TAYLOR Madaline F. Taylor (interred 9 Mar. 1913, Grand daughter of
        Sgt. Michael Brady)

423A   TELMOS Baby Telmos, died 10 Feb. 1904 (interred 11 Feb. 1904)

967   TEMPLET Robert A. Templet, 18 Oct. 1951, Son of A. W. Templet, U.S.A.
        (interred 20 Oct. 1951)

459   TESAR Corp'l J. F. Tesar, Band, 14 U. S. Inf. (interred 9 July 1906)

1089   TESKE Isabelle Teske, 20 June 1936 (interred 23 June 1936, Mother-
        in-law of 1 Sgt. Wallace Kidd)

641   THOM Sophia B. Thom, 16 Mar. 1928 (interred 27 Mar. 1928, wife of
        William Thom)

642   THOM William Thom, 1846 - 1919 (interred 28 Mar. 1919)

---   THOM Wm. Thom, Co. H, 51 Wisconsin Inf. Vol. (**probably the same
             person as above with two stones)

---   THOMAS 1st Sgt. Carl Thomas, Co. M, 14 U. S. Inf. (interred 2
             Oct. 1914)

497   THOMAS Corp'l H. E. Thomas, 1 U. S. Engrs. (Harley E. Thomas, Cpl.,
             interred 23 Nov. 1908)

604   THOMSON Rob't C. Thomson, U. S. Army (Robert C. Thomson, Pvt., in-
             terred 7 Aug. 1918)

713   THOMPSON A. V. Thompson, 1845 - 1923, 44th Indiana Vols. Inf. (Pvt.,
             interred 25 Sept. 1923, Adolph V. Thompson)

1057   THOMPSON Dorothea Thompson, 10 Dec. 1933, Wife of Sgt. T. B. Thomp-
             son, U. S. A. (interred 12 Dec. 1933)

714   THOMPSON Frances Thompson, 1851 - 1929, Wife of A. V. Thompson (in-
             terred 27 Mar. 1929)

748   THOMPSON George E. Thompson, 31 May 1931, Washington, Corp., 14
             U. S. Inf. (interred 3 June 1931)

---   THOMPSON James S. Thompson, Pvt., 1882 - 1932 (interred 4 Aug. 1932)

509   THOMPSON Lillian Thompson, 1887 - 1967 (wife of Pvt. James Thompson,
             interred 12 Oct. 1967)

996   THOMPSON Lillian Thompson, 12 Oct. 1937, Wife of Pvt. James S.
             Thompson (interred 15 Oct. 1937 **these appear to be the same
             person although interment dates differ by several days and the
             grave number is different as is the year. Since James S. Thomp-
             son doesn't have a grave number, it is possible that one of
             these is actually his and some error was made in the records)

1082   THOMPSON Lincoln Morris Thompson, 8 June 1897 - 18 Feb. 1977, Sgt.,
             U. S. Army, WW I (interred 25 Feb. 1977)

1174   THORNTON Thomas J. Thornton, 5 May 1943, California, Staff Sgt.,
             362 Inf. (interred 12 May 1943)

919   TIBBETTS Sarah Matthews Ruiter Tibbetts, 1860 - 1931, Mother (in-
             terred 20 Jan. 1931, wife of Pvt. N. Tibbetts)

152   TIMMINS Emma E. Timmins, Born 10 Jan. 1854 - Died 11 Feb. 1879,
             Wife of C. Timmins, Gone But Not Forgotten (interred 12 Feb. 1879)

    1883R   TOOBITS _____ Toobits, Indian, died 5 Oct. 1873

370   TRENT Julia Trent (interred 24 Jan. 1895)

    1879R   TRIP Abel G. Trip, died 17 Sept. 1875

484   TRISSLER Joseph Trissler, Co. R, 1 Washington Inf. (Pvt., interred
             27 Feb. 1908, spelling on stone reads 'TRISLER')

918   TUCKER Alton Tucker, 20 Dec. 1930, Arkansas, Pvt., 7 Inf. (in-
               terred 28 Dec. 1930)

401   TURNER Ellis Turner, Co. L, 24th U. S. Inf. (Pvt., interred 10
               Oct. 1900)

471   UNASH J. W. Unash, Co. F, 14 U. S. Inf. (Joseph W. Unash, Pvt.,
               interred 16 July 1907)

373   UNDERWOOD David Underwood, Co. A, 14 U. S. Inf. (Pvt., interred
               6 Nov. 1895)

1137   UNSELT Carl H. Unselt, 9 Dec. 1940, Indiana, Master Sgt., U. S.
               Army (interred 12 Dec. 1940)

1138   UNSELT (Lot reserved Mrs. Carl H. Unselt)

548   VAN FLEET Clara I. Van Fleet, (interred 30 Mar. 1930, wife of
               George F. Van Fleet)

09   VAN HORN J. Raymond D. Van Horn, 22 Jan. 1900 - 7 Jan. 1974, Wash-
               ington, M. S. G., U. S. Army, WW I & II, Korea

    1879R   VANWINKLE Jane Vanwinkle died 16 July 1874

    1879R   VANWINKLE J. C. A. Vanwinkle died 3 Jan. 1874

493   VENIN Eliza B. Venin, 1836 - 1908, Mother, Sleeping (interred
               27 Nov. 1908, Mother-in-law of P. T. Kelly)

939   VITOU Benjamin Vitou, 22 Mar. 1931, Florida, Master Sgt., U. S.
               Army (interred 24 Mar. 1931)

938   VITOU Benjamin Wallace Vitou, 9 Sept. 1938, Oregon Lieut. (JG),
               U. S. Army (interred 24 Oct. 1938)

937   VITOU Jean Margaret Vitou, 20 Nov. 1889 - 2 May 1965, Wife of Sgt.
               Benjamin Vitou, U. S. A. (interred 5 May 1965)

440   VOELKER John Voelker, Born 8 Feb. 1848 - Died 14 May 1905 (inter-
               red 16 May 1905)

154   VOHWINKEL Jane Vohwinkel, Died 16 July 1874, aged 49 years, Wife
               of J. C. A. Vohwinkel, Erected by their son, Ed August Vohwinkel
               (interred 17 July 1874)

---   VOHWINKEL J. C. A. Vohwinkel, Died 3 Jan. 1874, Aged 49 yrs.
               (interred 4 Jan. 1874)

414   VON KUROWSKY Olga Mary Von Kurowsky, Born 14 Sept. 1890, Entered
               Into Rest 3 Apr. 1903, Blessed are the pure in heart (interred
               4 Apr. 1903)

403   VOSBURG J. J. Vosburg, Co. A, 28 U. S. Inf. (John J. Vosburg, in-
               terred 11 Aug. 1901)

1056   WADDELL Eva Waddell, 13 Mar. 1933, Wife of Pvt. R. F. Waddell, U. S.
               A. (interred 16 Mar. 1933)

1101   WADE   Charles J. E. Wade, 11 May 1937, Oregon, Pvt., 7 Inf. (inter-
            red 24 Aug. 1937)

334   WAITE   Edward Thomas Waite, 22 Apr. 1876 - 5 July 1887, Son of G. B.
            & S. A. Waite, May He Rest In Peace (interred 6 July 1887, son
            of George Waite)

474   WAITE   Ellen M. Waite, Born 25 Apr. 1890, Drowned 17 Aug. 1907, A
            Little Time On Earth She Spent, Till God For Her His Angels
            Sent (interred 19 Sept. 1907, Daughter of 1 Sgt. George Waite)

339   WAITE   Frank Waite, Born 26 Jan. 1886 - Died 14 Apr. 1888, In Life
            Beloved, In Death Lamented

480   WAITE   George B. Waite, 14 July 1848 - 4 Dec. 1907, At Rest, First
            Sargeant, Co. B, 14 Inf. (interred 6 Dec. 1907)

359   WAITE   Lula Edith Waite, Beloved Daughter of G. B. & S. A. Waite,
            Born Nov. 1881, Died 17 Jan. 1892, Suffer Little Children and
            Forbid Them Not To Come Unto Me, For Such Is The Kingdom Of
            Heaven.

542   WAITE   Sarah A. Waite, 8 Aug. 1859 - 3 Oct. 1912, At Rest, In Memory
            Of (interred 7 Oct. 1912, Wife of 1 Sgt. George Waite)

1879R   WAKER   John Waker, Maj. Paymaster, died 27 Jan. 1873

1883R   WALSH   John Walsh, Pvt., Co. G, 12th U. S. Inf.

1055   WALCH   William Carl Walch, 14 Dec. 1932, Washington, Seaman 2 Cl.,
            U. S. N. R. F. (interred 16 Dec. 1932)

395   WALDEN   J. M. Walden, Corp'l Co. E, 35th U. S. Vol. Inf. (John M.
            Walden, interred 18 Sept. 1899)

1201   WALKER   Richard Chamlee Walker, 15 Dec. 1925 - 28 May 1944, Washing-
            ton, S. 2, U. S. Navy, WW II (interred 5 June 1944)

---   WALLACE   Jas. Wallace, Co. G, 21 U. S. Inf.

1114   WALTERS   Della Walters, 21 Apr. 1943, Wife of Regt. L. Sgt. Major
            William Walters, U. S. A.

389   WALTERS   Francis D. Walters

1113   WALTERS   William Walters, 7 Dec. 1937, Regt. L Sgt. Major, 4 Cav.,
            Texas (interred 11 Dec. 1937)

757   WAMPLER   Wm. D. Wampler, Co. A, 146 Indiana Inf. (Pvt., interred 5
            Apr. 1926)

818   WARD   Electa A. Ward, 4 Aug. 1928 (interred 7 Aug. 1928, mother of
            Pvt. I. S. Ward)

817   WARD   Isaac S. Ward, 15 Sept. 1927, Pvt., 19 Inf. (interred 17
            Sept. 1927)

322   WARD   James Ward, Co. H, 14th U. S. Inf.

988   WARREN   William W. Warren, 8 May 1952, Oregon, Pvt., 1 Cl., Q. M.
                Corps   (interred 10 May 1952)

78   WARRINGER   Rob't Warringer, Co. F, 2nd U. S. Art.   (Robert Warringer,
                Pvt., interred 22 July 1867)

1000   WASSENAR   Simmon J. Wassenar, 1895 - 1933   (interred 4 Jan. 1933)

1001   WASSNER   John Oliver Wassner, 1924 - 1940   (interred 22 Mar. 1940)

3   WATSON   Lieut. Stephen Watson, Born in Saint Stephens, N. B. 15 May
                1828, Killed in battle with the Snake Indians near Crooked
                River, Oregon, 18 May 1864, 1st Oregon Cavalry, Erected to his
                Memory by members of the regiment   (interred 19 May 1864)

   1883R   WEBBER   L. Webber, Citizen

707A   WEBSTER   Alice Webster

79   WEBSTER   Chas Webster, Co. F, 2nd U. S. Art.   (Pvt., Charles Webster,
                Died 23 Aug. 1867, interred 24 Aug. 1967)

947   WEIGEL   Helen M. Webber Weigel, 29 Aug. 1921 - 2 Oct. 1974, PFC,
                U. S. Army   (interred 4 Oct. 1974)

489   WEISSGERBER   F. T. Weissgerber, Co. C, 1 U. S. Inf.   (Frank T.
                Weissgerber, Pvt., interred 28 July 1908)

573   WELCH   Geo. W. Welch, Co. C, 21 U. S. Inf.   (Pvt., George W. Welch,
                interred 28 Feb. 1915)

689   WELCH   MIchael Welch   (interred 10 Mar. 1922)

   1879R   WEINHART   Emma A. Weinhart, died 12 Aug. 1864

   1879R   WELFORTH   Dennis Welforth, Band, 1 U. S. Cav., died 8 July 1867

417   WELLS   Serg't Peter Wells, Co. F, 22 U. S. Inf.   (interred 12 Oct.
                1977)

1270   WELLS   Richard Junior Wells, 3 Oct. 1930 - 11 Oct. 1977, S. Sgt.,
                U. S. Air Force, Korea   (interred 15 Oct. 1977)

---   WELSON   John Welson, Co. E, 14 U. S. Inf.

511   WELTON   Sgt. Laban C. Welton, Co. H, 13 Wis. Inf.   (interred 24 Aug.
                1909)

586   WENZEL   Rob't C. Wenzel, Chf. Mechanic, Co. F, 1 U. S. Field Art.
                (Robert C. Wenzel, interred 25 June 1917)

1286   WERLINICK   Samuel Werlinick, 19 Dec. 1904 - 22 Feb. 1979, MSG, U. S.
                Army, WW II   (interred 5 Mar. 1979)

7   WESTERN   Charles B. Western, Born Clifton, New York, 12 Jan. 1844,
                Died Vancouver Barracks, Wash. 10 June 1890, In Memory Of, Capt.,
                14 Regt. Inf.   (interred 11 June 1890)

729   WESTOVER   Lester L. Westover, Co. F, 27 Michigan Inf.   (interred
              May 1924)

768   WHEATON   Anna L. Wheaton, 1875 - 1961, Mother   (interred 20 Apr.
              1961, Wife of Cpl. Walter S. Wheaton)

767   WHEATON   Walter S. Wheaton, 1878 - 1926, Father   (Cpl., interred 17
              Apr. 1926)

287   WHITE   B. L. White, Died 3 Dec. 1857, Aged 41 Years   (interred 4
              Dec. 1857)

565   WHITE   Ernest S. White, Co. E, 21 U. S. Inf.   E. S. White, An Only
              Son   (interred 1 Sept. 1914, Pvt.)

432   WHITE   Miles White, Co. E, 19 U. S. Inf.   (Pvt., interred 13 Dec.
              1895)

392   WHITE   Thos. White, Co. B, 24th U. S. Inf.   (Pvt. Thomas White,
              interred 18 July 1899)

1   WIGGINS   A. W. Wiggins, M. D., Born in Wakefield, N. H., Died Ft.
              Stevens, Oregon, 7 Mar. 1875, I Know That My Redeemer Liveth
              (interred 8 Mar. 1875)

953   WIBUR   Elmer Wilbur, 5 July 1931, Washington, Pvt., 3 Engrs.

1284   WILE   Charles Joseph Wile, 17 May 1920 - 23 Feb. 1979, M. Sgt., U. S.
              Air Force, WW II, Korea - Vietnam   (interred 29 Feb. 1979)

420   WILEY   F. A. Wiley, Co. I, 26 U. S. Inf.   (Francis A. Wiley, Pvt.,
              interred 7 Oct. 1902)

924   WILLIAMS   Infant Williams, 18 Feb. 1931   (interred 25 Feb. 1931, son
              of R. J. Williams)

337   WILLIAMS   Jno. Williams   (John Williams, interred 23 Nov. 1887)

393   WILLIAMS   Moses Williams, 23 Aug. 1899, Medal Of Honor, Ord. Sgt.,
              Co. I, 9 U. S. Cav., Indian Wars   (interred 24 Aug. 1899)

881   WILLIAMS   Russell J. Williams, Jr., 14 Apr. 1930, Son   (interred 16
              Apr. 1930, son of Sgt. Russell Williams, Sr.)

934   WILLIAMS   Zola E. Williams, 8 Apr. 1931, Wife of Pvt. Williams   (in-
              terred 11 Apr. 1931)

1147   WILSON   Arthur L. Wilson, 3 June 1941, Oregon, Pvt., 1st 6 Inf.   (in-
              terred 21 June 1941)

62   WILSON   Ezekial Wilson, Co. C, 3rd U. S. Art.   (Cpl., died 12 Aug.
              1860)

636   WILSON   Irving J. Wilson, Air Service, U. S. A.   (Pvt., interred 18
              Jan. 1918)

1088   WILSON Vivian Lucille Wilson, 1902 - 1936 (interred 20 Feb. 1936,
              wife of Cpl. Frank G. Wilson)

638   WINBERG Vivian Winberg, Infant (interred __ Jan. 1919)

601   WITT Sewell Witt, Co. G, 7 Wisconsin Inf. (Pvt., interred 18 May
              1918)

892   WODMAN Infant Wodman (son of Lt. Wodman)

135   WOHLGEMUTH Anna, died 19 Nov. 1875 (interred 2o Nov. 1875, in re-
   1879R   cords as Anne WHOHGEMUTH)

620   WOLFBRANDT John S. Wolfbrandt (interred 21 Nov. 1918)

1272   WOLFE Scott L. Wolfe, 5 May 1952 - 25 Oct. 1977, S.S.G., U. S. Army,
              Vietnam (interred 31 Oct. 1977)

85   WOLFORTH Dennis Wolforth, Band, 1st U. S. Cav. (interred 9 July
              1867)

575   WOLFGRAM Lst Sgt. Fred W. Wolfgram, Co. F, 1 U. S. Inf. (LSG, in-
              terred 18 June 1915)

322   WOOD James Wood (Pvt., interred 13 Apr. 1886)

---   WOODY Herschel A. Woody, 21 Sept. 1938, Oregon, Pvt. 1 Cl., 7 Inf.

   1879R   WORKMAN John Workman, 11 Sept. 1863

499   WORMWORTH Jos. Wormworth (Pvt., interred 23 Dec. 1908, Joseph Worm-
              worth)

499A   WORMWORTH Josephine H. Wormworth, 13 June 1936, Wife of Pvt. J.
              Wormworth)

   1879R   WRENKART Mary A. Wrenkart, died 25 Sept. 1862)

450   WRIGHT E. C. Wright, Sig. Corps, U. S. A. (Elmer C. Wright, Pvt.,
              interred 11 Oct. 1905)

481   WRIGHT Jack Wright, Co. B, 4 Field Art. (Pvt., interred 25 July 1918)

619   WRIGHT John S. Wright, U. S. Army (Pvt., interred 20 Nov. 1918)

   1879R   WRIGHT W. A. Wright, 15 Sept. 185C

   1879R   WURRINER Robert Wurriner, Co. F, 2 U. S. Art., died 21 July 1867

410   WYDER Jno. Wyder, Sgt., 26 Field Art. (John Wyder)

1102   YARDLEY Phillip J. Yardley, 1 July 1937, Son of Pvt. 1 Cl. P. Yardley
              U. S. A. (interred 2 July 1937, infant son)

466A   YOUNG George S. Young, 1854 - 1919, Colonel (interred 7 Jan. 1919)

621   YOUNG Gustave Young, 8 Trench Mortar Batty., U. S. A. (interred 10
              Nov. 1918)

466B   YOUNG Harold W. Young, 1887 - 1923, Capt. (interred 4 Oct. 1923)

585½   ZIEGLER Gustav Ziegler, Buglar, Co. H, 9 U. S. Inf. (interred 28
               May 1918)

835   ZIKE Howard H. Zike, 25 July 1928, Pvt., 7 Inf., Nebraska (interred
               30 July 1928)

1244   ZIMMERMAN Charles F. B. Zimmerman, 25 Nov. 1855 - 8 Nov. 1945, Wash-
               ington, Comsy., Sgt., U. S. Army (interred 14 Nov. 1945)

364   ZIMMERMAN Edna F. Zimmerman, Died 29 Mar. 1893, Aged 20 Yrs. 8 Ds.,
               Farewell, Wife of 1st Sgt. Chas. F. B. Zimmerman, Co. G, 14 Inf.

1245   ZIMMERMAN Jennie Zimmerman, 5 Jan. 1946, Wife of Comsy., Sgt. C.F.B.
               Zimmerman, U. S. A. (interred 9 Jan. 1946)

                              ✳✳✳✳✳✳✳✳✳✳

                                 ADDENDUM

1161   HAMMONDS   Nettie M. Hammonds, 12 Feb. 1888 - 30 July 1956, wife
                          of 1st Sgt. E. D. Hammonds (interred 1 Aug. 1956)

239   LA FRAMBOISE   Joseph La Framboise, Civilian (interred 12 Sept
                          1918)

1109   RASPPERRY   Sumiko Ikeda Raspperry, 19 June 1925 - 16 Feb. 1976,
                          Wife of MSG-K.B. Raspperry U.S.A. (interred 20
                          Feb. 1976)

735   SAFRANEK   John Safranek, 1841 - 1925, Band Master 12th Minnesota
                          Vols. 1898 - Chief Musician 34th U.S. Inf. 1899,
                          Honorably Discharged 1900, Member of Wash. Lodge
                          #4 F + AM, Vancouver, Wa. (interred 12 Feb. 1925)

Headstone notes medalist

Copy, April 4, 1980
Vancouver, Wash.

The COLUMBIAN

An Army headstone honoring the second Medal of Honor winner at the Vancouver Barracks post cemetery was erected Thursday.

It honors Herman Pfisterer, a Brooklyn, N.Y., native who won his medal in combat in Cuba on June 22, 1899, during the Spanish-American war.

Pfisterer died here on Aug. 8, 1905, while serving with Company D, 14th U.S. Infantry, at Vancouver Barracks. He lies next to his wife, Sarah P. Hahn, who changed her name after remarring.

Pfisterer's medal was unknown here until last November, when the Veterans Administration tracked down his burial place and notified Army authorities here.

A headstone recording his honor was ordered. On hand when the headstone was erected was Pfisterer's grandson, David King of Vancouver.

Few details are known yet of Pfisterer's life. His citation was for "gallantry while assisting in the rescue of wounded men from in front of his lines while under heavy enemy fire." He was a musician with Co. H, 21st U.S. Infantry, in Cuba.

The Army has requested more information from National Archives.

The other Medal of Honor winner buried at the cemetery on Fourth Plain Boulevard opposite the Veterans Hospital is Moses Williams, a black cavalryman who won his medal fighting Apache Indians.

61

Medal of Honor

Wednesday, Dec. 12, 1979
Vancouver, Wash.   The COLUMBIAN

2nd winner lies here

A second Medal of Honor winner is buried at the Vancouver Barracks post cemetery, the Veterans Administration has discovered.

The medal was won June 22, 1899, by Herman Tfisterer, originally of Brooklyn, N.Y., during combat in Cuba during the Spanish-American War.

Tfisterer has been buried in Vancouver since Aug. 8, 1905, when he died while serving as a private with the 14th Infantry here. He had not been identified as winning the nation's highest military decoration until two weeks ago, when the Veterans Administration tracked down his burial place and notified military authorities here.

The other Medal of Honor winner buried at the cemetery on Fourth Plain Boulevard opposite the Veterans Hospital is Moses Williams, a black cavalryman who won his medal fighting Apache Indians.

Tfisterer was a musician with Co. H, 21st U.S. Infantry, while in Cuba. His citation was for "gallantry while assisting in the rescue of wounded men from in front of his lines while under heavy enemy fire."

The name of the battle or other details are not known. Barracks administrators have asked for more information from a private group which searches out records on Medal of Honor recipients.

1,224 laid to rest in barracks cemetery

The low and mournful sounds of Taps have drifted over this quiet parcel of Clark County land 1,224 times — once for every person buried here.

Most of those who now rest in the Vancouver Barracks Post Cemetery, on Fourth Plain Boulevard just east of Interstate 5, were soldiers who served here when it was the Army's Pacific Northwest headquarters.

But there are family members also, as well as 196 graves marked only "Unknown."

And resting with American soldiers are two German prisoners-of-war from World War II, an Italian POW from the same conflict and two Soviet soldiers.

Local records do not reveal what made this the final resting place for the two Soviets. But every Memorial Day, when national flags of the men buried here are placed on the graves, two small red Soviet flags flutter in the breeze among the rows of stars and stripes.

"Someone usually calls" when they see the Soviet flags, said 1st Sgt. Frank Villa, who helps maintain the cemetery. Sometimes they think it's some kind of cruel joke, he said.

"We tell them that they are buried here and they were our allies in World War II."

Established in 1848, this is the oldest active Army cemetery in the Pacific Northwest. Tombstones here speak of battles long faded into history.

The oldest marker records the death of John Charles June, "who unfortunately lost his life by the accidental discharge of a gun in the hands of his companion and fellow travelor on the 21st of October,

1849."

Four Congressional Medal of Honor winners are buried here. One fought in the Civil War, one in the Indian Wars and two in the Spanish-American War.

On another marker are the names of five members of an infantry company. They were killed in 1877, during the north Idaho campaign against the Nez Perce that immortalized Chief Joseph.

The nation's immigrant roots also are clearly visible, with tombstones telling of soldiers born in County Cork, Ireland; Friedersdorp, Germany; Paris, France; and other locations thousands of miles distant.

Five or six persons a year are still buried here, Villa said. The cemetery has 795 remaining spaces, he said.

David H. Morrissey

Blacks fought

By DAVID H. MORRISSEY
The Columbian

They were cheated, robbed and sometimes killed by the persons they were sworn to protect.

Their valor and bravery were exceptional but were often ignored or mocked in official reports.

Their role in history was intentionally forgotten or distorted while others, often less deserving, received a nation's praise.

They were the "Buffalo Soldiers," all-black cavalry units of the U.S. Army that served on the nation's Western frontier in the late 19th century.

The plains Indians thought "the soldiers' hair resembled the 'wool' sprouting between a buffalo's eyes, and . . . respected their fighting prowess enough to name the soldiers for their sacred animal," wrote Marian T. Place in "Rifles and War Bonnets," a study of America's black cavalrymen. The soldiers adopted the nickname with pride.

Despite fearsome prejudice, one of the Buffalo Soldiers — 1st Sgt. Moses Williams — became one of the few black cavalrymen to win the Congressional Medal of Honor, awarded in 1896 for extraordinary heroism.

Today Williams is largely forgotten. His simple grave in Vancouver Barracks Post Cemetery draws almost no visitors. There is no memorial there telling of 32 years of service to his country. Only the gold inlay on the modest, white marble headstone identifies it as the final resting place of a soldier who received his nation's highest military honor.

While the aging cemetery at Fort Vancouver marks where Williams' story ended, no one knows for sure when it began. Even his place of birth remains obscure. While some records on Williams can be found in the National Archives, their content is sketchy and incomplete.

In 1896, no one worried too much about gathering facts on a black man in the Army — even one who won the Congressional Medal of Honor.

Army records show Williams first enlisted in the 9th U.S. Cavalry on Oct. 2, 1866. He listed his age as 21 and his civilian occupation as farmer. His home was somewhere in Carroll County, Louisiana, the records show.

Williams may not have realized he was part of a great social experiment.

Black soldiers died serving Gen. Washington and fought bravely with Gen. Jackson at the Battle of New Orleans. In the Civil War, 180,000 fought for the North, and 33,380 of those died for the Union that promised them liberty.

But their position in the military had always been tenuous. Harsh prejudice existed among officers as well as civilians. Many opposed giving blacks a permanent place in the Army.

But 1866's reconstruction-era Congress, which included a fair number of radical Republicans, vowed to change the status of black Americans. Congress, realizing a permanent place in the armed forces was a major step in elevating the status of former slaves, on July 26, 1866, authorized the creation of six regiments of black troops.

Nine weeks later, Williams abandoned farming for a career with the 9th U.S. Cavalry.

The experiment wasn't a total success. The all-black units were assigned white officers. Some of those officers, fearing that commanding black troops would ruin their chance for promotion, refused their appointment.

Historian William H. Leckie, in his study of black Army units, "The Buffalo Soldiers," noted that "George A. Custer refused a lieutenant colonelcy with the 9th and wangled the same rank in the newly formed 7th Cavalry — a decision that was probably a stroke of good fortune for the 9th and launched Custer on the road to the Little Big Horn and a dubious niche in history."

The attraction Williams felt for the 9th Cavalry is easily understood. When the unit was organized in New Orleans, he was just one of thousands of poor farmers in a war-ravaged region.

The $13-a-month Army pay wasn't much. Many whites rejected it out of hand. But it offered former slaves a way out, a chance to make something of their lives.

There was yet another promise the Army offered. Most blacks who enlisted were the illiterate product of the pre-war South. Again, the radicals in Congress took a novel step, assigning special chaplains to each black unit. These chaplains were charged with more than just moral instruction; they were responsible for teaching black soldiers the basics of reading, writing and math.

For blacks with a thirst for education, the Army was a rare opportunity. Many, like Williams, took advantage of the offer.

Records in the National Archives show Williams was illiterate when he enlisted, signing his Army papers with an "X." Five years later, when he re-enlisted with the 9th, Williams signed his name.

Was Williams a slave? Records are unclear on the point, said William E. Lind, a National Archives official. "He probably was a slave," Lind said. "You had very few free blacks in the South, and most would be in North Carolina and Virginia."

Records in Louisiana are also sketchy. Carroll Parish (county) no longer exists, and Williams' exact birthplace is unknown.

Life in the black units, while an improvement over what blacks might expect in the post-Civil War South, was still not easy.

Black soldiers were often issued shoddy uniforms and sometimes cheated by those provisioning the Army. White units frequently received better food. There was also intense civilian prejudice against blacks in the newly settled West, and some black troopers were killed in frontier-town disputes.

At times, horses assigned black troopers were old or lame — a factor of vital importance to cavalry.

Despite the prejudice and problems, the 9th U.S. Cavalry became a solid fighting unit, proving its worth on the Western frontier. Initially few expected the Indian Wars to amount to much. Almost no one realized the Western tribes would fight for 20 years defending their

without glory

lands and people.

The 9th was assigned to Fort Griffin, Texas, where Williams and the other troopers campaigned against Apaches.

Few more tenacious enemies existed.

Writes historian Place: "For over 300 years Apaches had fought Spaniards and Mexicans and Americans so viciously that even the mention of their name made men's blood run cold."

On Aug. 16, 1881, Williams and the men of the 9th's Company I were in New Mexico, resting after days of chasing Apaches.

2nd Lt. George R. Burnett would recall, years later, it was almost noon when a near-hysterical man raced into camp, screaming Apaches had attacked a nearby ranch, murdering the ranch owner, his wife, their two children and two sheepherders.

Burnett and 12 men immediately rode off in search of the Apaches. Shortly after spotting the Indians, both sides began shooting. Troopers and Apaches dismounted and took cover in the hilly, rocky country.

Williams and several soldiers arrived soon afterward and charged the Apaches on their right flank, forcing them to retreat. This began a running gun battle that continued for several hours over eight or 10 miles.

At one point in the battle, Burnett's startled horse broke free and raced away. Troops in the rear assumed the officer had been killed. They panicked and began retreating, leaving the men still facing the Apaches to almost certain death.

Exposing himself to hostile fire, Williams quickly rode after the deserters, rallied them and brought them back to the battle. The Apaches, even though they probably outnumbered the troopers, were forced to turn back.

But as the battle raged, officers became convinced they didn't have enough men to dislodge the Apaches. A retreat was ordered and Williams, Burnett and Pvt. Augustus Walley gave covering fire as the other men crawled to safety.

After the men were safe, and as the three prepared to abandon their position, a voice suddenly cried out from several hundred yards away. "Lieutenant, please, for God's sake, don't leave us here!"

Three men, one of whom was wounded, had been cut off during the battle and were now trapped precariously behind a low hill. Although outnumbered by perhaps as many as 30 Indians and in an exposed position themselves, Williams and Burnett quickly started a covering fire, allowing Walley to rescue the wounded man while the other endangered men crawled to safety.

All three would receive the Congressional Medal of Honor for their actions that day.

In recommending Williams for the medal, Burnett wrote "I . . . recommend him for a Medal of Honor for his bravery in volunteering to come to my assistance, his skill in conducting the right flank in a running fight of three or four hours, his keensightedness in discouraging the Indians in hiding and which probably prevented my command from falling into a trap, for the skill and ability displayed by him in rallying my men when I was dismounted and unable to reach them and lastly for his coolness, bravery and unflinching devotion to duty in standing by me in an open position under a heavy fire from a large party of Indians at a comparatively short range, and thus enabling me to undoubtedly save the lives of at least three of our men."

Two years after receiving the medal, Williams retired from the Army after 32 years in the 9th Cavalry. He came to live in Vancouver, then the Army's Pacific Northwest headquarters. The reasons Williams came to Vancouver aren't entirely clear, although near the end of his military career he had been assigned to a post in Oregon.

Williams, like many other retired professional troopers, may have felt that Vancouver's large contingent of soldiers made it a good place for an Army veteran to retire.

He died in Vancouver the following year, at the age of 54.

His passing drew a terse, five-line notice in the Aug. 25, 1899, Columbian. The following week the newspaper reprinted a short account, initially published in a rival newspaper, of the battle that led to Williams' receiving the Congressional Medal of Honor.

The commanding officer of Vancouver Barracks reported Williams' death to Army headquarters in Washington, D.C., adding the sergeant "died alone and without friends."

The **COLUMBIAN**

Friday, September 7, 1984

Dead Lake (or Fallen Leaf) Cemetery

Dead Lake Cemetery, also known as
Fallen Leaf Cemetery, is now abandoned.
It was located adjacent to the then existing St. Thomas Catholic Church at the
southern tip of LaCamas Lake northwest
of Camas on N.E. Lake Road. Burials
have been relocated.

DEAD LAKE CEMETERY

HOOD   Elizabeth Hood, died Jan. 7, 1872, aged 29 yrs 11 mos 29 days

MARREN   Maria Marren, died Feb. 18, 1860, aged 32 yrs 9 mos 14 days

MARREN   Martin Marren, died May 10, 1899, aged 59 yrs

MARREN   Maggie Marren, died Nov. 16, 1892, aged 6 yrs 1 mo 6 days

BANFIELD   Avis Banfield (no dates available)

BANFIELD   John Isaac Banfield, 1845 - 1923

RUBENS   Joseph Rubens, Dec. 10, 1918 to Aug. 3, 1920

NEGRETTO   Joe Negretto, 1868 - 1921

GRAVE MATTER—What to do with eight bodies left in the abandoned Catholic cemetery at Fallen Leaf Lake is the question Father Ron Belisle of St. Thomas Catholic Church in Camas is trying to resolve. Seen here examining a gravestone in a neglected, overgrown family plot, Belisle would like to have survivors of those buried there give permission for their relatives to be removed to another cemetery where their graves can be cared for.

Church asks to move old graves

The Corporation of the Catholic Archbishop of Seattle has asked Clark County Superior Court for permission to transfer bodies buried in the old Camas Catholic Cemetery.

In a petition filed here Thursday, the church said it will pay for new graves and markers. Bodies found in unmarked graves will be reburied and separately designated as graves of "Clark County Pioneers," according to the court petition.

The church acquired the land near the southern tip of Lacamas Lake in 1881. It was used as a Catholic cemetery adjacent to the then existing St. Thomas Catholic Church. That church is now at 324 N.E. Oak St.

Late last year, the Rev. Ronald Belisle, pastor at St. Thomas, said he wanted to bring back dignity to those buried in the old cemetery, which has long been neglected. State law says bodies may be removed from a cemetery with the consent of the cemetery authority and the written consent of a survivor.

However, the Camas Catholic Cemetery, as it is known, never was dedicated formally as a cemetery. Like many Catholic cemeteries of the time, it was merely part of the church yard.

The law provides that a superior court also may give permission to transfer remains.

Belisle has said the site may have had 15 to 20 graves at one time. At least eight people are known to have been buried there. There are additional gravesites for which the monuments have been lost.

New graves will be marked with the deceased's name, date of birth and date of death, if known, according to the church's petition. The church will pay for the costs of the transfers and for the new markers.

Belisle said this morning the bodies probably will be moved to another Catholic cemetery in the area, unless relatives specify another site.

A Superior Court hearing must be held before permission to exhume the bodies is given.

● BODIES ORDERED: The Corporation of the Catholic Archbishop of Seattle Friday won a court order to remove bodies buried in the old Camas Catholic Cemetery.

Superior Court Judge J. Dean Morgan granted the order, which permits the church to transfer the bodies to other cemeteries, at the church's expense.

The church acquired the land near the southern tip of Lacamas Lake in 1881. It was used as a Catholic cemetery adjacent to the then existing St. Thomas Catholic Church, now at 324 N.E. Oak St. Late last year, the Rev. Ronald Belisle, pastor at St. Thomas, said he wanted to bring back dignity to those buried in the old cemetery, which has long been neglected.

Under the court order, the church will provide new markers for the transferred graves, identifying dates and names. The few unmarked graves will be designated as graves of Clark County pioneers.

Concern over cemetery

Priest seeks relatives

FORGOTTEN DEAD—Since Joe Necretto was laid to rest more than 60 years ago, the Catholic cemetery at Fallen Leaf Lake has become a virtual jungle. Necretto's is one of eight graves still left amongst the trees and encroaching brush.

By JIM GERSBACH

The eight remaining graves at the abandoned Catholic Cemetery near Fallen Leaf Lake are almost buried beneath encroaching vegetation.

With autumn adding dead leaves to the litter, the few weathered tombstones will soon be nearly hidden.

Many bodies have already been dug up and taken to cemeteries where their graves will be cared for. Father Ron Belisle of St. Thomas Catholic Church wants to do the same for the eight people still believed to lie in the hillside cemetery.

But before Joe Cecretto, John Isaac Banfield, Avis Banfield, Joseph Rubens, Martin Marren, Maria Marren, Maggie Marren and Elizabeth Hood can be placed in new homes, their next of kin must give permission.

Since all of the people buried in the cemetery died before 1924, finding a living relative could be difficult. If none can be located, the church will probably seek an order to move the bodies and close the cemetery, said Father Belisle.

He said the cemetery was run by the first Catholic church in Camas, started in 1870 as a mission of St. James Church in Vancouver.

Many Catholic pioneers were buried in the little cemetery beside the church on 1.7 acres donated by the DeLeat family. Even after the church moved in 1901 to 13th Avenue and Birch Streets in town, burials continued for another 30 years.

Father Belisle said St. Thomas is also looking to close the four-acre Holy Cross Cemetery in Washougal. Maintaining the 82-year-old Holy Cross Cemetery would be financially difficult for the church, he said.

Once bodies are exhumed, the cemetery land would probably be sold and the proceeds used to cover the cost of the reburials in other Catholic cemeteries, he said.

Anyone who might be related to the deceased should call Father Belisle (834-2126).

68

The Rev. Ronald Belisle deciphers the dates on one of the old headstones in the abandoned Camas Catholic Cemetery.

Forgotten cemetery may get new life

By WENDY REIF
The Columbian

CAMAS — Deep in some dark, dank woods near the southern tip of Lacamas Lake eight graves lie in obscurity.

At this Catholic cemetery dating back to the 1920s 1890s, nobody has been buried since the 1920s and nobody has maintained it for just about as long. Several of the sites have been exhumed and the remaining ones are grown over with ivy, moss and ferns.

The Rev. Ronald Belisle, pastor of the St. Thomas Catholic Church, wants to bring back a little dignity to those buried there by closing the cemetery and moving the remaining graves to other sites, where they can be cared for.

"There's an obligation of the parish to maintain them," he said.

Located near Fallen Leaf Lake — also known as Dead Lake — and behind a rental property, the hillside cemetery is no longer accessible without trespassing.

Since July, Belisle has used informal channels, such as the local historical society, in his search for relatives of the deceased.

He has found one relative — who gladly gave permission for the grave's relocation — and has a lead on one other descendant. But nothing will be moved until Belisle has exhausted all efforts to find relatives of the remaining deceased.

If other relatives cannot be found, he will advertise the names in the newspaper.

Normally, the authority for any disinterments would have to be sought through Clark County Superior Court. But the law only speaks to dedicated cemeteries and the Camas Catholic Cemetery, as the overgrown parcel once was called, was never dedicated.

Like many other old Catholic cemeteries, it was merely a church yard. St. Thomas Catholic Church was established by the cemetery's site in 1870, as a mission of the St. James Church in Vancouver.

It has moved twice since then and is now at 324 Oak St.

Parish archives offered Belisle few clues as to the cemetery's history. The last recorded reference came in 1942, when Bishop Gerald Shaughnessy of the Seattle Archdiocese directed the pastor to forward a plat of the cemetery to comply with a new state law.

"If the order had been carried out, it would be in the archives," said Belisle. It isn't.

Five years earlier the bishop, on his parochial visitation, observed the abandoned cemetery and wrote: "Bodies have been exhumed from this cemetery without any permission whatsoever from the Bishop. I spoke to the pastor about this and he told me that it was done just through the undertakers, and he promised, at my admonition, that he would inform the people that hereafter absolutely no exhumations may be made except by permission of the Bishop."

Even in 1937, the Bishop referred to it as an "old" cemetery.

At one time, the site may have had 15 to 20 graves, Belisle said. The eight people who still are buried there are:

Joe Negretto, 1868-1921.
John Issac Banfield, 1845-1923.
Avis Banfield, no dates available.
Martin Marren, 59, died May 10, 1899.
Maria Marren, 32, born Feb. 18, 1860.
Maggie Marren, 6, born Nov. 16, 1892.
Elizabeth Hood, 29, died Jan. 7, 1892.
Joseph Rubens, Dec. 10, 1918 to Aug. 3, 1920.

Belisle said the Banfields had two sons, both of whom were bachelors. The Marrens homesteaded east of Washougal and the Hood family lived on Government Island. Beyond that, he knows little about any of the people except Negretto, whose relative he located.

Those whose descendants can be found will be moved according to the relatives' wishes, he said. The remainder probably will be relocated in the Camas Cemetery.

If he manages to succeed in this effort, Belisle said he will attempt to close the 82-year-old Holy Cross Cemetery in Washougal, which was by the old St. Andrew's Church, near where Jemtegaard Middle School is located. Although some attempts have been made to maintain that, blackberry vines run over the abandoned site.

Bethel Lutheran Cemetery

Bethel Lutheran Cemetery is next to the Bethel Lutheran Church, 159th Street, Brush Prairie, Wash.

BETHEL LUTHERAN CEMETERY

ABERNATHY	Anna, 1872-(11 October 1954)
ABERNATHY	Samuel M., 1864-(14 May 1948)
ABERNATHY	Vivian Carolyn, November 13,1935-April 11, 1946
ADAMS	Leslie V., 1910-(29 August 1974)
ADAMS	Walter O., 1921-(6 March 1975)
AHOLA	Lillian B., 1906-(24 April 1985) (records show 2nd marr. to Carlson)
AHOLA	William I., 1896-1968
AKRE	Ryan Alan; birthdate September 1, 1983
ANDERSON	Ellen M., 1912-1969
ANDERSON	John A., 1884-(4 June 1958)
ANDERSON	Ruby W., 1891-(24 July 1958)
ARNTZEN	Augusta, 1890-(18 June 1942)
AUSTRENG	Walter L., October 17, 1897-February 1, 1970
BATES	Leon A., 1891-(15 April 1973)
BATES	Lillian (Lilly) E., 1892-(12 February 1986)
BAXTER	Jesse R., 1911-(22 September 1951) U.F.K.B.T.S., Odd Fellows
BENNETT	Clio Roth (Cleo) 1880-1935
BERGREN	Glenn V., January 25, 1933-December 16, 1985
BJELDE	Tygve O., August 1, 1912-June 2, 1971; Washington, Pfc, 333 Inf., 96 Div., W. W. 2
BJURK	John, d. June 1, 1925
BRATSBERG	Nette J., 1856-1930
BRATSBERG	Ole J., 1865-(15 June 1924)
BRIDSTON	Samuel O., 1866-(9 March 1939)
BRITZMAN	Edna L., 1904-(24 December 1968)

BETHEL LUTHERAN CEMETERY

BRITZMAN	Robert H., 1901-(19 July 1983)
BRITZMAN	Wallace G. (d. 16 April 1981)
BRITZMAN	William H., 1899-(19 March 1954)
BROWN	Albert M., August 27, 1875-May 18, 1946
BROWN	Alma B., 1884-(6 June 1926)
BROWN	Anna O., 1855-1929
BROWN	Emil Kykyri, 1885-(29 August 1972)
BROWN	Ole A., 1843-1934
CARLSON	Gust, 1870-(11 August 1948)
CARLSON	John P., August 3, 1902-April 19, 1951, Washington, Pfc, QM Corps, W. W. 2
CHARLSTON	Edith Hjertaas, February 12, 1894-February 12, 1973
CHARLSTON	Gustave A., November 22, 1891-February 28, 1960
CHRISTENSEN	Anne, 1850-(21 October 1923)
CHRISTIAN	Bernt, October 24, 1846-November 15, 1925
COLFELT	Henry J., 1902-(4 April 1972)
COOK	Anna S., 1864-1946
COOK	Edward, 1905-
COOK	Henry, 1863-1930
COOK	Jake, 1896-(6 January 1972)
COOK	John Henry, 1891-(26 October 1926)
COOK	Olga E., 1897-(14 May 1962)
COOK	Suoma Mary, 1906-(10 May 1968)
DAGGETT	Gertrude Olive, 1892-(30 July 1981)
DAGGETT	Roy William, 1893-(20 June 1982)
DAGSLAND	Agnes Bertina, 1912-1918
DAGSLAND	John E., 1874-(6 March 1960)

73

BETHEL LUTHERAN CEMETERY

DAGSLAND   Marie B., 1884-1966

DAGSLAND   Ralf Meidell, 1914-1918

DANNAT   Lydia, April 27, 1877-December 28, 1962

DANNAT   Walter M., March 17, 1870-February 28, 1949
                  Pvt. 1 Mont., Inf., Sp. Am. War

DRAKE   Eva Elizabeth, 1908-(January 1973)

ELLERTSON   Joan G., February 13, 1934-August 27, 1976

ELLINGSON   Arthur, 1907-1939

ELLINGSON   Patria O., 1861-(9 December 1947)

ERKHILA   Ellen S., 1911-(5 August 1984)

FAEH   Leah, July 19, 1907-October 21, 1985

FAEH   Otto, 1905-(8 August 1973)

FERGUSON ·   Harold Eugene, August 20, 1925-February 2, 1986

FINSETH   Andrew, July 19, 1884-July 26, 1970

FINSETH   Emma C., January 19, 1887-January 12, 1943

FINSETH   Ivar, January 12, 1879-December 29, 1961

FORSEL   Anna, 1851-(21 November 1943)

FOSSAND   Alfred, 1901-(4 March 1976)

FOSSAND   Millie J., 1902-

FOSSUM   Martin A., 1893-(1 April 1972)

FRIEDRICH   Ida H., 1885-(1 August 1946)

FROST   Elizabeth M., January 13, 1904-July 28, 1986

FROST   Russell W., 1903-(22 March 1975)

GEHRING   Paul O., 1916-(25 November 1942)

GRANFORS   Anna, 1855-(28 January 1939)

GRANLUND   Anna Elizabeth, 1884-(6 August 1963)

BETHEL LUTHERAN CEMETERY

GRANLUND	George H., 1884-(3 September 1970)
GRANLUND	George J., 1906-(August 1930)
GRAUE	Carl T., 1900-(24 July 1953)
GRAUE	Gunda Sausville, 1909-1974
GRAUE	Palmer K., November 17, 1907-July 31, 1983
GRIFFELS	Infant Daughter, May 11, 1933
GRIFFELS	Bernice, d. August 1, 1928 (1929)
GRONROOS	Laurie J., March 16, 1917-September 23, 1974
GRONROOS	Leslie W., Sept. 6, 1904-June 13, 1956; Wash. Cpl.,U.S.A., W. W. 2
GRONROOS	Lillian, 1915-(29 February 1984)
GRONROOS	Tillie, 1880-(23 May 1931)
GRONROOS	Walter, 1878-(27 April 1949)
GULBRANSON	Amund, 1860-(20 April 1921)
GULBRANSON	Bertha, (dates illegible)
GULBRANSON	Gilbert, d. May 14, 1942
GULBRANSON	Josephine, d. April 12, 1942
GUSTAFSON	Anna H., 1860-(20 June 1952)
GUSTAFSON	August Carl, 1853-1937
GUSTAFSON	Peter S., 1899-(11 January 1968)
HALSTEIN	Henry, d. November 15, 1927
HALVERSON	Bertha, d. October 28, 1924
HANNUS	Ida, 1874-1935
HANNUS	Jacob, 1869-(17 January 1946)
HARD	Infant, no dates
HAUTALA	Antti A., 1888-(22 March 1971)

BETHEL LUTHERAN CEMETERY

HAUTALA	Matilda, 1886-(1 January 1958)
HEIKKINEN	Herman, 1884-(6 November 1972)
HEIKKINEN	Ida Marie, 1893-(7 April 1950)
HEINONEN	John, 1877-(2 December 1942)
HENDRICKSON	Andrew, d. November 4, 1930
HENDRICKSON	Augusta, 1867-(16 July 1954)
HENDRICKSON	Eino, 1912-1961
HENDRICKSON	John, April 28, 1851-October 9, 1934
HENDRICKSON	John A., 1882-(14 June 1912)
HENDRICKSON	Mary M., 1877-(23 September 1942)
HENDRICKSON	Wilfred A., April 6, 1906-November 29, 1951
HESJE ·	Birger, 1892-(6 December 1929)
HILL	August E., Aug. 11, 1895-June 19, 1947; Wash., Pfc, 361 Inf., 91 Div., W. W. 2
HILL	Eli, 1864-(9 January 1942)
HILL	Hilda, 1873-1960
HILL	Oscar, 1904-(18 October 1962)
HJERTAAS	Rev. Hans, 1857-(February 1922)
HJERTAAS	Indiana, 1858-1939
HOKKA	John, d. October 26, 1924
HOLMSTROM	Fred E., d. October 25, 1985
HUHTALA	August, 1886-1941
HUHTALA	Elizabeth, 1880-(8 July 1953)
HUHTALA	Ilma I., 1903-
HUHTALA	John J., 1905-(24 May 1976)
HUHTALA	Maria K., 1883-(12 January 1977)

BETHEL LUTHERAN CEMETERY

HUHTALA	Nikolai J., 1877-(28 March 1948)
HYRYLA	William A., January 24, 1891-December 28, 1941
ISAAK	Edwin S., July 18, 1897-Dec. 15, 1972; Wash., Pvt, U.S.A., W. W. 2
ISAAK	Jessie E., 1898-(1 January 1982)
IVARIE	John J., 1878-(18 March 1954)
IVARIE	Sophie C., 1877-(28 February 1963)
IVARIE	Wilbert J., 1916-(14 July 1980)
JACOBSON	Bartine G. "Jake", 1917-(15 November 1980)
JACOBSON	Erik, d. June 3, 1927
JACOBSON	Gust, d. July 25, 1929
JENSON	George P., 1883-(10 August 1965)
JENSON	Tina S., 1891-
JOHANSEN	Anna Martha, 1888-(6 September 1972)
JOHANSEN	Just P., 1906-(December 1969)
JOHANSEN	Mary A., 1912-
JOHANSON	Christian, February 7, 1889-August 31, 1947; N. Dakota, Pvt 83, Spruce SQ., W. W. 1
JOHANSON	Rev. Jens H., 1856-(2 September 1925)
JOHANSON	Johanna, 1881-(1 January 1945)
JOHNSON	Albert M., August 23, 1889-December 2, 1976
JOHNSON	Alma H., January 3, 1896-April 5, 1980
JOHNSON	Andrew, 1879-1947
JOHNSON	Anna, 1879-(31 October 1968)
JOHNSON	Charles J., 1872-1942
JOHNSON	Charles W., December 23, 1915-January 20, 1977
JOHNSON	Harold, d. March 3, 1959

BETHEL LUTHERAN CEMETERY

JOHNSON	Hulda M., 1886-(20 September 1958)
JOHNSON	Ida, 1875-(31 December 1942)
JOHNSON	Isak, d. August 26, 1960
JOHNSON	Jacob, d. November 2, 1948
JOHNSON	John A., 1877-(d. April 1940)
JOHNSON	Katherine, 1872-1938
JOHNSON	Martin E., 1876-(21 March 1940)
JOHNSON	Mary, 1856-(2 June 1943)
JOHNSON	Pauline, no dates
JOHNSON	Peter H., 1874-(27 February 1947)
JOHNSON	Peter J., 1850-1930
JOHNSON ·	Ruth A. C., October 19, 1893-July 4, 1984
JOHNSON	Sophie A., November 20, 1898-October 1, 1968
JOHNSON	Walter H., Aug. 29, 1894-Apr. 4, 1950; Wash., Pvt 37 FA, 13 Div., W. W. 1
JUOLA	Sophie M., 1892-1941
KAIVOLA	Herman, 1887-1930
KANANEN	Albert J., 1906-(24 February 1970)
KANANEN	Mamie E., 1906-
KANANEN	Mary J., 1884-1947
KANANEN	Matt, 1877-1936
KARI	Emily, 1891-(10 April 1959)
KARI	George A., 1889-(18 June 1962)
KERANEN	Eino A., Jan. 10, 1909-May 26, 1969; Wash., Sgt. U.S.A., W. W. 2
KLASSON	Knut H., 1898-(13 April 1968)
KREBS	Lillian E., April 14, 1915-September 18, 1973

BETHEL LUTHERAN CEMETERY

KROLL	Helen, d. 1921
KYTOLA	Armas Sam, 1910-(1 June 1970)
KYTOLA	Edla M., 1880-(1 June 1959)
KYTOLA	Ellen M., 1913-(14 May 1982)
KYTOLA	Samuel, 1882-1952
LARSON	Caroline, 1870-1961
LARSON	Gabriel, 1874-1960
LARSON	Leonard, 1863-(20 February 1947)
LARSON	Nillo, 1898-(buried 3 March 1978)
LARSON	Sophia, 1863-1936
LASSILA	Ina Martha, 1908-1967
LEE	Marlene C., May 22, 1935-February 4, 1963
LEFSTAD	Christian, 1873-(25 December 1942)
LEMATTA	Edward, 1892-1966
LEMATTA	George W., 1928-(18 July 1973)
LEMATTA	Hilda E., 1898-(18 December 1976)
LILLEBO	Bertha, 1864-(22 January 1948)
LILLEBO	Elias, 1860-1933
LILLEBO	Samuel B., 1928-1941
LINDBERG	Edwin J., 1886-(20 May 1962)
LINDBERG	Marie N., 1906-(16 June 1963)
LINDEN	Henry L., 1900-(28 November 1981)
LINDEN	Ida E., 1902-(3 July 1968)
LINDLAND	Jacob T., 1879-(19 February 1950)
LINDLAND	Josephine A., 1889-(27 October 1950)
LINDSTROM	Charles, 1883-(16 August 1955)

BETHEL LUTHERAN CEMETERY

LINDSTOM	Emil, 1885-1937
LINDSTOM	Milga, 1895-(14 May 1969)
LINDY	Hilma S.,1886-3 March 1962)
LINDY	Otto H., 1885-(7 June 1956)
LOBERG	Clara, 1890-1970
LOBERG	M. Dedrick, 1888-1958
LUND	Jacob L., 1900-(29 July 1976)
LUKARIVA	John, no dates
LUOTO	Ansel, 1887-(24 November 1962)
LUOTO	Hilja, 1888-(21 January 1985)
MAHLE	Edwin D., 15 June 1887-19 July 1966; Washington, Pvt, U. S. Army, W. W. 1.
MAKI	Fiina, 1892-(7 February 1972)
MAKI	Vaino E., 1913-(20 October 1981)
MARTIN	John A., 1883-4 November 1956)
MARTIN	Verna, 1917-(January 1945)
MATTILA	Maria S., 1879-(27 November 1939)
MATTILA	William J., 1873-(23 December 1946)
MATTSON	Baby Girl, d. July 12, 1952
MC LARTY	Pearl Belle, 1890-1946
MELBO	Anders H., 1860-1942
MELLAND	Nels C., 1877-(22 January 1937)
MELBO	Anders H., 1860-1942
MELLAND	Nels C., 1877-(22 January 1937)
MICHELSON	Henry C., 1900-(15 April 1974)
MICHELSON	John A., 1864-1930

BETHEL LUTHERAN CEMETERY

MICHELSON	Sophia, 1861-1947
MOEN	Elene E., 1860-(5 July 1930)
MOEN	Lewis A., 1864-(1 January 1937)
MONGILLO	Leonard L., (baby) b. & d. March 4, 1967
MONGILLO	Tracie R. (baby), February 10, 1968-February 3, 1969
NEHR	Ailone D., 1905-(13 April 1977)
NELSON	Albert, 1888-(30 October 1961)
NELSON	Mary L., 1891-(3 August 1974)
NELSON	Walter E., 1915-(15 September 1980)
NIELSEN	Sigurd C., 1907-(10 October 1976)
NOLTENSMEIER	Florence N., 1911-
NOLTENSMEIER	Floyd S., 1906-(16 December 1963)
NYLUND	Emelia L., 1887-(13 June 1955)
NYLUND	Oscar, 1882-1964
OFVERBERG	Elmar, 1884-(2 January 1946)
OGLE	Infant baby, b. & d. September 3, 1928
OLSEN	Albert F., 1894-(3 October 1979)
OLSEN	Christine I., 1861-(7 November 1950)
OLSEN	Lauritz H., 1855-(27 June 1938)
OLSEN	Thora, 1878-(29 April 1943)
OLSON	Brian, July 22 1967-May 18, 1986
OLSON	Christine, 1852-1938
OLSON	Ludwig, 1868-(8 August 1947)
OLSON	Ole J., 1859-1938
OLSON	Peter J., 1866- (8 October 1920)
OLSTEAD	Emma Marie, 1898-(November 1957)

BETHEL LUTHERAN CEMETERY

ONEGG	Flora E., 1887-1938
OSTGAARD	Ane S., 1860-(18 February 1934)
OSTGAARD	Ole P., 1861-(31 January 1937)
OSTREM	Bertha M., 1885-(14 August 1944)
OSTREM	Svend O., 1878-1931
OTRANEN	Albin, 1883-1970
OTRANEN	Helena K., 1884-(13 June 1963)
PAPPAN	Jeffrey David, April 20, 1960-January 13, 1961
PARIS	Charles E., 1929-(19 July 1974)
PARVI	Andrew, 1855-1941
PARVI	Greda Matilda, 1863-1937
PERNELA	Olaf John, February 5, 1914-December 28, 1983
PERNELA	John A., 1876-(30 July 1955)
PERNULA	Laura K., 1878-(21 December 1960)
PIETILA	Anna S., 1869-(buried 9 October 1927)
PIETILA	Frederick A., 1901-1947
PIETILA	John A., 1870-(7 May 1924)
PIETILA	Judith, d. December 2, 1942
PIETILA	Waino, 1907-1982
PIETZ	Gettlieb, 1882-1937
PIETZ	Mathilda, 1882-1962
PIETZ	Mickey
PIIRAINEN	Henry, 1878-(19 January 1955)
PIIRAINEN	Sandra Lena, 1880-(11 February 1971)
PRESTHUS	Gunnar,1900-(10 December 1979)
PRESTHUS	Selma A., 1911-(11 March 1974)

BETHEL LUTHERAN CEMETERY

PROUTY	Forde W., 1900-(16 May 1968)
PROUTY	Florence, 1913-
QUAST	Christian F., June 7, 1895-Nov. 6, 1972, Wash., Pvt, Bty E., 124 FA, W. W. 1
QUAST	Daniel H., 1901-(8 September 1964)
QUAST	Esther, May 26, 1906-January 19, 1986
QUAST	Hazel E., October 3, 1906-November 6, 1977
REINERTSON	Dolores Louise, August 5, 1929-November 22, 1929
REINERTSON	Johnnie Alvin, 1931-1933
REINERTSON	Josephine, 1906-(21 May 1952)
REINIKKA	Albert Norman, 1915-1935
REINIKKA	Clifford C., August 9, 1914-June 24, 1978
REINIKKA	Edward M., May 1, 1877-September 29, 1939
REINIKKA	Effie M., January 6, 1877-May 15, 1964
REINIKKA	Hilda G., 1890-(28 February 1947)
REINIKKA	J. H. C., 1918-1921
REINIKKA	William, 1891-1964
RING	Konrad, 1873-(25 September 1955)
ROTSCHY	Edwin, 1898-(3 November 1959)
SAARI	Ida, 1869-1941
SAARI	Isaac, 1870-(22 March 1951)
SALMELA	Arthur P., 1898-(13 November 1940)
SAMMOEN	Albert D., 1918-(21 August 1940)
SAMMOEN	Christian J., 1870-(30 January 1926)
SAMMOEN	Emma D., 1881-1966
SAMUELSON	Mary, d. March 23, 1924

BETHEL LUTHERAN CEMETERY

SAUKO	Edwin S., 1902-(11 January 1947)
SAUKO	Liisa Sofia, 1859-1932
SAUKO	Victor, 1887-(23 March 1955)
SAUSVILLE	Gunda Graue, 1909-(26 June 1974)
SCHAFFER	Arthur, August 5, 1922-January 8, 1982
SCHAFFER	Joseph, 1894-(18 August 1983)
SCHAFFER	Rosina, 1897-(29 January 1979)
SCHENEGGE	Flora E. Abernathy, 1896-1938
SCHOONUSON	James, d. October 9, 1931
SCHULD	Fred J., 1889-(1 July 1964)
SCHULD	Lena, 1890-(26 April 1969)
SCHULZ	Wilhelmina, 1860-(30 November 1942)
SCHULZ	William P., 1862-1947
SCHULTZ	Carrie, 1854-1934
SCHULTZ	Herman, 1864-(25 October 1946)
SHOLSETH	John Alfred, 1915-(23 October 1921)
SHOLUND	Annie, 1882-(3 June 1947)
SHOLUND	Erik, 1877-(26 December 1962)
SHOLUND	Harold, 1907-(4 February 1934)
SHOLUND	Milton, 1908-(20 June 1933)
SIMONSON] SIMONSON] SIMONSON]	Three Simonsons in records w/no further information.
SODERBERG	George, d. September 25, 1959
SODERBERG	Toini, d. September 6, 1978
SOLBERG	Carl, 1862-(29 November 1944)

84

BETHEL LUTHERAN CEMETERY

SOLBERG	Mary J., 1871-(11 October 1951)
SOLBERG	Ole Oscar, December 17, 1899-April 12, 1957
SOMMERVOLD	Hilma, 1909-
SOMMERVOLD	Peter Ludvig, 1906-(1 November 1973)
SONNTAG	Otto C., 1884-(21 April 1959)
STALCUP	John M., 1875-(20 October 1962)
STALCUP	Lulu E., 1895-(4 August 1984)
STENEHJEM	Albert A., 1875-1937 (Church Records- bur. June 24, 1938.
STENEHJEM	Emma I., 1875-(8 February 1960)
STENEHJEM	Marion P., d. June 10, 1978
STENEHJEM	Thomas, buried October 11, 1976
SUNDBY	David Chester, 1902-(27 December 1974)
SUNDBY	Violet Fern, 1908-(15 December 1974)
SUOMI	Charles, 1888-1935
SWINEHART	Eleanor J., January 29, 1929-February 12, 1982
TAYLOR	Denise Rae, (baby) b. & d. November 28, 1955
TAYLOR	Evelyn, April 6, 1938-June 1, 1986
THRONDSEN	Donald C., 1912-(27 January 1978)
THRONDSEN	John T., February 10, 1948-October 21, 1983
THRONDSEN	LaFern R., 1915-(11 July 1980)
TISTEL	John Edward, 1878-(29 October 1954)
TISTEL	Matilda, 1878-(16 November 1958)
TOMBERG	Selma, 1873-(3 July 1950)
TOMBERG	Waino, 1884-(11 May 1929)
TOTTEN	Edward L., 1897-(28 March 1934)
TOTTEN	Mabel, 1902-1929

BETHEL LUTHERAN CEMETERY

TROMMES	Harold, d. January 24, 1932
TROMMES	Hilda, no dates
USKOSKI	Alma C., 1887-1941
USKOSKI	Axel E., 1886-(24 October 1954)
USKOSKI	Bonnie Ann, April 24, 1949-December 6, 1949
WALZ	Kathy Marie, b. & d. August 18, 1975
WAUGH	Millie S., 1898-(18 June 1959)
WOOD	Anna, 1879-(6 December 1962)
WUOLLE	Albertina Ring, 1886-(25 September 1979)
ZINKEN	Sophia, 1854-1932

Washougal Catholic Cemetery

Washougal Catholic Cemetery is now abandoned and overgrown. It is located on S. E. Evergreen Highway and Sunset View Road, Washougal, Wash.

WASHOUGAL CATHOLIC CEMETERY

ALLEN,   Mary Ellen   1868 - 1922   Mother

BARNES,   Anna Mary   21 Sept. 1870 - 21 June 1947   Mother

BEAUREGARD,   Elizabeth   1878 - 1952

BEAUREGARD,   John J.   1861 - 1919

BEAUREGARD,   Jules   Born 1902 - Died 14 Dec. 1906   aged 4 yrs.

DANFIELD,   Katherine   15 ___ 1935   aged 37 yrs. 4mos 27 ds.

DOHERTY,   Anthony   1832 - 1910

EAUREGA,   Julius T.   Died 14 Dec. 19__   aged 4 yrs

HENRIKSEN,   [Large Plot, No Names]

HOWELL,   Mary   1877 - 1938   Beloved Wife

LEFEBVRE,   Albert D.   Died 24 Oct. 1906   Aged 24 yrs. 11
          mos. 2 ds.   Forever my wife, dear O'dear,
          I am not dead but sleeping here, and if her m--
          c---?   no sorrow take, but love each other for
          my sake.

MANNHART,   Andrew   1855 - 1918   Father

MANNHART,   Katherina   1855 - 1921   Mother

MERTZ,   Magdalene m.   1861 - 1937   Mother

McALLISTER,   George   1876 - 1906

Mc CUE,   Julia   1853 - 14 Dec. 1922   aged 69 yrs.

McCUE,   Peter   1843 - 1911   Aged 68 yrs.

NELSON,   Frieda   1864 - 1930

NELSON,   Hans E.   1868 - 1926

NOLAN,   Hugh   Died 21 Jan. 1911   Aged 55 yrs   R.I.P.

PEDRANTI,   Joseph V.   25 Oct. 1874 - 6 Jan. 1933   Father

PEDRANTI,   Joseph V.   18 Dec. 1904 - 24 Jan. 1926   Son

ROTH,   Katharine   Born Nov. 11, 1848   Died 7 Sept. 1916

ROTH,   Theodore   Born 9 May 1836,   Died 24 Sept. 1908
          Aged 72 yrs; Remember friends as you pass by
          That all mankind are born to die, Then let your
          cares on Christ be cast, That you may dwell with
          Him at last.

WASHOUGAL   CATHOLIC   CEMETERY

ROTH,   Theodore   1873 - 1939

RUEDE,   Marie   1832 - 1915

SHIELDS,   Maurice   1889 - 1934   Aged 45 yrs.

WAGENER,   Alois J.   Born 2 June 1891 - Died 10 Apr. 1911
          In Memory Of
          Weep not for my death, Know that I now live in Heaven
          near Him who upon the earth was my only love.
                                  St. Agnes

WAGENER,   Dominick   1841 - 1926

WAGENER,   Margareth K.   1848 - 1928   His wife [Dominick]

WHITE,   Frances   1900 - 1924   Daughter

Sara Union Cemetery

Sara Union Cemetery is located next to the Independent Apostolic Lutheran Church of the Northwest, at 18416 N.W. 41st Ave., Ridgefield, Wash.

A place of rest

Sara Union Cemetery was established during the 1880s.

SARA — It is a quiet place, shaded by large oak and elm trees and with many of the hard stone edges of the tombstones softened with moss. It is the Sara Union Cemetery, the burial ground of many of Clark County's earliest settlers.

Once the site of a booming logging camp, Sara is now one of the few really quiet rural areas left within a short distance of Vancouver. Not much is left from those halcyon timber days — just the old town name and a residence that once was a general store.

Located next to quiet Whipple Creek, Sara was founded late in the last century when the Lake River Lumber Co. built a mill on Whipple Creek. Three different theories as to how the town got its name exist, but the most plausible one is that Sara was named for Sara Emmons, the wife of the operator of a large logging camp there.

There likely were high times during the boom years of Sara, but now the old town and cemetery lie quietly, awaiting future growth as Vancouver spreads northward.

Only an occasional visitor disturbs the peace at the cemetery, which forms the churchyard for the little Lutheran church in Sara. Those who do stop by can read the names of those who helped shape this county. The time-darkened tombstones are like the pages of a history book in this quiet place of rest.

Photographs by Reid Blackburn

—of The Columbian

North County News, Wednesday, January 2, 1980

SARA UNION CEMETERY

ADAMS, Fred R.   1868 - 1937   Husband

ADAMSON, Kingsley   1910 - 1967

ALEXANDER, Albert V.   1861 - 1933
            [Husband of Laura B.]

ALEXANDER, Laura B.   1865 - 1928
                  [Wife of Albert V.]

ANDERSON, Jack D.   1929 - 1976

AXTELL, Marcia I   1862 - 1905   [Wife of Samuel]

AXTELL, Samuel   1849 - 1929   (Husband of Marcia]

BABCOCK, Edith C.   1899 - 1952   [Wife of Lucius A.]

BABCOCK, Florence L.   1870 - 1953

BABCOCK, Lucius A.   1897 - 1974   [Husband of Edith C.]

BADE, Alfred H.   4 July 1900 - 7 Feb. 1961
        Washington   Pvt.   U.S. Marine Corps   W. W. I

BARNETT, Esther (Page)   1894 - 19___

BARR, Merle G.   1901 - 1930   Son

BEALL, Chester   25 March 1920 - 27 May 1978
                Tec. 5   U.S. Army   W.W. II

BEALL, Cowin M.   1871 - 1963   [Husband of Madie E.]

BEALL, Gerald T.   4 April 1916 - 19 Dec. 1948
        Washington   509 Ord. HV Maint. Co.   W.W. II

BEALL, Madie E.   1884 - 1947   [Wife of Cowin M.]

BEAVERT, John   1875 - 1934

BENNETT, Wilford B.   1917 - 1918

BEYELER, Benjamin   1864 - 1950   [Husband of Eda A.]

BEYELER, Eda A.   1871 - 1949   [Wife of Benjamin]

BOWER, Fred   1868 - 1957   Father
            [Husband of Hulda K. Bower]

BOWER, Gladys   28 April 1920 - Jan. 7 1921

BOWER, Hulda K.   1883 - 1940   Mother
            [Wife of Fred Bower]

BROWN, Bryant   1822 - 1910
            Co. H.   49 Ind. Vol. Inf.

SARA   UNION   CEMETERY

BRYANT,   Ferrel   A.   1906 - 1953

BUCK,   Charles   A.   1869 - 1923

BUSH,   Albert   1815 - 1908   [Husband of Alvira]

BUSH,   Alvira   1819 - 1908   [Wife of Albert

BUSH,   A.   Rolla   1849 - 1921   [Husband of Rosnette]

BUSH,   Bessie   C.   1884 - 1957   [Wife of Clarke   E.]

BUSH,   Clarke   E.   1880 - 1963   [Husband of Bessie   C.]

BUSH,   F.   Rosnette   1853 - 1937   [Wife of A. Rolla]

BUSH,   J.   Edgar   1850 - 1913   [Son of Alvira & Albert]

BYERS,   Charles   O.   1890 - 1976

BYERS,   George Kendell   28 Nov. 1922 - 9 Aug. 1952
         Washington   S1   U.S.N.R.   W.W.   II

BYERS,   Harry   1880 - 1906

BYERS,   Myrta   1897 - 1942

CAMERON,   Martha   C.   1848 - 1923   [Wife of William R.]

CAMERON,   William   R.   1843 - 1911   [Husband of Martha C.]

CHAMPLIN,   Amos Clarke   1894 - 1974   [Husband of Fannie Belle]

CHAMPLIN,   Fannie Belle   1894 - 1958   [Wife of Amos Clarke]

CHAPMAN,   Edith   L.   1923 - 19___   [wife of Ralph W.]

CHAPMAN,   Ralph W.   1920 - 1977   [Husband of Edith L.]

CIRCLE,   C.   F.   1873 - 1937

CIRCLE,   D.   S.   14 Sept. 1844 - 28 Nov. 1913

CIRCLE,   R.   L.   6 July 1849 - 23 Jan. 1922

CLARK,   Sadie   A.   1874 - 1948

CLARK,   Earl   L.   8 May 1895 - 17 July 1949
            Iowa   Pfc.   8 Co.   Coast Arty   W.W. I

CLENDENNING,   G.   Byron   1877 - 1969   [Husband of Mary L.]

CLENDENNING,   Mary   L.   1871 - 1962   [Wife of G. Byron]

CONZELMAN,   Mary   1881 - 1941   Mother

SARA UNION CEMETERY

COWANS, Rilla A.   1878 - 1919

CUSTARD, Clara S.   1859 - 1931   [Wife of James M.]

CUSTARD, Helena M.   1903 - 1931   [Wife of Philip]

CUSTARD, James M.   1856 - 1954   [Husband of Clara S.]

CUSTARD, Meridith M.   1901 - 1966

CUSTARD, Philip B.   1895 - 1958   [Husband of Helena M.]

CUSTARD, Philip S.   1865 - 1941

DALEN, Aaron L.   1876 - 1942

DALEN, Alfred T.   1922 - 1930   Son

DASHER, Clyde W.   1897 - 1970
              [Laynes Funeral Home Marker]

DASHER, Ethel M.   1877 - 1961   [wife of Ira C.]

DASHER, Coleman   Co. F.   Illinois   Cav.

DASHER, Ira C.   1876 - 1954   [Husband of Ethel M.]

DAVENPORT, John L.   13 Aug. 1921 - 20 July 1977
            Cpl.   U. S.   Army   W.W.   II

DAVENPORT, Jasper A.   19 June 1905 - 11 June 1955
     Washington   Tec.4- 2618   Prov. Qm. Trk. Bn.   W.W.   II

DAVENPORT, Henry   1880 - 1949   [Husband of Laura S.]

DAVENPORT, Laura S.   1884 - 1957   Mother
           [Wife of Henry]

DAVIS, Silas L.   1850 - 1918

DAVIS, Susan May   1855 - 1921
       [Vancouver Funeral Home Marker]

De BUHR, Martin   1911 - 1933

DIETRICH, A. F.   1863 - 1915

DIETRICH, Edward L.   1899 - 1904

DIETRICH, Loyd C.   1903 - 1904

DITMER, Frank M.   1865 - 1945

DOBBINS, Lola M.   1870 - 1928   Mother

EBERMAN, Flora (Neilson)   1895 - 1953   Daughter

SARA UNION CEMETERY

ELLIS, Fred M.   1901 - 19___   [Husband of Henrietta L.]

ELLIS, Henrietta L.   1896 - 1972   [wife of Fred M.]

ELSENSOHN, Dorothy P.   1882 - 1955   [Wife of Joseph L.]

ELSENSOHN, Joseph L.   1881 - 19___   [Husband of Dorothy P.]

ELSENSOHN, Murl E.   1909 - 1941
          [Vancouver Funeral Home Marker]

ERTZ, Margaret Pauline   Died 11 May 1936   Aged   39 years
                    Mother

FALCONER, David   1854 - 1939

FALCONER, James David   1892 - 1926

FALCONER, Mildred Lydia   Aged 3 Mos. [Grave next to James D.]

FARIN, Antone   1876 - 1943

FITZ, Alice Carrie   4 May 1883 - Kansas
              Died 20 Aug. 1979   [Widow of Colonel James Fitz.]

FITZ, Colonel James .   1879 - 1964   [Husband of Alice Carrie]

FITZ, Fred   24 Feb. 1923
       Washington   Pvt. 1st Class   Med. Dept.

FLEMING, David L.   1860 - 1951

FRADENBURG, Hugh A.   1876 - 1963   [Husband of Maisy H.]

FRADENBURG, Maisy H.   1887 - 1976   [Husband of hugh A.]

FRADENBURG, Rollin A.   1913 - 1914

FROSH, Albin W.   1900 - 1918   [Son of John F. & Augusta C.]

FROSH, Augusta C.   1867 - 1956   [Wife of John F. -
          Mother of Frank - Albin - Henry - Theo.]

FROSH, Frank E.   1889 - 1918   [Son of John F. & Augusta C.]

FROSH, Henry L.   1898 - 1918   [Son of John F. & Augusta C.]

FROSH, John F.   1859 - 1924 [Husband of August and
        Father of Frank - Albin - Henry - Theo.]

FROSH, Theo M.   1903 - 1920   [Son of John F. and Augusta C.]

FRYDENBERG, Myrtle   1917 - 1932

FULLMER, Chester W.   1858 - 1938

SARA UNION CEMETERY

GRAHAM, Leslie C.   1952 - 1969   Son

GRIFFITH, Amos   1874 - 1956

GRIFFITH, William   [no dates]
                    Sgt. Co. D. 26 Missouri Inf.

GUNDERSON, A. J.   8 July 1861 - 15 July 1909

GUNDERSON, Ingaborg Dorothy   Died 18 May 1930
                    Aged 67 yrs.   Mother

GUNDERSON, Ingwald   1887 - 1956

HAINES, George H.   1912 - 1962

HAMPTON, Cyrus D.   1856 - 1937

HAMPTON, Hannah S.   1861 - 1938

HAMPTON, Margaret V.   1835 - 1917

HANCOCK, Eliza J.   27 Nov. 1886 - 21 Sept. 1967   Daughter

HANIFIN, Tracey   1966 - 1966

HANSEN, Ray Julius   1912 - 1974

HAROLD, Sarah   1886 - 1978   Mother

HARRIS, John T.   1866 - 1952   [Husband of Lucy E.]

HARRIS, Lucy E.   1867 - 1910   [Wife of John T.]

HARRIS, Mathew   1903 - 1914

HATHAWAY, Anna   1865 - 1914   [Wife of Heil B.]

HATHAWAY, Heil B.   1852 - 1948   [Husband of Anna]

HELLINGSON, Charles A. 1894 - 1959   Father
              [Husband of Lucy C.]

HELLINGSON, Hans J.   1854 - 1918   [Husband of Inga K.]

HELLINGSON, Inga   1867 - 1940   [Wife of Hans J.]

HELLINGSON, John   1905 - 1943

HELLINGSON, Lucy C.   1896 - 1927   Mother
              [Wife of Charles]

HELLINGSON, Stephen H.   1900 - 1918

HEMMING, William Edward   16 May 1940 - 19 May 1940

SARA   UNION   CEMETERY

HENDERSON,   Martha   (Brazeal)   1869 - 1961

HOAGE,   Clyde   E.   1887 - 1963   Father

HOFF,   Florence   11 Oct. 1858 - 1 Aug. 1925
      [Wife of John and Mother of Howard, William, Maurice]

HOFF,   Frances   29 May 1912 - 31 Jan. 1920
      [Daughter of Mary and Wm. Hoff]

HOFF,   Howard   L.   27 July 1884 - 25 June 1906
      [Son of John and Florence Hoff]

HOFF,   John   M.   27 July 1849 - 27 Oct. 1925
      [Husband of Florence J. Hoff]

HOFF,   Maurice   M.   1887 - 19___
            [Son of Howard L. and Florence J. Hoff]

HOFF,   William L.   1882 - 1965
            [Son of Howard L. and Florence J. Hoff]

HOLCOMB,   Carrie   M.   1883 - 19___
            [Wife of Henry Holcomb]

HOLCOMB,   Henry   H.   1890 - 1958
            [Husband of Carrie M. Holcomb]

JOHNSON,   Alfred   6 Jan. 1894 - 8 Sept. 1971
            Kansas   Pvt.   U. S.   Army   W.W.   I

JOHNSON,   August   23 Sept. 1848 - 31 May 1915
            [Husband of Emma Johnson]

JOHNSON,   Emma   7 May 1860 - 28 Jan. 1942
            [Wife of August Johnson]

JOHNSON,   Emma   E.   1865 - 1933   [Wife of George M.]

JOHNSON,   George M.   1861 - 1925   [Husband of Emma   E.]

JOHNSON,   William   F.   1872 - 1941

KAMMER,   Joseph   1907 - 1971

KERN,   Robert   E.   1923 - 1935   Son

KRIEGER,   Frank   1855 - 1929   Husband

KRIEGER,   Louise   1873 - 1946   Mother

KRIEGER,   Max   L.   1906 - 1943

KREBSER,   Frieda   (Ryf)   1903 - 1928   Mother

KROMINGA,   Renard   1883 - 1925

98

SARA   UNION   CEMETERY

LAWSON,   Edith   R.   1878 - 1966   [Wife of Norman P.]

LAWSON,   Norman   P.   1876 - 1958   [Husband of Edith R.]

MADSEN,   Konrad   1855 - 1953

MALBORG,   Svenegan   1906 - 1970

MARTIN,   John   1893 - 1904   [Son of John B. & Mary Ann]

MARTIN,   John   B.   1853 - 1919
        [Husband of Mary Ann and Father of John]

MARTIN,   Mary Ann   1861 - 1951   [Wife of John B.]

MATHEWS,   Leander   1837 - 1910

MITCHELL,   John Frederick   Died 2 Jan. 1958
            Aged 48 years 11 mos. 7 days

MEYER, Lillian H.   Died 14 Nov. 1936   Aged 44 yrs.   Mother

Mc CANN,   D. Oscar   1875 - 1955   [Husband of Marian P.]

Mc CANN,   Marian   P.   1880 - 1961   [Wife of Oscar]

Mc CLELLAN,   Rose Marie   1886 - 1969   [Wife of Rollie I.]

Mc CLELLAN,   Rollie   I.   1883 - 1929   [Husband of Rose Marie]

McGEE,   Janice K.   1870 - 1943   [Wife of William W.]

McGEE,   William   W.   1862 - 1926   [Husband of Janice K.]

McIRVIN,   Earl J.   1892 - 1953   [Husband of Maude L.]

McIRVIN,   Herbert L.   1929 - 1938

McIRVIN,   Maude L.   1896 - 1969   [Wife of Earl J.]

Mc WILLIAMS,   Frank   Free   1885 - 1949

Mc WILLIAMS,   Florence (Page)   1890 - 19___

NAGELY,   George   1925   Aged 17 days

NICHOLS,   Edward   J.   1838 - 1917

NICHOLS,   Harriet Adeline   1866 - 1958

NICHOLS,   John Colfax   1868 - 1942

NICHOLS,   Kenneth L.   11 Feb. 1885 - 3 Dec. 1907

NICHOLS,   Sally (White)   1843 - 1941   Little   Mother

SARA UNION CEMETERY

NICKELS, Jacob Abraham   Died 1929

NICKELS, Jacob   1850 - 1929

NICKELS, Johanna   1876 - 1943

NICKELS, Robert W.   31 Dec. 1923 - 28 Jan. 1967
      Washington   EM2   U.S. Navy   W. W. II

NICKELS, Peter   1860 - 1945

OGBURN, Helen   1917 - 1918   [Daughter of W. A. & Nora]

OGBURN, Marian Jane   1852 - 1925

OGBURN, Walter Rustin   1888 - 1943   [Husband of Marian J.]

O'NEAL, Mary Helen   1891 - 1970

O'NEAL, Orson Henry   1882 - 1944   [Husband of Ray Hermion]

O'NEAL, Ray Hermoin   1887 - 1919   [Wife of O. H. O'Neal]

PAGE, Frances Adell   March 1863 - Oct. 1944
                  [Wife of George]

PAGE, George   June 1856 - Nov. 1937
            [Husband of Frances Adell]

PAGE, James   5 Feb. 1844 - 12 Dec. 1908

PAGE, Robert A. Jr.   1913 - 1939
            [Son of Robert A. & Willota F. Page]

PAGE, Robert A. Sr.   26 Dec. 1888 - 20 Sept. 1959
            [Husband of Willotta]

PAGE, Willotta F.   31 Dec. 1893 - 26 Nov. 1956
      [Wife of Robert A. Sr.   and Mother of Robert A. Jr.]

PETERSON, Alice M.   1876 - 1945   [Wife of Perry]

PETERSON, Perry B.   1867 - 1953   [Husband of Alice M.]

PHILLIPS, Leota M.   1890 - 1939   Mother

PHINNEY, Dora E.   1876 - 1950   [Wife of Jacob E.]

PHINNEY, Jacob E.   1863 - 1946   [Husband of Dora]

PHINNEY, Julia A.   1818 - 1906   [In the Hampton plot]

PLOTTS, Robert B.   1902 - 1966

PLUMMER, Walter W.   1864 - 1925   [Husband of Rozella A.]

100

SARA UNION CEMETERY

PLUMMER, Rozella A.   1862 - 1937   [Wife of Walter W.]

POE, Mabel E.   1894 - 1940

POWELL, Mamie M.   Born 17 April 1895 - Died 17 Aug. 1979
                    Aged 84 yrs.

PRY, August   1871 - 1922

PRY, Caroline   1848 - 1939

PRY, Herman   1845 - 1915

RANDALL, Elizabeth L.   1946 - 1979   Mother

RATHBONE, Adeline   1840 - 1925   [Wife of Albert R.]

RATHBONE, Fred N.   1883 - 1912

RATHBONE, Melba R.   1858 - 1938

RATHBONE, Eugene   Died 4 Dec. 1917   Aged 66 yrs.

RILEY, Mintie (Wilson)   1874 - 1970   Mother

ROBB, Edward Winton   1862 - 1935   [Husband of Minnie]

ROBB, Fred O.   1898 - 1976

ROBB, Howard W.   1901 - 1965

ROBB, Minnie   1873 - 1954   [Wife of Edward Winton]

ROBB, Wallace E.   1893 - 1937

ROBB, Walter Stanley   1896 - 1930   Son

ROBINSON, William F.   1865 - 1942

ROLOFF, Ethel W.   1893 - 1947

ROLOFF, Fred A.   1894 - 1964   [Husband of Ethel W.]

ROOS, Edwin   1910 - 1976

ROYLE, M. Cloe   23 Nov. 1895 - 11 May 1978   Wife and Mother

ROYLE, Walter R.   16 Feb. 1893 - 17 April 1954
                    Husband and Father

RUTHERFORD, Samuel   1852 - 1947

RYF, Ida   1880 - 1957   [wife of Jacob]

RYF, Jacob   1872 - 1961   [Husband of Ida]

SARA UNION CEMETERY

RYLAND, Mary (Page)   12 July 1887 - 17 Nov. 1969

SANTEE, Alice (Penlington)   1881 - 1970
          [Wife of Joseph F.]

SANTEE, Alva E.   17 June 1888 - 15 Feb. 1962

SANTEE, Ella   1865 - 1938   [Wife of James]

SANTEE, James   1863 - 1946   [Husband of Ella]

SANTEE, Joseph Frederick   1884 - 1956
          [Husband of Alice (Penlington)]

SCHELLER, John   1864 - 1921   Brother

SCOTT, John   1873 - 1946   [Husband of Mabel P.]

SCOTT, Mabel P.   1878 - 1939   [Wife of John]

SECRIST, Frances   1852 - 1940   [Wife of George W.]

SECRIST, George W.   1841 - 1917   [Husband of Frances]

SEYMOUR, Eva J.   1882 - 1948   [Wife of Otto B.]

SEYMOUR, Otto B.   1884 - 1959   [Husband of Eva J.]

SHIPP, Jean & Dean   (Twins)   1 June 1943

SHIPP, Velma B.   1906 - 1967   Mother

SIMONSON, James   11 Sept. 1864 - 28 Nov. 1947

SKEEL, Agness V.   7 May 1898 - 24 Dec. 1902

SMILEY, Louisa   1869 - 1944

SMITH, Flossie M.   1882 - 1952   [Wife of Frank E.]

SMITH, Frank E.   1873 - 19___   [Husband of Flossie]

SNEAD, Thomas B.   1879 - 1960   Father

SNEAD, Thomas E.   1844 - 1921   Civil War Veteran

STONE, Anna M.   1867 - 1922   [Wife of C. E.]

STONE, Chas. E.   1864 - 1939   [Husband of Anna M.]

STONE, Sol. C.   1860 - 1933

STOVER, Abigail   1836 - 1920   [Wife of Andrew J.]

STOVER, Andrew J.   1834 - 1929   [Husband of Abigail]

SARA   UNION   CEMETERY

STOVER,   Elizabeth Jane   1829 - 1913

SUTER,   Hazel (Bonebrake)   1927 - 1945

SUTTON,   Julia D.   1882 - 1965   [Wife of Alva P.]

SWAGER,   Alfred Lee   1870 - 1960   [Husband of Diantha A.]

SWAGER,   Diantha Anna   1875 - 1919   [Wife of Alfred Lee]

SWAGER,   Hamilton   Feb. 1828 - Nov. 1904

SWANK,   Charles F.   1863 - 1951   [Husband of Lillie M.]

SWANK,   Lillie M.   1872 - 1938   [Wife of Charles F.]

SWICK,   F. H. & C.W.   [No dates - Marker in bad condition]

TAYLOR,   Hannah F.   15 June 1844 - 19 Feb. 1927

THOMPSON,   Frederick   1861 - 1934   [Husband of May C.]

THOMPSON,   James   1850 - 1940

THOMPSON, May C.   1871 - 1952   [Wife of Frederick]

THOMPSON,   Worthy   Died 9 Dec. 1939   Age 71 yrs. 10 mos 2 dys
                              [1868 - 1939]

THURMAN,   Amanda   1855 - 1935   Mother

THURMAN,   Etta C.   1895 - 1963   [Wife of Leslie R.]

THURMAN,   Leslie R.   1887 - 1967   [Husband of Etta C.]

TOWER,   Franklin   23 Jan. 1894 - 18 Dec. 1942

TOWER,   Jay L.   1901 - 1941

TOWER,   Jennie E.   6 July 1892 - 7 March 1907

TOWER,   Mabel   [No dates]   Mother

TOWER,   Madeline J.   1 Aug. 1898 - 11 Aug. 1928

WALE,   Hjalmer   1914 - 1914

WALTER,   Lillian E.   1874 - 1956

WALTER,   Wilma R. (O'Neal)   1917 - 1977   Mother

WARD,   Burton D.   1888 - 1952

WARD,   Ellen P.   1859 - 1937   [Wife of John W.]

WARD,   John W.   1853 - 1934   [Husband of Ellen P.]

SARA   UNION   CEMETERY

WARD, John W.   1853 – 1934   [Husband of Ellen P.]

WEAVER, Weldon W.   5 July 1913 – 9 July 1913

WEAVER, Melvin E.   2 Sept. 1921 – 24 Mar. 1945
          Washington   2nd Lieutenant   379 A.A.F   Bomb Gr   W.W. II

WEAVER, Ervin E.   1883 – 1958·   [Husband of Ava N.]

WEAVER, Ava N.   1889 – 19___   [Wife of Ervin E.]

WEBB, Mabel   1906 – 1914

WEE, Carl   1877 – 1952   [Husband of Ida S.]

WEE, Ida S.   1868 – 1945   [Wife of Carl]

WEE, Ole   1883 – 1912   Brother

WHEELER, Alice E.   1884 – 1947   [Wife of Leon L.]

WHEELER, Leon L.   1874 – 1960   [Husband of Alice E.]

WILLIAMS, Chester A.   1886 – 1973   [Husband of Clara E.]

WILLIAMS, C. L.   1821 – 1906   [Husband of Mary A.]

WILLIAMS, Clara E.   1891 – 1972   [Wife of Chester A.]

WILLIAMS, Margaret A.   1913 – 1977

WILLIAMS, Mary A.   1848 – 1931   [Wife of C. L.]

WILLIAMS, Winton L.   1912 – 19___   [Husband of Margaret A.]

WILSON, Nancy Jane   1854 – 1934   [Wife of Thomas M.]

WILSON, Thomas M.   1847 – 1933   [Husband of Nancy Jane]

WINDERS, Rose (Frosh)   1887 – 1973

WRENN, Byron Thomas   1902 – 1965   [Vancouver Funeral
          home Marker]

WRENN, Charles L.   1871 – 1950   [Husband of Margaret B.]

WRENN, Margaret B.   1878 – 1965   [Wife of Charles L.]

WRIGHT, Ferda L.   1902 – 1967

YANN, Barbara   5 Feb. 1847 – 22 July 1921
          [Wife of Christian]

YANN, Christian   30 Oct. 1838 – 8 March 1920
          [Husband of Barbara]

SARA   UNION   CEMETERY

YANN,   Lewis   G.   1889 –   1974   [Husband of Mary G.]

YANN,   Mary G.   1893 – 1973   [Wife of Lewis G.]

St. Mary of Guadalupe Cemetery

The Shrine was erected in Memory of
ANNA MARY CARTY SCHOEN

St.Mary of Guadalupe Cemetery is located south
St.Mary of Guadalupe Catholic Church.
28309 N.W.11 th.Ave. Ridgefield.Washington, 98642
$\frac{1}{4}$ mile East & 1 mile North of Ridgefield Junction.

ST.MARY of GUADALUPE CHURCH & CEMETERY.

St.Mary's was the first of the Clark County Mission Churches. Its history takes us back to the days when it was established in the community known as West Pioneer, near what is now the Ridgefield Junction. Before buildings were erected, mission priests celebrated Mass in homes or schoolhouses.

Early records of the Most Rev.Augustine Blanchet, Bishop of Nisqually, notes: "On the 5th.day of September, 1869, we blessed the Chapel of the Lewis River Mission, and put it under the the patronage of the Blessed Virgin Mary Immaculate in honor of her Holy name.

Mr.Johm Mays donated the land for the Chapel . This land donation extends behind the Church across the creek and includes the present church, cemetery & the woods south of the where the first chapel was.

The second church was built across the street from the present church in 1902, on land donated by Valentine Kapus. Mr.Kapus helped build the church. Others helping were; John Kane, Edward R.Dullea, James Carty, Philip Lee & Patrick Meany. The alter was hand carved by Joe Kapus of redwood brought from California by boat and unloaded at Pekin Ferry. The pews were made by Joe Gretsch, Sr.and Mrs.James Carty donated the red sanctuary rug. Stations had been brought from the Nisqually Mission in 1869. The first Mass in the new church was celebrated by Fr.Wm.Palmer on October 11, 1902.

John Malley, son of Casper & Catherine Malley of Spencerville, (now known as Enterprise) , celebrated his first mass at St.Mary's on Jan.1, 1904. A reception was held in the pioneer home of Valentine & Johanna Kapus. The first marriage ceremony performed by Fr.Malley was for his uncle, Joe Gretsch, Sr.and his bride Katherina Koppl. It was held at the home of James & Annie Carty.

Some of the earliest burials in St.Mary's cemetery were people with Irish names; Connell, Carty, O'Leary, Conway, Costello, Carr, Cunningham, Lynch, O'Brien, Riordan, Ryan, McCarthy, and many more.

****

107

ST.MARY of GUADALUPE CEMETERY.

ACKLEY: Forest K.   1898-1977   row 1-lot.9

ALARIG: Lois   d.March 1924 age 83 yrs.   r.12-lot 9

ANDRE: Margaret M.-b.14 Dec.1907-d.3 Feb.1985
          w/ Eugene R. - b.16 Oct.1906

ANDRING: Christina 1879-1965   r.9-lot 4
          Donald J. 1916-1931   r.9-lot 3
          Luon A.   1935-1936   r.9-lot 2
          Peter F.   1877-1950   r.9-lot 4

BARRON: Nicholas   23 Feb.1828 - 27 May 1897   r.7-L.29
                     born in Co.Kilkenny,Ballyloque,Ireland

BELLOWS: Marion (Grus) 1904-1957   r.4-L.3
          Paul M.   1906-1977   r.4.L.4

BIRON: Louis J.   1874-1940   r.6-L.21
          Mary (Conway) 1877-19   r.6-L.20

BJUR: Joseph   1895-1969   r.1-L.26
          Mary   1905-1969   r.1-L.25

BOYS: Edward W. 1886-1955   r.7-L.3
          Elizabeth J.   1889-1972   r.7-L.2

BRADY: Viola C.   1911-1986   r.8

BROOD: Adolph P.   d.28 Aug.1972 age 63 (funeral home
                                                    marker)
          Lydia Mary   d.15 June 1964 age 55   "   "
          Michael Ray - buried 6 Dec.1961   "   "

BROOKS: Sophie M. b.6 Oct.1926- Minot,No.Dakota
                     d.16 June 1986 -home-Ridgefield,Wa.
                     bur.20 June 1986 -r.2-lot 7
          w/Ed Brooks

BROSS: Baby   1902   r.8-lot 4

CARR: Anne   1849-1931 mother   r.7-lot 35
          George   1883-1943   r.7-lot 33
          James,Sr. 1846-1921 father   r.7-lot 36
          James,Jr. 1879-1900   r.7-lot 34

108

ST.MARY of GUADALUPE CEMETERY.

CARROL: Bridgett- d.17 April 1907   age 58 yrs.   r.7-L-25
            John   b.24 June 1847-d.29 March 1899-r.7-L.26
                        born in Co.Kilkenny,Ireland   w/Bridgett
            Mary   b.1836-d.1921   r.11-L.9

CARTY: Anna E.   1859-1937   r.10-L.36
            James N.   1839-1913   r.10-L.37
            Mary E.   1894-1975   r.10-L.38
            William   1894-1962   r.10-L.39

CHESTER: Leland R.   1911-1980   h/ Alice C.

CONNELL: John   b.Ballyolla Clonara,Ireland,Co.Clare,Ireland
                    d.11 Dec.1880 age 39 yrs.   r.9-L.32

CONNERY: Edmond b.Co.Limerick,Ireland-d.7 march 1890
                    age 67 yrs.-headstone erected by
                    Julia Connery,in memory of her beloved
                    husband.   r.8-L.30

CONWAY: Abbie (Bonner) 1883-1919   r.6-L.22
            Joanna A.   1872-1927   r.6-L.23
            Johanna   -   Juanita - Abbie --Baby B.

CONWAY: Katherine J. 1885-1896   r.7-L.24
            Mary Anne   1845-1918   r.7-L.21
            Maurice D.   1851-1901   r.7-L.20
            Patrick J.   1880-1889   r.7-L.22
            William T.   1882-1896   r.7-L.23
                (One headstone for above 5 graves)

COX: Eileen L.   1923-1982   w/Forest Cox
                    (sister of Opal Renner)

CRAIG: Benjamin Wesley b.29 Dec.1974-d.20 June 1977
            (picture of father holding benji)   r.1-L.12

ST.MARY of GUADALUPE CEMETERY.

CREAGON: Bernice E.   1906-   r.6-L.1
             David M.   1908-1967   r.6-L.2

COSTELLO: James   b.12 May 1825-d.30 May 1898   r.7-L.38
                     b.Co.Limerick,Ireland
             John   (no dates)   r.7-L.37

CUNNINGHAM: John   d.16 May 1898 age 83 yrs.   r.9-L.20
             Mary   d.31 Aug.1888 (natives /Co.ClareIreland

DAILY: William H.   d.11 Oct.1925(funeral home marker)
                                                    r.12-L.11

DAUGHERTY: Gertrude   1890-1972   r.11-L.14

DEAKO: .   Leonora d.16 May 1912 age 24 yrs.21 da.
             Thomas   d.20 April 1894-3 yr.8 mo.20 da.
             Willie   d.11 Nov.1906 7 yr.4 mo.16 da.
             (the above Deako' are in O'Leary plot 10-25 thru
                                                    27)
De BRUYNE: Robert J. - 1888-1963   r.4-L.21

DOBLER: U.J.   b.Switzerland 31 Jan.1844-d.3 Nov.1888
                                                    r.9-L19

DOLAN: John B.   24 April 1935-Washington Pvt.14 Inf.
                       19 Div.   r.7-L.9
             James Wm.   1860-1937   r.7-L.10
             Rosetta E. 1867-1942   r.7-L.10

DORNER: Clara   1909-19   r.8-L.21
             John   1892-1972   r.8-L.22

DOW: George   1909-1911   r.9-L.7

ST.MARY of GUADALUPE CEMEMTERY.

ERLER: Frank   b.3 Jan.1819-d.3 May 1891   r.8-L.20

              Joseph L.   1880-1923   r.6-L.37

              Mary   b.3 Sept.1832-d.14 March 1895   r.8-L.20

FAHEY: Nicholas Francis -b.1922-d.1979   r.4-L.2
              Lt.Col.-U.S.Army-W.W.2
              Norma (Sellers) b.1921-d.1984   r.4-L.1

FASLER: Mary   b.1900-   r.11-L.3
              Melchior (Mike) 1896-1950   r.11-L.4

FINNIGAN: Bridgètt Mary -6 June 1839-21 Jan.1922   r.11-L24
              Nora M.   1885-1973   r.11-L22
              Peter (son) b.25 Oct.1921-d.1 Dec.1921   r.11-L20
              Peter J.   22 June 1882-21 Sept.1967   r.11-L.21
              Thomas W.   1880-1951   r.11-L23

FITZPATRICK: Beulah V. 1904-1969   r.11-L.39
              Lawrence H.   29 July 1906- 14 April 1962- r.11-L40
              Vincent J. -16 Dec.1898-2 June 1960   r.11-L38
                   Oregon,Sgt.-Batry.A. -W.W.1

FLAHERTY: James   1852-1936   r.10-L.12
            John Leonard- 11 Sept.1891-16 April 1901   r.10-L.14
               b.Portland,Oregon- d.Douglas,Alaska
            Mary E.   1852-1938   r.10-L11
            Michael   1887-1930   r.10-L13

FLYNN: Bridgett b.24 June 1853-d.16 April 1908
                   native of Pollaugh,Ireland   r.10-L9
             Michael C. b.27 Feb.1844 -Co.Meath,Ireland
                   d.14 Aug.1913-Portland,Oregon   r.10-L.9

FOX: Alphonse P. b.11 July 1913-d.13 Dec.1978   r."A"L.9
             Frances J.-b.20 July 1922-d.25 Dec.1981

ST.MARY of GUADALUPE CEMETERY.

FOX: Chris T.   1909-19
          Edna M.   1911- 19
          Clarence Paul -b.30 Nov.1914-d.7 Aug.1972   r.3-L.7

FUCHS: Aquinas   1907-1977   r.11-L.17
          David   b.5 July 1919-d.15 Feb.1920   r.11-L15
          John J.   1870-1941   r.11-L.19
          Mary L.   1883-1961   r.11-L18

GATZ: Ann   1897-1942

GILLEN: Baby girl-d.9 July 1962 (funeral home marker-r.6-L36
          Irene E.   1926-1964   r.6-L37

GILLESPIE: Edward E.   10 Aug.1946- 8 April 1970   r.8-L.37
                  Oregon-Sgt.U.S.Marine Corp-Vietnam

GEORIG: Carl   1875-1927   r.10-L.17

GOERIG: Christina J.-d.29 June 1903-age 72 yr.8 mo.14 da.
                                                  r.10-L18
          F.N.   b.9 Feb.1824-d.10 March 1904   r.10-L19
          Lawrence H.-   1869-1941   r.10-L20
          William Walter   1871-1946   r.8-L11
          Emma Mary   1884-1965   r.8-L10

GREEN: Rosa B. -b.10 Mar.1884-d.13 Feb.1907   r.6-L.15

GRETSCH: John J. (father) 1906-1970   r.7-L15
          Rose M. (mother) 1910-19   r.7-L14
          Betty Jean (daughter) 1933-19   r.7-L16
          Joseph   1867-1953   r.7-L18
          Katherina 1878-1969   r.7-L19
          Peter S. b.19 May 1909-d.8 Jan.1982

GRIFFITH: Gwen Dawn -b.15 Oct.1965-d.28 Dec.1978   r.9-L.1

ST.MARY of GUADALUPE CEMETERY.

GODDARD: James   1878-1942   r.4-L.11
            Marion   1882-1962   r.4-L.11

GROSNIK: Michael (Mike) 1897-1979   r.6-L-8
            Mary

GRUS: Clara K.-b.24 May 1878-d.27 Sept.1963 r.5-L-6
         William G.-b.13 May 1871-d.25 April 1954- r.5-L6

HABERMAN: Florence M.   1892-19   r.8-L-26
          John J.   1892-1963   r.8-L.27

HAGEDORN: Infant girl   1963

HANNAN: Michael   1841-1908 (in Fleming lot)   r.11-L.11

HASTINGS:Sanford W. (Sandy) 1930-1985
          Jo Ann   b.1930

HELLEY: Max W. 22 Jan.1924-19 Dec.1962   r.5-L.11
        married 18 March to Dorothy F.-b.25 Dec.1925

HERZ: Valentine -b.3 Dec.1924-d.30 Jan.1973   r.9-L6
        Washington Pfc.-Co."C"-85th.Inf.-W.W.2

HiiM: Ordin A.   1892-1954   r.9-L.9
         Jack   1903-1977   r.10-L10

HILTON: Alan A.   1929-1983 (same grave as R.M.Imhoff)
                                                 r.3-L.13

HOGEVAR: Michael -native /Austria-d.25 Dec.1915
                age 74 yr.3 mo.   r.8-L.38

HOLBROOK: Melbourne   1925-1968   r.7-L.32

ST.MARY of GUADALUPE CEMETERY.

| HOLLOWAY: | Lois N. | 1911-1971 | r.3-L25 |
| | Merritt E. | 1903-1983 | r.3-L.25 |

| HUEBEL: | Joseph P. | 1889-1956 | r.12-L15 |

| IMHOFF: | Rose Marie | 1909-1972 | r.3-L13 |

| JACQUES: | Arthur | 1863-1927 | r.12-L7 |
| | Eugenie | 1854-1923 | r.12-L 6 |

KANE: Anna (Flanagan) w/Michael,b.in Ireland   r.10-L30
              d.2 March 1894-age 52 yrs.
       Ellen ,w/ Thomas -d.23 June 1899-age 53 yrs.
         b.New Castle West,Ireland-Co.Limerick r.11-L.30
       James C.   1874-19 59   r.10-L.29
       Johanna   1881-1938   r.11-L.34
       Katherine T. 1874-1965   r.10-L.28
       Mary B.   1885-1964   r.12-L.31
       Mary E.   1875-1939   r11-L.33
       Julia   1877-1953   r.11-L 35
       Michael H. 1880-1932   r.11-L.29
       Robert   1923-1931   r.12-L.30
       Thomas F.   b.Co.Clare,Ireland   r.11-L.31
              b.6 Jan.1838-d.8 Aug.1927
       Thomas   1878-1961   r.11-L.28
KAPUS: Anton   1886-1954   r.5-L.13
       Anton V.   17 June 1923-14 Feb.1963   r.5-L.10
       Frances   1895-1977   r.5-L.12
       Frank (brother) 1893-1952   r.6-L.14
       Johanna (Mother) b.Veldes,Austria-7 April 1850
              d.24 April 1900   r.6-L.16
       Joseph   1877-1945   r.6-L.12
       Lloyd J.   1908-1931   r.6-L.13
       Rose B.(Green) 10 Mar.1884-13 Feb.1907   r.6-L 15
       Valentin (father) b.Veldes,Austria   r.6-L16
              14 Feb.1838 - 30 June 1900
       Valentine   1874-1929   r.6-L.17

114

ST.MARY of GUADALUPE CEMETERY.

KARNIS: Anthony (Tony) 1904-1979   r.4-L.16
         Frank G.   1939-1965   r.4-L.17

KASPER: Adam J.   1907-1978   r.4-L.23

KEMPER: Infant   1961-1961   r.5-L.22

KENNY: James   b.Co.Kilkenny,Ireland-d.29 Aug.1908
                 age 82 yrs.   r.7-L30

KRAUSE: Robert Allen -b.7 Aug.1951 -d.17 July 1975
         Pfc.U.S.Army-Vietnam   r.2-L.3
         (son /Donald C.Krause & Geneva Stemmerman)

KREBSER: Raymond M.   1900-1952   r.7-L.5
          Florence   1917-1920   r.7-L.6
          Mary O.   1895-1961   r.7-L 7
          Frank A.   1888-1958   r.7-L.8
          Edward O.   1916-1976   r.8-L.3
          Mary A.   1921-19   r.8-L.2
          John   b.26 March 1898-d.3 July 1980-r.8-L4
          George   1890-1911   r.8-L.6
          Frederick J. 1910-1911   r.8-L.7
          George   1859-1916   r.8-L.8
          Emma   1867-1934   r.8-L.9
          Albert V.   1893-1942   r.8-L.34
                   Pvt.22nd.Mg.Bn.8 Div.
          Cora   1891-1966   r.8-L.35

KOESTER: Anna M.   1870-1951   r.10-L.3
          Bernard M. 1867-1950   r.10-L.4

KOPPL: Henry - b.12 Sept.1903- d.19 Dec.1971 - r.6-L24
             Washington-Pvt.-Co.B.-119 TD-Bn.-W.W.2

KOSHER: J.   no dates   r.8-L.18

ST.MARY of GUADALUPE CEMETERY.

KUCKENBERG: William (father) 1863-1938   r.5-L.18
              William P. (son) 1892-1914   r.5-L.17
              Katie (mother)   1871-1954   r.5-L.16

LAWS: Cecil b.12 Nov.1902- d.15 March 1981   r.11-L.13

LEARY: John   1877-1942   r.10-L.7
        Michael   1842-1927   r.10-L.8
        Annie   1845-1908   r.10-L.8
        Lawrence   1879-1950   r.11-L.6
        Annie   1882-1972   r.11-L.7

LEHNER: Albert F.   1888-1972   r.4-L.24
        Bertha K.   1900-1963   r.4-L.25
        Bertha M.   14 June 1917-16 Nov.1970   r.5-L26
        'Grace   1875-1964   r.5-L.24
        Michael J. 1858-1938   r.5-L.25
        Herman A.   25 March 1911-31 Oct.1968   r.5-L-27
                 Washington-Tec.5-U.S.army W.W.2
        William   1911-1984

LUTZENBERGER: John   1904-1975   r.9-L.33
        George R. 2 Dec.1916-1 March 1960   r.9-L.34
        Veronica E.- 1884-1954   r.9-L.35
        John   1880-1956   r.9-L36
        William   1914-1934   r.9-L.38
        Mary ANN   1906-1931   r.9-L39
        Veronica C. 1917-1945   r.9-L 37

LYNCH: William B.   native /Co.Limerick,Ireland
            d.18 Feb.1907-age 72 yrs.   r.9-L.27
        Honora (wife) b.Co.Limerick,Ireland   r.9-L28
            d.5 Sept.1914-age 82 yrs.
        Mary Ann Katherine (daughter) 1862-1883- r.9-L.29
        Ellen   1872-1883   r.9-L.29
        William   1870-1943   r.9-L.30

ST.MARY of GUADALUPE CEMETERY.

MAIN: Pauline   d.13 March 1981-age 66 yrs.   r.7-L.1

MALSEY: Robert O.(Bert) b.3 April 1919-d.29 Nov.1980
          T.Sgt.-U.S.Army

MANNIX: Patrick   1847-1920 -b.Co.Kerry,Ireland-r.6-L31
        Margaret   1831-1898-b.St.Johns,New Brunswick,Canada
                                              r.6-L.31

MARTIN: Abraham B.   1882-1937   r.1-L.3
                (moved from Oregon cemetery)   .
        Emma   b.21 March 1890-d.18 May 1979- r.1-L.4

MAUL: Elizabeth   1874-1943   r.6-L.33

Mc Carthy: Martha May   1883-1976   r.9-L.23
           John D.   1884-1939   r.9-L.23

Mc GUIRE: Patrick -b.Co.Meath,Ireland-   r.6-L30
                d.8 April 1903-age 74 yrs.

MILLER: Rhoda M.   1923-1979 -w/George (b.1920) r."A"-12

MYHRE: Mary H.   1890-1976   r.9-L.10
        Leslie L. 1903-1980

NARY: single marker for 4 graves. inscribed "Nary"
                          r.9-L.24 thru 26

NELSON: Garett Lloyd -3 Aug.1974-1 Oct.1975   r.5-L.19
        Betty C.   1911-1983
        Lester   1908-1983   Betty & Lester marr.18 June 1933

NOLL: George -native /Germany-d.age 69 yrs.   r.8-L.28

O'BRIEN: Alice- d.23 Sept.1910-age 55 yrs.   r.10-L 21
          native/Waterford Co.,Ireland
        Thomas   1843-1918   r.10-L 21
        James - b.Leller Kelly,Co.Clare,Miltown Malboy,Ireland
             d.age 67 yrs.on 14 Sept.1907   r.10-L.22

OCHSNER: Joseph Edward -b.17 May 1958-d.18 May 1958-r.6-L 29

O'CONNELL: Mary E. - 19 Dec.1888-11 Jan.1969   r.5-L.5

ST. MARY of GUADALUPE CEMETERY.

O'LEARY: Mary-d.14 Feb.1912-age 76 yr.3 da.   r.10-L.25

Dennis-27 Feb.1893-age 72yr.9 mo.16 da.   thru

John -d.11 July 1892-11mo.12 da.   L.27

Nellie - 30 Nov.1895-age 5 yr.7 mo.16 da.

Edward -d.7 Oct.1891-age 7 mo.3 da.

John   1869-1940   r.11-L.23

Dennis A.   1876-1936   r.11-L.24

Joseph   1912-1926   r.11-L.25

Thomas   1866-1918   r.11-L.26

Patrick -d.26 Jan.1892-78 yrs.   r.8-L.23

b.Rosscarberry,Co.Cork,Ireland.

O'ROURKE: Katherine E. - 1863-1931   r.10-L.35

PECHIN: Delima E.- 1904-1969   r.6-L.11

PFEIFER: no name - d.1960

PLAMONDON: George R.-b.29 Sept.1914-d.8 Jan.1969- r.3-L.27

Calif.-Cpl.-Medical Dept.-W.W.2

Mary G.   1887-1957   r.6-L.4

Isadore J.- 1887-1957   r.6-L.5

George L. -b.29 July 1928-d.21 Dec.1951-- r.6-L.6

Washington-Pvt.-7 Tank Bn.-3rd.Armored Div.

Kathleen Ann - 21 Oct.1961   r.4-L.8

Leonard J. -b.10 Nov.1923-d.10 Feb.1962--r.4-L.9

Washington-Tec.5-2 Basc P.O.-W.W.2

POWERS: John T. -b.11 April 1923-d.4 Dec.1970   r.5-L.4

Washington-Cox-U.S.Navy-W.W.2

PROM: George N.-b.6 Sept.1895-d.29 March 1968--r.9-L21

Washington-Pvt.U.S.Army-W.W.1

RASHFORD: Walter 1843-1901   r.10-L.24

Ellen   1847-1948   r.10-L.23

RAU: Ernest A.   1917-1986

Mary Ann   1916-1984

ST.MARY of GUADALUPE CEMETERY.

RAYMER: George M.   b.1932-1953   r.12-L.16
        (son /Giles & Laura(Chenette)Raymer)

REARDON: Anna (Fitzpatrick) 1871-1956   r.11-L.37

RENNER: Amanda Kae b.17 Feb.1978-d.31 Dec.1978--r.1-L.13
        Hubert E. -3 May 1922-d.21 June 1980   r.10-L.2
            (husb./Opal Carlson Renner)

        Joseph E.- 1882-1966   r.10-L.6
        Maud L.   1893-1985 (12 May)   r.10-L.5

REESE: Amelia M.   1905-19
       Charles H.   1903-1969   r.6-L.18
                                                   r.6-L.19

RIORDON: Michael J.   1855-1932   r.9-L.12
         Margaret   1864-1941   r.9-L.12
         Jeremiah -b.Ballingeary,Co.Cork,Ireland
                  d.6 Aug.1891 age 40   r.9-L.14
         Jere D.   1888-1932   r.9-L.13

RIPP: Mary Helen - d.23 May 1961-age 38yrs.   r.4-L.7

RYAN: Maggie d.1898 age 2 yrs.   r.8-L.25
        Albert d.1893 "   16 mos.   r.8-L.25
        Analiza (Carty) d.on Union Ridge-27 Nov.1888
            age 42 yrs.-w/ Joseph Ryan - b.in Black Water,
            Waxford co.,Ireland   r.9-L.17

SANNA: Steve   1889-1966   r.6-L.26

SANSFACON: Joseph L.   1881-1938   r.5-L.7

SHOEN: Anna Mary (Carty) b.20 May 1922-d.4 May 1957
            beloved wife of Leonard S.Shoen -- r.8-L.14
            mother of/ Samuel William -- Mark Vincent
                        Michael Leonard -- Mary Anna
                        Edward Joseph   -- Paul Francis
        Hendrick b.29 July 1913-d.16 Jan.1984

    (The Shrine in front of the Cemetery was erected in
      memory of Anna Mary Carty Shoen.)

ST.MARY of GUADALUPE CEMETERY.

STANEK: Frank E. (father) 1886-1943   r.12-L.25
         Eugene T. (son)   1924-1939   r.12-L 25
         Deloris T. (daughter) 1932-1937   r.12-L 26

STARRS: Eliza   1860-1943   r.12-L.13
        ? no name   r.12-L.14

SCHULTZ: Bertha F.   1883-1972   r.7-L.39
         Bernard   1880-1975   r.7-L.40

TEMME: Ramon Stephen -b.3 March 1977-d.28 April 1977
                                                 r.1-L.10

THOMAS: Alice E.   1894-1963   r.4-L 18
         Harry   1888-1975   r.4-L 19

THOMPSON: Laura P.   1910-1969   r.11-L.36

TORKER: Anton   1875-1954   r.5-L 14
         Annie   1879-1978   r. 5-L15

UNGEMACH: Georgianna L.   1901-19   r.5-L.8
           Richard C.   1880-1959   r.5-L 9

VAN STIPHOUT: Peter 1876-1943   r.6-L.9
        Delima   1882-1913   r.6-L.10
        Helen   1901-1914   r.6-L.10

WALKER: Minnie E.   1890-1967   r.12-L.4
        John Patrick 1885-1966   r.12-L.5

WARNER: Jerrold R.   1950-1964   r.3-L 3

WASER: Remy   1889-1936   r.12-L 39
        Calvin   1935-1946   r.12-L 35

WELLS: Mary C.   1883-1932   r.5-L 20
        "Luke" T.L. 1873-1938   r.5-L 21

WHITE: Henry   1895-19   r.8-L.40
        Mary R.   1889-1932   r.8-L 39

WHEELER: Clara L.   1887-19   r.3-L.18
         Darcy V.   1885-1969   r.3-L.19

120

ST.MARY of GUADALUPE CEMETERY.

WINES: Josephine   d.Dec.1926   r.12-L.8

WRIGHT: Elmer S.   1908-1971

WULF: Frances K.   1898-19   r.3-L.13
        John C.   1901-1980   r.3-L. 4

ZONTER: Martin   1855-1940   r.6-L.7
 (Zontar)

Unknown grave - marker says "Mother" 1849-1897 - r.7-L.28

****

Families who have reserved plots in the above Cemetery.

Chester   Boys   Fassler   Gretsch
Krause   Powers   Carty
Pfeifer   Krupicha   Fuchs
Brooks   Creagan   Effinger
Fox   Krebser   Van Rosky
Warner   Torker   Wheeler

****

St.Mary of Guadalupe Cemetery was read by members of the
Clark County Genealogical Society in October of 1978. It
was checked again for additional burials in Oct.1986.
The cemetery reading was checked with the person in charge
of lot sales,(Martha Krebser) in 1978.The Pastor of St.Mary
of Guadalupe Catholic Church,Fr.Ronald Knudsen, gave
permission to publish the Records.

****

Row & Lot numbering begin in front nearest the Church side.
"r"means row number. "L"refers to lot number.

****

Mr. and Mrs. John Lutzenberger

Mr. and Mrs. John Fox, Sr.

Mr. and Mrs. Michael Lehner, Sr.

Michael and Margaret Riordan
and family

Fr. John Malley with newlyweds
Joe and Katherina Gretsch

St. Mary of Guadalupe

The Krebser Family

Above: Joe & Katherina Gretsch
        and sons
Above right: Valentine & Johanna
             Kapus & family
Middle: James & Anna Carty & son
        William
Middle right: Mr. & Mrs. Thomas
              Kane
Below right: Mr. & Mrs. Simon
             Gretsch

Ridgefield Cemetery

Ridgefield Cemetery was originally two cemeteries, I.O.O.F. and Valley View Cemetery. It was owned by the I.O.O.F. and the First Presbyterian Church, and deeded over to the town of Ridgefield in 1915.

It is located in south Ridgefield on Cemetery Road just off Hillhurst Road.

RIDGEFIELD   CEMETERY

ABRAMS,   Daniel Kendrick   1 June 1829 - 26 Aug. 1911
                    A Friend To All

AHRENS,   Gertrude A.   1917 - 1936

AHRENS,   Ida   1878 - 1920   [Wife of William P.]

AHRENS,   Paul W.   1918 - 1975   U.S. Army   W.W. II

AHRENS,   William P.   1873 - 1935 [Husband of Ida]

ALBEE,   Zelda Mae   1930 - 1975

ALBRECHT,   August   1840 - 1908

ALBRECHT,   Frank   1867 - 1950

ALLEN,   Arthur N.   1883 - 1936

ALLEN,   Elizabeth J.   1848 - 1928

ALLEN,   Ernst L.   1880 - 1958

ALLEN,   Lulu B.   1 June 1876 - 17 Aug. 1893
              Beloved daughter of W.G. & Mary A. Allen
              "God be with you till we meet again"

ALLEN, Nathaniel S.   1845 - 1926   [Husband of Elizabeth J]

ALVIN,   Sophia A.   6 Dec. 1873 - 7 Sept. 1917

AMACHER,   Jacob   1883 - 1920
               Empor Zuin Lirhl.

ANDERSON,   Ada M.   1877 - 1954   [In Pearson Plot]

ANDERSON,   John   25 Feb. 1822 - 17 Sept. 1896
              I have fought a good fight
              I have finished my course
              I have kept the faith   2 Timothy 4:7
         O, how sweet it will be in that beautiful land
       When free from all sorrow and pain, With sons on
              our lips and with harps in our hand--
       To meet one another again.

ANDERSON,   Paul A.   1877 - 1948   [In Pearson Plot]

ARMSTRONG,   George   1863 - 1930   Father
                 [Husband of Virginia]

ARMSTRONG,   Ruth Ann   1830 - 1904   [Wife of William]

ARMSTRONG,   Virginia   1870 - 1951   Mother
                 [Wife of George]

ARMSTRONG,   William   1829 - 1916   [Husband of Ruth Ann]

126

RIDGEFIELD   CEMETERY

ATTERBURY, Claude G.   29 Nov. 1897 - 10 Sept. 1955
        Washington   Cpl.   Co. B. 2 Military Police Co. WW I

BADGER, Sylvia   1845 - 1903   [Wife of Ephriam]

BAGLEY, Chester J.   1887 - 1969   [Husband of Loretta H.]

BAGLEY, Loretta H.   1888 - 1967   [Wife of Chester J.]

BALES, Allen King   1858 - 1927

BALES, Allen K.   1885 - 1957

BARLEY, Christa (Nay)   1885 - 1964   [Wife of Lloyd B.]

BARLEY, Lloyd B.   1884 - 1963
                    [Husband of Christa Nay]

BARNES, Abner Allen   28 Feb. 1894 - 14 Oct. 1969
        Washington   Pfc MG. Co. 355 Infantry   W W 1

BARNES, Esther M.   1882 - 1946   [Wife of Hiram H.]

BARNES, Hiram H.   1883 - 1927   [Husband of Esther M.]

BARTLETT, George H.   1906 - 1964

BATES, Glen A.   1915 - 19___

BATES, Ella   1868 - 1930

BEHYMER, Ray   1890 - 1969   [Husband of Ola]

BELL, William Munger   1904 - 1919

BEMIS, George   1896 - 1963

BEMIS, Isabel   1906 - 19___

BEMIS, Ted M.   1939 - 1952

BENNETT, David   1 June 1830 - 15 Oct. 1908
        Aged 78 yrs. 4 mos. 14 days
                [Husband of Margaret Ann]

BENNETT, Florence M.   1878 - 1961   [Wife of Thomas]

BENNETT, John W.   1868 - 1954
                    [Husband of Lillian E.]

BENNETT, Lillian E.   1876 - 1940   [Wife of John W.]

BENNETT, Margaret Ann   2 April 1832 - 2 Sept. 1905
            [Wife of David]

BENNETT, Thomas   1866 - 1928   [Husband of Florence M.]

RIDGEFIELD CEMETERY

BERNARDO, Edgar L.   1890 - 1936

BISHIR, Charles Lundy   1887 - 19___
                                        [Husband of Mary K.]

BISHIR, Mary K.   1893 - 19___
                                              [Wife of Charles Lundy]

BJUR, Albin   1902 - 1973   Dad
              [Husband of Maud]

BJUR, Maud   1907 - 19___   Mother
              [Wife of Albin]

BLACKBURN, John W.   1870 - 1950   [Husband of Lulu]

BLACKBURN, John Ward [Infant]   12 Nov. 1904 - 13 Nov. 1904
                  Son of J.W. & Lulu B. Blackburn

BLACKBURN, Lulu   1879 - 1933
                                        [Wife of John W.]

BLACKBURN, Samuel H.   16 July 1842 - 20 Sept. 1912

BLACKBURN, Sarah Ellen   23 May 1833 - 8 April 1909
                  Wife of S. H. Blackburn

BLACKSTONE, Martha H.   1884 - 1952   [Wife of Thomas H.]

BLACKSTONE, Thomas H.   1872 - 1938   [Husband of Martha H.]

BLAUVELT, Allan J.   1862 - 1920   [In Funhouser Plot]

BLAUVELT, Euphemia   1863 - 1945
              [Wife of Allan J. - In Funkhouser Plot]

BLISS, Edith A.   1888 - 1908

BLUM, Ruth E.   1899 - 1936

BOCHART, Dorothy M.   1900 - 1963   Mother
              [Wife of William A.]

BOCHART, Herman   1856 - 1938   Father
              [Husband of Regina]

BOCHART, Regina   1857 - 1938   Mother
              [Wife of Herman]

BOCHART, William A.   1891 - 1959   [Husband of Dorothy M.]

BOGHILD, Ted M.   1939 - 1952

BONE, Laverne V.   1902 - 1969   [Wife of William B.]

BONE, William B.   1896 - 1964   [Husband of Laverne V.]

128

RIDGEFIELD CEMETERY

BOOSE, Hattie E.	1853 – 1947	[Wife of Peter M.]
BOOSE, Peter M.	1849 – 1932	[Husband of Hattie E.]
BOYER, A. (Mrs.)	2 Feb. 1831 – 5 July 1899	[Wife of Z. Boyer]

BOYER, Z. (Mr.) 29 Oct. 1822 – 16 Aug. 1898
[Husband of A. Boyer]

BRAMHALL, Albert A. 27 March 1894 – 28 Nov. 1922

BRATLIE, James H. 1909 – 1946

BRATLIE, John Louis 1880 – 1951

BRATLIE, Hans J. 1878 – 1943

BRICE, Agnes M. 1899 – 1908

BRICE, Charles E. 1877 – 1940

BRICE, Effie O. 1881 – 1964 [Wife of William T.]

BRICE, Gordon L. 1913 – 1960

BRICE, Jane B. 1857 – 1916 [Died 3 Nov. 1916]
[Wife of Wm. O.]

BRICE, Laura 28 July 1881 – 15 Sept. 1907
Rest in Peace

BRICE, Robert W. 1871 – 1920

BRICE, Truman C. 6 April 1847 – 16 April 1913
Rest in Peace

BRICE, Wm. O. 1845 – 1917 [Husband of Jane B.]

BRICE, William T. 1875 – 1934 [Husband of Effie O.]

BROWN, Benjamin G. 1881 – 1946 [Husband of Carrie M.]

BROWN, Carrie M. 1879 – 1971 [Wife of Benjamin G.[

BUCKBEE, Elizabeth A. 1874 – 1954 [Wife of James F.]

BUCKBEE, James F. 1866 – 1954 [Husband of Elizabeth A.]

BUKER, Martha Ellen 1840 – 1922 [Wife of William E.]

BUKER, Mary E. 1875 – 1966 [Wife of George W.]

BUKER, William E. 1847 – 1922 [Husband of Martha Ellen]

BUTLER, James F. 1875 – 1936 Father

BUTLER, Louis B. 1872 – 1945

RIDGEFIELD   CEMETERY

BURNS,   Joseph   C.   1867 - 1946

BURROW,   Etta   A.   1856 - 1940

BURROW,   George W.   1881 - 1954   [Husband of Minnie M.]

BURROW,   John   4 Sept. 1841 - 1 April 1898

BURROW,   Minnie   M.   1885 - 1973   [Wife of George W.]

CALL,   Mildred   V.   1904 - 1964

CLARK,   Carl V.   1 July 1894 - 20 April 1944
          Washington   Pvt 1Cl.   Med. Dept.

CLARK,   Florence [Edmonds]   1872 - 1937   Mother
                [Wife of Myron   H.

CLARK,   Myron   H.   1866 - 1925 [Husband of Florence Edmonds]

CARLSON,   Nettie   1895 - 1937   Mother [Wife of Oscar]

CARLSON,   Oscar   1883 - 1953   Father [Husband of Nettie]

CARMACK, Marcia   O.   1861 - 1942

COLEY,   George   V.   1906 - 1945

COOK,   Alonzo   R.   10 Mar. 1898 - Born in Saratoga, New York-
          Aged 68 yrs. 8 days   [2 March 1830]

COOK,   Telitha   1887 - 1933

CUNNINGHAM,   Eva E.   1880 - 1955   Daughter

DAHL,   Edward   1886 - 1942   [Husband of Hilda M.]

DAHL,   Hilda M.   1886 - 1948   [Wife of Edward]

DANIELSON,   Enoch   1881 - 1959

DAVENPORT,   Abraham   Co. A.   17 Indiana Inf.   [no dates]

DAVIDS,   Winnie   H.   1896 - 1924   Mother

DAVIS,   John William   1881 - 1952
                [Husband of Birdie (Shobert) Davis]

DAVIS,   Ida   E.   1878 - 1934

DEACON,   Ernest   H.   3 May 1904 - 11 May 1966   Father

DEARBORN,   Earnest   W.   1850 - 1926   At   Rest
                [Husband of Maude (Cook) Dearborn]

RIDGEFIELD CEMETERY

DEARBORN, Maude (Cook)   1867 - 1945   [wife of Earnest W.]

DICKERSON, Audrey M.   17 March 1903 - 19___
                                [Wife of George L.]

DICKERSON, George L.   22 Feb. 1894 - 8 June 1960
          Washington   Pvt.   103 Spruce Sq.   W.W. I

DIXON, Laura E.   1892 - 1969   [Wife of Nelson G.]

DIXON, Nelson G.   1886 - 1953
                                [Husband of Laura E.]

DOTSON, Antionette   1893 - 1947

EARL, Lena   1890 - 1929   Mother
                    [Wife of Simon]

EARL, Simon   1877 - 1962   Father
                    [Husband of Lena]

EATCH, Alexina (Pearson)   1884 - 1948   [In Pearson Plot]

EATCH, Leo Francis   1887 - 1942   [In Pearson Plot]

EATCH, Louise   25 Oct. 1925   [In Pearson Plot]

EATON, Thomas J.   1882 - 1961

EDINGER, Emma   1892 - 1935

EDMONDS, Albert M.   1867 - 1937
                                [Husband of Elmina A.]

EDMONDS, Albert M.   1912
          Sgt.   Co. F   6 Kansas Cav.

EDMONDS, Elmina A.   1868 - 1957   [Wife of Albert]

EDMONDS, Erma V.   1907 - 19___   [Wife of Ralph M]

EDMONDS, Everett E.   23 Jan. 1866 - 9 June 1946
                [Husband of Lida]

EDMONDS, George E.   30 March 1904 - 15 Jan. 1967
          Washington   Captain   U.S. Army   W.W. II

EDMONDS, H. Frederick   1878 - 1966
                [Husband of Sylvia Brice]

EDMONDS, Lida M.   10 Aug. 1880 - 24 Jan. 1920
                [Wife of Everett E.]

EDMONDS, Ralph M.   1908 - 1959
                [Husband of Erma V.]

33333

3333333333333333

333

RIDGEFIELD CEMETERY

EDMONDS, Sylvia (Brice)   1873 - 1945
[Wife of H. Frederick]

EGGLESTON, Harold G.   1950 - 1966   Son and Brother
Gone But Not Forgotten

ELDER, Charles   1885 - 1953

ELDER, Marion   1862 - 1941   [Husband of Xanthia]

ELDER, Xanthia   1862 - 1938   [Wife of Marion]

ELLIOT, Marie C.   25 Nov. 1881 - 25 Aug. 1963

EMERICK, Minnie J.   1873 - 1951   Mother
[Wife of William T.]

EMERICK, William T.   1864 - 1958   Father
[Husband of Minnie J.]

ERIKSSON, Emanuel   1868 - 1953   Father

FAIRBROTHER, Frederick H.   1884 - 1944

FEAK, Hattie Mae   12 Sept. 1872 - 20 June 1962
[Wife of James Erwin]

FEAK, James Erwin   2 Aug. 1865 - 24 Feb. 1955
[Husband of Hattie Mae]

FERRELL, Greta S.   1894 - 1961   [Wife of Otis C.]

FERRELL, Otis C.   1888 - 1957   [Husband of Greta S.]

FISHER, Baby   1908 - 1908   Our Beloved Baby

FISCHER, Mabel   29 Jan. 1914 - 26 Jan. 1933

FLEMMING, George F.   1882 - 1941
Sleep on dear son and take thy rest;
God called thee home when he thought best.

FLEMMING, Walter James   11 Dec. 1919 - 13 Dec. 1919

FORCIA, James   1850 - 1936   [Husband of Mary]
[One stone for family   James - Mary - Lela - Pearl]

FORCIA, Lela   1880 - 1898   [Daughter of James & Mary]

FORCIA, Mary   1851 - 1924   [Wife of James]

FORCIA, Pearl   1888 - 1903   [Daughter of James & Mary]

FORSBERG, Carrie H.   1887 - 19__   Mom
[Wife of Nels C.]

FORSBERG, Floyd C.   1916 - 1952

132

RIDGEFIELD   CEMETERY

FORSBERG,   Mary Joyce   1924 - 1928

FORSBERG,   Nels C.   1878 - 1959   Dad
                                          [Husband of Carrie H.]

FORSBERG,   Robert R.   13 May 1928 - 15 June 1970

FRAZIER,   Infants   Died 12 Dec. 1925   Son and Daughter
             Son and Daughter of S.J. and Mary Frazier

FRENCH,   Geraldine Z.   Died 24 July 1976   Aged 63 yrs.

FREWING,   Albert F.   1900 - 1977
             Pfc.   U.S.   Army   W.W. I

FREWING,   Isabel M.   10 Feb. 1885 - 10 March 1940   Mother
                          [Wife of Philip J.]

FREWING,   Philip J.   18 March 1882 - 2 July 1950   Father
                          [Husband of Isabel M.]

FREWING,   Robert P.   1857 - 1928   Father

FRINK,   Ellen   1849 - 1926
                                      [Wife of Lyman]

FRINK,   Lyman   1848 - 1922
                                      [Husband of Ellen]

FRY,   Lucy A.   1871 - 1961
                                      [Wife of Nelson J.]

FRY,   Nelson J.   1872 - 1950   [Husband of Lucy A.]

FUNKHOUSER,   E.   30 March 1839 - 6 Sept. 1915
                [In Funkhouser Plot]

FUNKHOUSER,   George P.   1874 - 1939
             Funkhouser plot - One stone bearing the following
             names: George - Georgia E. Funkhouser - Mary Ellen -
             Allan Blauvelt - Euphemia.

FUNKHOUSER,   Georgia   1875 - 1965
                [Wife of George   In Funkhouser Plot]

FUNKHOUSER,   Mary Ellen   1842 - 1933
                                      [In Funkhouser Plot]

FUNKHOUSER,   S. R.   1859 - 1926

GARDNER,   Rose M.   1894 - 1968

GARRISON,   Selma M.   17 Dec. 1906 - 14 Feb. 1969

GAUKEL,   Bradford L.   1874 - 1944
                                      [Husband of Margaret J.]

RIDGEFIELD   CEMETERY

GAUKEL,   Margaret   J.   1874 - 1950   (Wife of Bradford L.]

GIBBENS,   Alice   1862 - 1931

GIBBENS,   Charles H.   1861 - 1940   Father

GIBERSON,   Caroline   1887 - 1952   [Wife of Elijah]

GIBERSON,   Elijah   1876 - 1918
                                                     [Husband of Caroline]

GIBERSON,   James   William   1866 - 1961
          [Husband of Susan I.   In Giberson Family Plot]

GIBERSON,   John   1914 - 1930
                                                    [Husband of Mildred]

GIBERSON,   John O.   1868 - 1904
                                                    [Husband of Sarah]

GIBERSON,   Mildred   May   1910 - 1950
                                                    [Wife of John]

GIBERSON,   Sarah   1876 - 1958
                                                    [Wife of John O.]

GIBERSON,   Susan   I.   1858 - 1942
          [Wife of James   William   In Giberson Family Plot]

GILBERT,   Frank   H.   1859 - 1923

GILBERT,   Fred   T.   Died 1942   Father

GILBERT,   John   30 Oct. 1817 - 1 April 1901
          [Husband of   Sarah (Ball) Gilbert]   At   Rest

GILBERT,   Sarah (Ball)   15 Dec. 1824 - 14 May 1919
                      [Wife of John]

GILBERT,   Sarah J.   1864 - 19___   [Wife of Fred T.]

GLUTH,   Paul   G.   28 Jan. 1887 - 15 July 1923   Father

GOODLOW,   Edith M.   1880 - 19__
                                          [Wife of Roscoe   C.]

GOODLOW,   Roscoe C.   1880 - 1941
                                          [Husband of Edith   M.]

GRIFFITHS,   Ellen   26 June 1837 - 14 Sept. 1912
              [Wife of Griffith   Griffiths]

GRIFFITHS,   Griffith   1830 - 1913
                      [Husband of Ellen]

GUSTAFSON,   Mary E.   1886 - 1973

RIDGEFIELD   CEMETERY

GUTHRIE,   Elsie   30 Jan. 1889 - 16 Aug. 1912
                          [Wife of Stephen L.]

HALE,   Allen W.   19 March 1934
        Washington   Pvt 1Cl   148 Field Art. 41st Div.

HALE,   Anna G.   1867 - 1951

HALE,   George D.   1858 - 1916
                          [Husband of Anna G.]

HALL,   Carrie (Packard)   Died 24 Jan. 1899 - Aged 50 years
                  We miss thee from our home, dear
                  We miss thee in thy place,
                  We miss the sunshine of thy face.

HALL,   Infant Son and Daughter of N.C. and May Hall

HALL,   May C.   1874 - 1956   [Wife of Newman C.]

HALL,   Newman C.   1864 - 1933   [Husband of May C.]

HALTINER,   Anna   1888 - 1973   Mother
                  [Wife of Rudolph]

HALTINER,   Rudolph   1889 - 1973   Father
                  [Husband of Anna]

HANSEN,   Peter W.   25 Aug. 1885 - 22 June 1943

HARDT,   August   1865 - 1948   Father
                  [Husband of Minnie]

HARDT,   Minnie   1869 - 1937   Mother
                  [Wife of August]

HARRIS,   Jessie G.   1866 - 1948

HARRIS,   Johanna   1875 - 19___

HASCALL,   Arthur E.   1872 - 1951   [Husband of Maggie P.]

HASCALL,   Maggie P.   1874 - 1942   [Wife of Arthur E.]

HASKELL,   Myrtle E.   1899 - 1957   [Wife of Harry C.]

HASSING,   Anna H.   17 April 1912 - 6 Dec. 1973
                  Wife   and   Mother

HAWKINS,   Charles A.   1855 - 1922   [Husband of Emma]

HAWKINS,   Emma   1867 - 1936   [Wife of Charles A.]

HAWKINS, Virgelee   7 Nov. 1923 - 28 May 1959
          Washington   S1   U.S. Navy   W. W. II

RIDGEFIELD CEMETERY

HAWKINS, Clyde   1898 – 1960   [Husband of Hattie M.]

HAWKINS, Hattie M.   1904 – 1952   [Wife of Clyde]

HAWKINS, Baby Boy   11 Dec. 1912
                                   [In Hawkins Plot]

HAWKINS, Emma   1867 – 1936
                                       [Wife of Charles A.]

HAWKINS, Charles A.   1855 – 1922
                                       [Husband of Emma]

HAWKINS, Clayton   1905 – 1949   Our Daddy

HAWKINS, Owen   6 Oct. 1915 – 18 Sept. 1972
                    In Memory Of Husband Owen

HAWKINS, Mona G.   29 Jan. 1893 – 11 March 1951
                  In Loving Memory Of Mother

HAWKINS, Barnie H   1 July 1890 – 21 Feb. 1958

HAYDEN, Dana Paul   21 May 1955 – 14 June 1976

HAYDEN, Mary L.   1887 – 1971   Mother

HEASLEY, Bernice   1906 – 19___
                Married to Earl Heasley on 8 Feb. 1925

HEASLEY, Earl   1903 – 1968
                  Married to Bernice on 8 Feb. 1925

HEISER, Mary V.   1879 – 1952
          [Name on same stone with George F. Zepernick]

HEITHMAN, Henry   1838 – 1918
              [Husband of Sarah]

HEITHMAN, Sarah L.   1843 – 1911
                  [Wife of Henry]

HELDMAN, Abel M.   1976 – 1976

HENKLE, Elbert E.   1872 – 1921

HERBERT, Fred   1876 – 1954
              [Husband of Gertrude]

HERBERT, Gertrude   1879 – 1959
                ] Wife of Fred]

HEWETT, Alfred W.   1853 – 1920

HEWETT, Clara   1895 – 1897   At Rest

HEWETT, Edith A.   1899 – 1977   [Wife of Rowland]

RIDGEFIELD   CEMETERY

HEWETT,   Martha   L.   1832 - 1908

HEWETT,   Rowland   26 March 1896 - 30 April 1961
        Washington   Eng. 1   U.S.   Navy   W.W.   I

HIBBARD,   Clara   5 April 1873 - 18 April 1898
        Aged 25 yrs.   13 days   Wife of J.N. Hibbard

HIBBARD,   James   N.   1860 - 1939
        [Husband of Wilhelmina   E.]

HIBBARD,   Wilhelmina   E.   1875 - 1944   [wife of James N]

HIBBARD,   James   J.   1883 - 1911

HILL,   Anna   G.   1867 - 1951   [Wife of George D.]

HILL,   Bertha H.   1890 - 1929

HILL,   Frederick   15 March 1865 - 30 Dec. 1919

HILL,   Pauline   (Olson)   1933 - 1954

HIXON,   Lilian   1889 - 1915

HOARD,   Eleanor   O.   1893 - 1973
        [Wife of Horace   A.   Mother of M. Nadine]

HOARD,   Horace   1895 - 1975
        [Husband of Eleanor   Father of M. Nadine]

HOARD,   M. Nadine   1922 - 19
        [Daughter of Horace and Eleanor Hoard]

HOBERT,   Mary A.   1848 - 1932

HOLDEN,   Baby Fisher   1908 - 1908

HOLDEN,   Sophia   J.   (Fisher)   16 June 1885 - 31 July 1962

HOLMES,   Robert   C.   1920 - 1940

HOLLAND,   Betty C.   1923 - 1978   Mother

HORN,   Albert   F.   31 May 1910 - 6 Aug. 1965

HORN,   Amelia   6 Sept. 1844 - 20 Nov. 1908
        [In Horn Plot]

HORN,   August   10 Aug. 1837 - 13 Feb. 1927
        [In Horn Plot]

HORN,   Bobby   26 May 1954 - 13 Nov. 1972
        [Son of Robert and Nacia Horn]

HORN,   Charles   1864 - 1954   Father
        [Husband of Josephine]

RIDGEFIELD   CEMETERY

HORN,   Chris   1877 - 1942   Uncle
                    [In   Horn   Plot]

HORN   [In   Horn   Plot   -   no dates]   Father

HORN,   Fred J.   22 Sept. 1886 - 24 July 1918
                    [Horn   Plot]

HORN,   George   1880 - 1958   [Husband of Tilda]

HORN,   Gestine   1 Feb. 1855 - 16 Feb. 1902
                    Truly my soul waited upon God
                    From Him cometh my Salvation.

HORN, Gustave William   1868 - 1937   [Swank Memorial Marker]

HORN,   Herman   13 Aug. 1882 - 13 Sept. 1908
                                      [In Horn Plot]

HORN,   Josephine   1866 - 1956   [Wife of Charles]

HORN,   Mother   [In Horn Plot -   no dates]

HORN,   Orlando   1902 - 1938   [Laynes Funeral Home
                                              Marker]

HORN,   Sylvia Ann   1879 - 1961 [Swank Memorial Marker]

HORN,   Tilda   1881 - 1931   [Wife of George]

HORTON,   Mildred (Stinson)   1921 - 1966   Wife

HOYT, O. A.   1844 - 1917   [Husband of Jane]

HUGHES,   Ellen (Blackburn)   1868 - 1958
                              [Wife of Evan Peris Hughes]

HUGHES,   Evan Peris   1863 - 1923
                    [Husband of Ellen (Blackburn Hughes]

HUGHES,   John W.   1862 - 1914
                    Gone but not Forgotten

HUMPHREY,   Arlie Eldon   25 Oct. 1896 - 4 Mar. 1961
          Washington   Pvt.   Co. E.   5 Bn. Relp. Tng. Gen. WW I
                    American   U.S. Legion

HUMPHREY,   Irene M.   7 May 1907 -
                    [Wife of Arlie Eldon]

HUTCHINS,   Edna Ruth   1900 - 1976

HUTCHISON,   Elizabeth   1844 - 1918   [Wife of John]

HUTCHISON,   Eunice Ann   1903 - 1964   Mother

138

RIDGEFIELD   CEMETERY

HUTCHISON, John   1837 - 1911   [Husband of Elizabeth]

HYLLA, Imogene   13 Aug. 1928 - 4 April 1959
                    In Loving Memory   [Wife of Steven L.]

HYLLA, Steven L.   20 April 1949 - 9 April 1960
                    In Loving Memory   [Husband of Imogene]

JACKSON, Peter W.   1876 - 1947   Father
                    [Husband of Regina B.]

JACKSON, Regina B.   1876 - 1953   Mother
                    [Wife of Peter W.]

JACOBSON, Arthur W.   2 May 1910 - 7 Feb. 1951
              Washington   Pfc.   289 Inf.   W. W. II

JEWETT, Alfred W.   1853 - 1920

JEWETT, Martha L.   1832 - 1908

JOHNS, Clarence M.   1903 - 1964   [Husband of Clytie]

JOHNS, Clytie   1902 - 1978   (Wife of Clarence M.]

JONES, Laura E.   31 Oct. 1848 - 16 Aug. 1913
                    Beloved Wife of T. W.   Jones

JOHNSON, Ainer G.   1895 - 1946
                                    [Husband of Dollie D.]

JOHNSON, Amelia   1892 - 1969

JOHNSON, Carl Peter   Born 3 Jan. 1853 in Vekadal, Sweden
                           Died 8 Feb. 1908 in Elma, Washington
                    At   Rest

JOHNSON, Charles A.   1880 - 1969   [Husband of Hattie L.]

JOHNSON, Dollie D.   1897 - 1972
                                    [Wife of Ainer G. Johnson]

JOHNSON, Hattie L.   1878 - 1964   [Wife of Charles A.]

JOHNSON, Maxine D.   1919 - 1946   Wife

JOHNSTON, Doris I.   1904 - 1978   [Wife of James C.]

JOHNSTON, James C.   1881 - 1954   Father
                    [Husband of Mabel]

JOHNSTON, James C.   1907 - 19___   [Husband of Doris I.]

JOHNSTON, Mabel   1884 - 1976   Mother
                    [Wife of James C.]

RIDGEFIELD CEMETERY

KANZIER, Andrew   4 Sept. 1837 - 23 Feb. 1914
          [Husband of of Barbara]

KANZIER, Barbara   20 oct. 1836 - 3 May 1908
          [Wife of Andrew]

KAUFFMAN, Augusta Newman   1890 - _____

KAUFFMAN, Ella H.   1892 - 1930
          Beloved Wife and Mother

KAUFFMAN, Emil A.   1894 - 1972

KAUFFMAN, Grace S.   1914 - 1947   Mother

KAUFFMAN, John   1887 - 1950   Father

KAYE, Abel   25 Aug. 1839 - 14 Nov. 1916

KEENEY, Monica Ann   18 Oct. 1969 - 24 Oct. 1969
               Our Baby

KELLER, Elizabeth M.   1881 - 1956   [Wife of Henry F.]

KELLER, Henry   1880 - 1966   [Husband of Elizabeth M.]

KELLER, Gottfried   1853 - 1927   [Husband of Louise B.]

KELLER, Louise B.   1858 - 1937   [Wife of Gottfried]

KEMPER, Clara   1890 - 1946   Mother
          [Wife of Howard A.]

KEMPER, George N.   1892 - 1968   [Husband of Maybel]

KEMPER, Howard A.   1881 - 1953   Father
          [Husband of Clara]

KEMPER, Irvin I.   1890 - 1959   Dad

KEMPER, Maybel   1896 - 1964   [Wife of George N.]

KEMPER, Newton A.   1860 - 1937   Father
          Safe With Jesus   [Husband of Sarah M.]

KEMPER, Robert L.   1921 - 1937   Son
          Safe With Jesus

KEMPER, Sarah M.   1860 - 1950   Mother
          Safe With Jesus   [Wife of Newton A.]

KLICKMAN, Agnes   1866 - 1948   Mother

KLICKMAN, John Albert   23 Aug. 1895 - 11 Feb. 1973
          Washington   U.S. Navy   GM 1   W.W. I
          [Husband of Opal Violet]

KLICKMAN,   Louis A.   11 Feb. 1893 - 26 Sept. 1952
        Washington   Pvt   213 Engineers   13 Div. W.W. I

KLICKMAN,   Opel Violet   9 Feb. 1902 - 19___
                    [Wife of John Albert]

KNOX,   Alfred Alonzo   1837 - 1920

KOETHE,   Albert J.   1897 - 1955

KRAMER,   Judy Ann   1942 - 1946   Daughter

KOEPKE,   Frances J.   1879 - 1943   [Wife of Frank L.]

KOEPKE,   Frank L.   1868 - 1939   [Husband of Frances J.]

KRAUS,   Don   4 June 1961 - 6 April 1975   Son

KRAUS,   Marie   1913 - 19___

KRAUS,   Nargus   1906 - 19___

LANGDALE,   Melvin   28 Oct. 1889 - Oct. 22. 1963
        Washington   Pvt.   U.S. Marine Corp   W. W. I

LANGSDALE,   Ida Julia   29 Nov. 1886 - 3 July 1914

LANGSDALE,   Systa Josephine   9 July 1893 - 10 May 1912

LAYNE   Beda   1889 - 1963   [Wife of Bert]

LAYNE,   Bert   1886 - 1971   [Husband of Beda]

LAYNE,   Mary J.   1869 - 1955   Mother
            [Wife of Samuel E.]

LAYNE,   Samuel E.   1862 - 1931   [Husband of Mary J.]

LAYNES,   Gertrude L.   1898 - 1953   Mother
              [Wife of Thomas V.]

LAYNES,   Thomas V. Sr.   1889 - 1967   Father
              [Husband of Gertrude L.]

LARSON,   Bruce R.   1954 - 1975   Son

LAWS,   Franklin   1870 - 19___   Father

LAWS,   George   6 Sept. 1865 - 22 May 1896

LAWS,   Polly   19 Oct. 1841 - 13 Sept. 1885

LAWS,   Rachel   1884 - 1947   Mother
              [Wife of Franklin]

LAWSON,   Goldie E. (Kemper)   1912 - 1973

RIDGEFIELD   CEMETERY

LEE,   Borghild   M.   1915 - 1965

LEE,   Virgil   1881 - 1942

LEHNER,   Alice   M.   14 Nov. 1908 - 11 July 1975
            Minnesota   [Wife of Michael   J.]

LEHNER,   Michael   J.   27 Aug. 1906 - 22 July 1976
        Sgt.   U.S. Army   W.W.   II   [Husband of Alice M.]

LENGEL,   Charles   E.   1868 - 1954   [Husband of Elmina]

LENGEL,   Elmina   J.   1873 - 1960   [Wife of Charles E.]

LENZ,   Emilie   Geb 1   Jan. 1840 - Gest 13 March 1908
        Rhue Sanet   Frau Von   [Wife of William Lenz]

LENZ,   William   1 January 1840 - 13 March 1908

LITTLER,   Donald   4 July 1910 - 17 Jan. 1913
    In Memory Of   Our Little Man   Son of E.L. and E. E. Littler

LITTLER,   Edward L.   1870 - 1953   [Husband of Ethel E.]

LITTLER, · Edward Neil   1903 - 1951

LITTLER,   Ethel E.   1884 - 1972   [wife of Edward   L.]

LOOMIS,   Alma   E.   1916 - 1934

LUNDQUIST,   Oscar F.   3 April 1943
            Washington   Pvt.   166 Depot Brig.

LUNDQUIST,   Willa C.   1896 - 1975

LUTTREL,   Robert L.   1888 - 1925

LYONS,   Leonard Earl   1887 - 1918

LYONS,   Willard Loren   1849 - 1923   Father

MACKEY,   Earnest Paxton   31 May 1882 - 2 April 1885
            Son of S.P. & Mary G. Mackey
        Suffer the little children and forbid them not
        to come unto me for such is the Kingdom of Heaven.

MAHER,   Lawrence   1900 - 1959

MAKI,   Amanda   1886 - 1950   At   Rest

MAKI,   Herman   1883 - 1919

MAINWARING,   David O.   4 Oct. 1906 - 9 July 1970
        Washington CHELEC,   U.S. Navy   W. W.   II

MAINWARING,   Helen L.   1909 - 1948   [Wife of David O.]
            American Auxillary Legion

RIDGEGIELD CEMETERY

MALKSON,   [no name]

MANSFIELD, Lester
              [Son of Margaret   In Horn Plot   no dates]

MANSFIELD, Margaret   1821 - 1911
              [Mother of Lester and Lena   In Horn Plot]

MATNEY, Elza Le Roy   28 Nov. 1920 - 21 April 1972
              Washington   Pfc.   U.S. Army   W. W. II

MAXON, James S.   1859 - 1955   [Husband of Laura A.]
              [In Giberson Family Plot]

MAXON, Laura A.   1871 - 1945   [Wife of James S.]
              [In Giberson Family Plot]

MAXON, Ruth   1898 - 1917   [In Giberson Family Plot]

MAYNARD, Annie (Malkson)   1873 - 1949

MILLER, Clifford   30 Jan. 1901 - 4 March 1974
              Oregon   E3   U.S. Navy   W.W. I

MILLER, Michael J.   1966 - 1966

MILLS, Ada   1883 - 1965   Mother
              [Wife of Thomas]

MILLS, Minnie R.   1880 - 1971

MILLS, Otha Belle   1920 - 1928
              [Near Thomas and Ada Mills Grave]

MILLS, Thomas J.   1876 - 1951   Father
              [Husband of Ada]

MINER, Betty Jo Ann   1947 - 1962   Beloved Daughter

MINER, Leo Elbe   28 Sept. 1926 - 21 Nov. 1962
              Oregon   AOMI   U.S.N.R.   W.W. II

MITCHELL, James   Mar. 1821 - Feb. 1908
              A Faithful Friend

MOORE, Annie   1870 - 1962

MOORE, Esther L.   8 Feb. 1907 - 9 Dec. 1967   Mother

MOORE, Joseph N.   21 Aug. 1875 - 18 May 1949
              Missouri   Master Sgt.   U.S. Army Retired   W.W. I

MORAN, George A.   1879 - 1966

MORRIS, Ru Lee   6 Nov. 1974 - 5 Jan. 1976   Our Baby

RIDGEFIELD   CEMETERY

MORTON,   J. H.   1846 - 1927   [Husband of Matilda]
   [Has a star badge with intials C A R in center of star]

MORTON,   Matilda   1849 - 1926   [wife of J.H. Morton]

MORTON,   Silas W.   1854 - 1926

MOSIER,   Clara C.   1885 - 1945   Mother

MUFFET,   Ida M.   1859 - 1936   [Wife of Robert B.]

MUFFET,   Robert B.   1864 - 1950   [Husband of Ida M.]

MUFFETT, Winfield F.   1 July 1890 - 9 April 1924
        Blessed are the pure in heart for they shall see God

MURRAY,   Andy   1855 - 1911   [Husband of Mary J.]

MURRAY,   Mary J.   1863 - 1931   [Wife of Andy]

Mac KENZIE, Angus (Rev.)   Died 7 Jan. 1911 Aged 71 yrs.
                 [Husband of Annie]

Mac KENZIE, Annie   Died 22 Oct. 1918   Aged 75 yrs
                 [Wife of Rev. Angus Mac Kenzie]

Mac KENZIE, Murdock   Died 5 April 1892
        [Son of Rev. Angus and Annie Mac Kenzie]

Mc ANDREW,   Amanda   1839 - 1914   Mother

Mc ANDREW,   Freddie   1916 - 1916
                 [Vancouver Funeral Chapel Marker]

Mc ANDREW,   Margaret E.   1884 - 1944   [Wife of Stephen F.]

Mc ANDREW,   Stephen F.   1873 - 1935
                 [Husband of Margaret]

Mc CLEARY,   M. Abraham   1857 - 1939   (Husband of Martha S.]

Mc CLEARY,   Martha S.   1855 - 1936   (Wife of Abraham]

Mc CORMACK, Alfonso W.   1856 - 1936
                 [Husband of Cora C.]

Mc CORMACK, Cora C.   1864 - 1951   [Wife of Alfonso W.]

Mc GROTTY,   James   1860 - 1929   Father
                 [Husband of Margaret A.]

Mc GROTTY,   Margaret A.   1858 - 1923   Mother
                 [Wife of James]

Mc KINNEY,   Paul C.   1906 - 1969 [Husband of Edna]

144

RIDGEFIELD CEMETERY

Mc PHATE,   Beverly L.   1912 - 1972
                                          [Wife of Fielding H.]

Mc PHATE,   Fielding H.   1893 - 1961
                                          [Husband of Beverly L.]

NEIL,   Babies   [No names or dates]

NEILL,   James R.   1855 - 1929   [Husband of Sarah L.]

NEILL,   Sarah L.   1865 - 1917   [Wife of James R.]

NELSON,   Albert   1892 - 1968
          [Husband of Ethel   Father of Lester]

NELSON,   Ethel   1896 - 1959
          [Wife of Albert   Mother of Lester]

NELSON,   Lester L.   1938 - 1950

NEVETRAL,   Clare (Ted)   1912 - 1961   Husband

NEVETRAL,   Norman   1869 - 1954   [Husband of Phoebe]

NEVETRAL,   Phoebe   1877 - 1972   [Wife of Norman]

NEWMAN,   Augusta (Kauffman)   1890 - 19__   [Wife of Emil A.]

NEWMAN,   Emil A.   1894 - 1972
          [Husband of Augusta Kauffman Newman]

NEUMAN,   Daughter   1888 - 1918
          [Daughter of Gottlieb and Ernestine-no given name]

NEUMAN,   Ernestine   1858 - 1931   [Wife of Gottlieb]

NEUMAN,   Gottlieb   1859 - 1934
          [Husband of Ernestine]

NILSEN,   Caroline   1871 - 1952
              The Lord is my Shepherd.

NILSEN,   Dagny E.   1910 - 1923
              He wanted her for his own.

NILSEN,   Inger   1845 - 1922   Mother
          Wife of Nils, Pioneer Missionaries to Madagascar
              I have kept the Faith.   II Tim. 4:7

NILSEN,   Nils   1834 - 1923   Father
          Husband of Inger   Missionaries to Madagascar
              I have kept the Faith   II Tim. 4:7

NILSEN,   Ommund   1873 - 1939
              Happy at home with the Lord

NILSEN, Sophia   1876 - 1957
        Well done, good and faithful servant.

NORDIN, Viola E.   1896 - 19___
        Well done, good and faithful servant.

NORDIN, Walter C.   1892 - 1969   [Husband of Viola E.]

NORTH, Virginia Lee   1881 - 1942

NORTHRUP, Darwin E.   1864 - 1944   [Husband of Hattie E.]

NORTHRUP, Edison R.   1894 - 19___   [Husband of M. Eleanor]

NORTHRUP, Hattie E.   1874 - 1964   [Wife of Darwin E.]

NORTHRUP, M. Eleanor   1901 - 1979   [Wife of Edison]

OLDHAM, George   1880 - 1950

OLIVER, Rose M.   1883 - 1956
        The Lord is my shepherd.

OLSON, Goldie (Stinson)   1903 - 1964   Mother

OLSON, Howard Earl   1900 - 1967

OSBORN, Chester E.   1899 - 1960   [Son of Hiram & Reba]

OSBORN, Hiram A.   1877 - 1948
        [Husband of Reba H.   Father of Chester]

OSBORN, Reba H.   1881 - 1975
        [Wife of Hiram A.   Mother of Chester]

OWENS, Laura V.   28 Aug. 1903 -

OWENS, Roy   26 June 1900 - 1 July 1952
        OM 2   U.S. Navy   W. W. I

PACKARD, Joseph, Captain   7 Sept. 1817 - 12 April 1892
        Born in Camden, Maine   A kind husband and loving father.

PACKARD, Joseph Leslie   1855 - 1924   Father
        [Husband of Melinda Babbidge Packard]

PACKARD, Melinda (Babbidge) 1859 - 1925   Mother
        [Wife of Joseph Leslie]

PACKARD, Sarah   Died 16 Jan. 1899 - Aged 78 yrs.
        In Loving Memory Of

        God in his wisdom has recalled the boon
            his love had given
        And though the body moulder here
            the soul is safe in heaven.

146

RIDGEFIELD   CEMETERY

PATEE, Alma D.   1884 - 1955   [Wife of Harold W.]

PATEE, Harold W.   24 March 1888 - 23 Aug. 1979
                Born in Idalia, Colorado
        [Husband of Margaret   Father of Harold W. Jr. and
                    Alma Jean Patee Wyckof]

PAULISSEN, Catherine   8 Feb. 1893 - 12 Mar. 1947
                    Mother

PAUTZ, Wilhelmina   1861 -1921   Mother
              [Wife of Frederick]

PAUTZ, Frederick   1859 - 1947   Father
              [Husband of Wilhelmina]

PAUTZ, Erna O.   1885 - 1970

PAXTON, Ernest   31 May 1882 - 23 April 1885
              [Son of S.P. and Mary C. (Mackey)]

PEARSON, Edwin Lyall   1879 - 1899
                [In Pearson Plot]

PEARSON,' _____   1838 - 1909   Father
              [In Pearson Plot]

PEARSON, James B.   1872 - 1932   [In Pearson Plot]

PEARSON, Jessie   1881 - 1946   [In Pearson Plot]

PEARSON, Marie O.   1894 - 19___   [Wife of Robert E.]

PEARSON, _____   1843 - 1922   Mother
                [In Pearson Plot]

PEARSON, Robert E.   22 June 1896 - 10 Jan. 1964
        Massachusetts   Mus. 2   U.S. Navy   W.W. I

PEFFER, Clara D.   1862 - 1949   [Husband Warren B.]

PEFFER, Lou M.   1870 - 1944   [Wife of Fred E.]
              [Broken Stone]

PEFFER, Warren B.   1863 - 1936   [Husband of Clara D.]

PEPPER, Harold I.   4 May 1902 - 16 June 1949

PIPPIT, Mary Edna   1871 - 1942

POTTER, Baby   Died 5 Nov. 1916
              [Buried in Potter Plot]

POTTER, Tilda   1882 - 1964   [Wife of William]

POTTER, William   1876 - 1827   [Husband of Tilda]

RIDGEFIELD CEMETERY

POWELL, Lela G.   1875 - 1967   [Wife of Samuel D.]

POWELL, Samuel D.   1867 - 1954   [Husband of Lela G.]

POWELL, Walter R.   1900 - 1920
        Gone but not forgotten   John 3:16

RATHBUN, Baby Boy   Jan. 1928

RATHBUN, Beulah D.   1910 - 1972   (Wife of Jake J.]

RATHBUN, Charles B.   1858 - 1948

RATHBUN, Carrie   1870 - 1942   [Wife of John G.]

RATHBUN, Fred Jr.   1885 - 1958   [Son of Fred and Mary]

RATHBUN, Hannahl   1847 - 1902   [Wife of John]

RATHBUN, Izola   1862 - 1947   Mother
                [Wife of John B.]

RATHBUN, Jacob B.   1861 - 1932   Father
                [Husband of Izola]

RATHBUN, Jake J.   1903 - _____

                                     [Husband of Beulah]

RATHBUN, John   1824 - 1877   [Husband of Hannahl]

RATHBUN, John B.   1887 - 1914

RATHBUN, Mary   12 April 1869 - 23 Sept. 1933
                [Wife of Fred W.]

RICE,   Ada C.   17 Aug. 1878 - 13 June 1969
                [Wife of Carl N.]

RICE,   Carl N.   28 July 1876 - 9 March 1944
                [Husband of Ada C.]

RICKMAN, Henry M. (Butch)   1884 - 1969

RIPLEY, Ernest A.   14 Aug. 1910 - 14 June 1916

RITCHIE, Elizabeth   Died 14 June 1905
                Wife of W.H. & M. Ritchie

RITENOUR, Charles H.   1853 - 1918
                [Husband of Phebe A.]

RITENOUR, Joseph C.   1893 - 1967   [Husband of Midge]

RITENOUR, Midge   1899 - 1979

148

RIDGEFIELD CEMETERY

RITENOUR, Phebe A.   1868 - 1957
                [Wife of Charles H.]

ROBY, Etta   1884 - 1962

RODGERS, Walter G. (Mickey)   1941 - 1964
                [In Loving Memory Of]

ROGERS, Jerry M.   1895 - 1973
                Safe in the arms of Jesus

ROSE, John   1828 - 1908   [Husband of Margaret]

ROSE, Margaret   1826 - 1911   [Wife of John]

ROUNDS, Alfred L.   1854 - 1929   [Husband of Ursula]

ROUNDS, Frances Lynde   1892 - 1950

ROUNDS, Nelson C.   1890 - 1944

ROUNDS, Ruth E.   1850 - 1932

ROUNDS, Ursula   1856 - 1929   [Wife of Alfred]

RUSSELL, Grace V.   1880 - 1970   Mother
                [Wife of William S.]

RUSSELL, Larry L.   1939 - 1972

RUSSELL, William S. 1876 - 1960   [Husband of Grace V.]

SCHENK, Ilione   [no dates - still living]
                            [Wife of John F.]

SCHENK, John E.   1870 - 1951   In Loving Memory Of

SCHENK, John F.   1900 - 1945   [Husband of Ilione]

SCHNEIDER, Loretta   Aug. 1918
          [Vancouver Funeral Home Marker]

SCOTT, Lucille M.   2 Feb. 1915 - 6 April 1977

SCOTT, Thomas   7 April 1890 - 24 Jan. 1971   Brother

SEAMAN, Ada   1863 - 1954   Mother
                [Wife of Judd J.]

SEAMAN, Judd J.   1858 - 1932   Father
                [Husband of Ada]

SEDERBURG, Albert A.   1904 - 1977   Father
                [Husband of Reta]

RIDGEFIELD   CEMETERY

SEDERBURG,   Herbert F.   3 Nov. 1909 - 22 Jan. 1978
                    [Son of John and Maggie]

SEDERBURG,   John P.   1872 - 1922
             [Husband of Maggie A.   Father of Herbert]

SEDERBURG,   Margaret M.   11 May 1914 - 23 May 1972

SEDERBURG,   Minnie A.   1881 - 1941
             [Wife of John P.   Mother of Herbert]

SEDERBURG,   Reta E.   1912 - 19___   Mother
                    [wife of albert A.]

SHANKLAND,   A. Elizabeth   1884 - 1957   [wife of Leon]

SHANKLAND,   Leon   1883 - 1938   [Husband of A.Elizabeth]

SHERMAN,   Mattie (Nay)   1864 - 1929   Mother
                    Christ is my Hope

SHERRILL,   Hannah   1885 - 1915   [Wife of John Sigfred]

SHERRILL,   John Sigfred   1894 - 1934   [Husband of Hannah]

SHOBERT,   Catherine C.   18 Feb. 1818 - 22 Oct. 1904   Mother
                 A Loving Mother and a Generous Friend

SHOBERT,   Napoleon B.   1823 - 1901

SHOBERT,   Oscar H.   1887 - 3 Feb. 1934
            Washington   Pvt   17 Bct. Co.   Gen. Ser. Inf.

SHOBERT,   Rawley   11 July 1886 - 3 Sept. 1886
                    [Son of S. & J. Shobert]

SHOBERT,   Susan Jane   1859 - 1948   [Wife of William H.]

SHOBERT,   William H.   1849 - 1942
                 [Husband of Susan Jane]

SIGRIST,   Juleen K.   1946 - 1967   Beloved Daughter

SIMMONS,   Annie   1867 - 1928   Mother
                 [Wife of Edward]

SIMMONS,   Edward   1864 - 1931   Father
                 [Husband of Annie]

SIMMONS,   George W.   1879 - 1957
                                 [Husband of Hattie L.

SITNER,   John A.   1856 - 1948 [Husband of Katherine M.]

SITNER,   Katherine M.   1861 - 1924   [Wife of John A.]

RIDGEFIELD CEMETERY

SITNER, Lydia   1888 - 1967   In Memory Of

SMITH, Anna M.   6 Feb. 1857 - 19 Jan. 1895
    Born in Sulivan Co., Missouri [wife of George F.]

SMITH, George F.   16 Jan. 1855 - 1 Jan. 1898
    Born in Burlington, Racine Co., Wisconsin
            [Husband of Anna M.]

SMITH, Lewis Clark   1 June 1900 - 14 Oct. 1904
            Son of F.C. & J.L. Smith

    A bud plucked from earth to bloom in Heaven.

SOUTHWICK, Harry C.   10 May 1888 - 28 Oct. 1912

STARKEY, Maurice R.   1882 - 1955   [Husband of Reba V.]

STARKEY, Reba V.   1898 - 1974   [Wife of Maurice R.]

STEIN, Gus A.   1888 - 1958   Father
            [Husband of Mabel H.]

STEIN, Mabel H.   1894 - 1953   Mother
            [Wife of Gus A.]

STEPHEN, Robert   1837 - 1923   Father

STEPHENSON, Andrew   1882 - 1971   Father
            [Husband of Anna]

STEPHENSON, Anna   1884 - 1961   Mother
            [Wife of Andrew]

STEVENSON, Walton A.   1877 - 1953   [Husband of Susie M.]

STINSON, Earl N.   1895 - 1962   Father

STEELMAN, Chas. D.   1895 - 1896

STOEBNER, W. F.   1884 - 1944   "Our Uncle Will"

STONER, Myrtle   1889 - 19___   [Wife of Edward]

STRICKLAND, Helen   1923 - 19___   Mother
            [Wife of Leslie L.]

STRICKLAND, Leslie L.   1922 - 1977   Father
            [Husband of Helen]

STUBBS, Fannie   1870 - 1927   Mother

SUTHERLAND, Rebecca I.   1835 - 1919

SUTTON, William   1839 - 1916

SWEARINGEN, N. B.   1867 - 1915

RIDGEFIELD CEMETERY

TALBERT, Abner Pearl   28 Oct. 1894 - 5 Jan. 1970
        Missouri   Pvt   Provost Guard Co.   W.W. I

TALLMON, Richard M.   1915 - 1944

TAYLOR, Curtis F.   1891 - 1919
                I have fought a good fight
                I have finished my course
                I have kept the faith
                Hence forth there is laid up for thee
                A crown of righteousness.

TAYLOR, Curtis F.   29 Aug. 1890 - 13 Oct. 1918
        Washington   Pvt.   3 Co. Coast Artillery   W.W. I

TAYLOR, Dona T.   1860 - 1930   Mother
                [Wife of E. Frank]

TAYLOR, Eddie D.   1881 - 1953   [Husband of Linnie M.]
            To live in God is to live forever.

TAYLOR, E. Frank   1855 - 1948   [Husband of Dona T.]   Father

TERRY, Charles A.   1877 - 1947   Father
                [Husband of Florence M.]

TERRY, Florence M.   1883 - 1943   Mother
                [Wife of Charles A.]

THOMPSON, Marian I.   _____ - 1975   Mother

TIM, Ada A.   28 Feb. 1890 - 18 Sept. 1974 [Wife of John]

TIM, Fred W.   26 Nov. 1860 - 25 Dec. 1910
                [Husband of Mary]

TIM, Fred, Jr.   1885 - 1958

TIM, John   1885 - 1959

TIM, Mary   12 April 1869 - 23 Sept. 1933

TOBEY, Leta P.   1885 - 1975

TOBEY, Wilbur   1875 - 1959

TRACY, F. Lavern   1889 - 1972   Father
                [Husband of Nellie P.]

TRACY, Henry Franklin   1871 - 1936

TRACY, Nellie P.   1895 - 19____   Mother
                [Wife of F. Lavern]
TRAVNICEK, Albert F.   1898 - 1975
                [Husband of Anna]

152

RIDGEFIELD CEMETERY

TRAVNICEK, Anna	1901 - 1974	[Wife of Albert F.]
UNGEMACH, Magdalene	1851 - 1934	[Wife of Richard]
UNGEMACH, Richard	1846 - 1938	[Husband of Magdalene]
VANDERGRIFT, Althea D.	1856 - 1934	[wife of Samuel R.]
VANDERGRIFT, Samuel R.	1865 - 1917	[Husband of Althea D.]
VOLTZ, William	1886 - 1966	Father

VRANNA, Kenneth G.   28 July 1948 - 11 Aug. 1977
              Pfc.   U.S. Army   Vietnam

WALKER, Charles E.   1890 - 1968   Dad
              [Husband of Verna I.]

WALKER, Bonnie E.   1903 - 1949   Beloved Wife and Mother

WALKER, Verna I.   1894 - 19___   Mother
              [Wife of Charles E.]

WARD, Myrtle	1889 - 19___	[Wife of Nichol A.]
WARD, Nichol A.	1889 - 1959	[Husband of Myrtle]

WARE, John   12 Nov. 1904 - 13 Nov. 1904

WARNEKE, Albert H.	1894 - 1969	Brother
WATERS, Anna Jane	1857 - 1934	Mother
WATERS, Bert O.	1886 - 1957	[Husband of Elizabeth E]
WATERS, Elizabeth E.	1885 - 1963	[wife of Bert O.]

WATERS, Grace N.   1916 - 1933
              Safe With Jesus

WEACKLER, Belle	1883 - 1966
WEACKLER, R.	1902 - 1967

WEACKLER, Susan Isabel   1883 - 1966   Mother
              [Wife of Leonard P.]

WEBB, George	1882 - 1948	[Husband of Rita]
WEBB, Rita	1894 - 1964	[wife of George]
WEBER, Frances	[no dates]	

WEBER, Frances   13 Nov. 1846 - 28 Sept. 1926

WEBER, Halsey F.   (Baby)   1919 - 1919

RIDGEFIELD CEMETERY

WEBER,   Harry E.   1890 – 1947   [Husband of Letha A.]

WEBER,   Homer H.   1883 – 1954   [Husband of Marie A.]

WEBER,   Kenneth   1908 – 1953

WEBER,   Marie A.   1886 – 1974   [Wife of Homer H.]

WEBER,   Letha A.   1899 – 19____   [Wife of Harry E.]

WEBER,   William   6 Sept. 1840 – 30 Oct. 1910
                        [Husband of Frances]

WELLS,   Clifford V.   1898 – 1918

WELLS,   Gwendolyn A.   1909 – 1935
         And Baby Thomas Robert   1935 – 1935

WELLS,   Joseph G.   1872 – 1957   [Husband of Loretta E.]

WELLS,   Loretta E.   1865 – 1937
                     [Wife of Joseph G.]

WEST,   Frank W.   1863 – 1943   [Husband of Lottie B.]

WEST,   Rena   1860 – 1935

WHITE,   Andrew Thomas   1855 – 1911   Father

WHITE,   Charles H.   1879 – 1963   Father
                     [Husband of Grace A.]

WHITE,   Franklin E.   1910 – 1978
                     W. W. II   U.S. Army

WHITE,   Grace   1889 – 1971   Mother
                     [Wife of Charles]

WILSON, Chancy   1869 – 1914

WILSON, Rebecca M.   1847 – 1923   Mother
                     [Wife of Robert]

WILSON, Robert   1842 – 1929   Father
                     [Husband of Rebecca]

WILSON, T. M.   Died 15 Oct. 1890   49 yrs.

WINGFIELD, Lee W.   1881 – 1930

WINGFIELD, Mayme   1877 – 1966

WINGFIELD, William A.   1876 – 1950

WINSLOW, Alton Clay   Died 3 Aug. 1907 Age 13 yrs. 21 days.

WISE,   Russell Melvin   19 April 1904 – 26 Sept. 1965

RIDGEFIELD CEMETERY

WITTER, Arthur W.   1876 - 1954   [Husband of Dora G.]

WITTER, Dora G.   1874 - 1958   [Wife of Arthur W.]

WOOD, Martha B.   1820 - 1918   At Rest

WRAY, Alice R.   27 Feb. 1897 - 19__   [Wife of Benjamin F.]

WRAY, Benjamin F.   11 May 1893 - 26 NOv. 1966
     Pfc.   3 Army Military Police   Bn   W.W.   I
                    [Husband of Alice R.]

ZEBRUN, Baby Boy   4 Nov. 1955
              [Grave next to Nicholas Zebrun]

ZEBRUN, Nicholas A.   25 March 1919 - 5 Nov. 1968

ZEBRUN, Nicholas (baby)   1 April 1947   Aged 1 day
              [Grave near Nicholas Zebrun]

ZEBRUN, Nicholette   14 Mar. 1949   Aged 7 mos. 12 days
              [Grave near Nicholas Zebrun]

ZEPERNICK, George B.   1863 - 1936
              [Name on same stone with Mary V. Heiser]

WEST, Lottie B.   1870 - 1938
          wife of Frank W.

An old grave marker at the Ridgefield Cemetery. *(Staff photo by Greg Lawler)*

Some markers are in disrepair.

In still, quiet places

They are scattered all over the county, many of them all but forgotten.

They are the stuff f that Halloweens are made of, and the places young children only go on dares. To some, they are places where the past is vividly recalled, with all its joy and sorrow.

They are old cemeteries. In a vivid way the history books often can't, they recount the history of Clark County and the names that were prominent during the settlers' early years here.

In recent years some people have tried to catalog and, if possible, restore the old cemeteries.

Mrs. Margaretta Zimmerman is one of those people. Beginning in in the early 1970s, she and her daughter, Mary, began searching out the old grave sites, hoping to preserve tha names and the places for future generations.

Thus far she has cataloged 47 old cemeteries, and she believes there may be more.

Some are quite new and easy to reach, others are buried under accumulations of leaves and dust, and can be reached only by foot.

Mrs. Zimmerman, 67, of 9504 N.E. 119th, said that there is much work to be done yet, "but at least it's a ' start."

Many of the records she has collected have been copied and donated to the Daughters of the Pioneers and the Clark County Genealogical Society.

Mrs. Zimmerman said that if records aren't made many family names in the area could be lost forever.

So whenever she has chance, she gets in her car and drives to the old cemeteries.

There, in those still, quiet places, she makes sure those who cannot speak for themselves will not be forgotten.

North County News, Wednesday, January 10, 1979

Chelatchie Prairie Cemetery

Chelatchie Prairie Cemetery was established in 1892. It is located 4 4 1/2 miles N. E. of Amboy on Highway 503, Amboy, Wash.

Donna Larsen recorded this cemetery and it has been compared with records of caretaker, Mary Campbell.

158

CHELATCHIE CEMETERY

Lot No.

77	ADAMS,	James Sr.	[No name on marker - Died 1923]
27	ALLEN,	Baby	[Son of Percy - no date]
98	ALLEN,	Alva	[No stone - Died 1940]
27	ALLEN,	Mary Emaline	1860 - 1932
27	ALLEN,	Miles Lee	[No stone - Grandchild of Miles-no dates]
27	ALLEN,	Miles Standish	1850 - 1921
27	ALLEN,	Percy	1902 - 1952 [No stone- Son of Miles]
27	ALLEN,	Vienettie L.	1893 - 1908

Beloved Daughter of M.S. & Mary E. Allen

77	ANDERSON,	Mr. [Inez's Husband - no stone - no date]
77	ANDERSON,	Inez P. (Gregory) [1886 - 1954 no stone]
72	AUSTIN,	Estella B. (Mc Kay) 1863 - 1942 At Rest
72	AUSTIN,	Minot 1853 - 1925 At Rest
73	BAGGETT,	Calvin C. 1895 - 1980
73	BAGGETT,	Esther A. 1896 - 1977 Mother
49	BAKER,	Adaline (Carlson) [No stone - Died 1935]
49	BAKER,	Baby [No stone - Died 1935]
79	BARNETT,	Ray [Baby No stone Died 1910]
54	BERNHARDT,	Richard D. 1895 - 1964
81	BLAIR,	Burt 1875 - 1952 [No stone]
81	BLAIR,	Elizabeth [No stone No dates]
62	BLAIR,	Enos 1882 - 1936
62	BLAIR,	George [No stone Died 1935]
62	BLAIR,	Tressie Died 1963
81	BLAIR,	Rhoda [1913 - 1918 Daughter of Bert & Elie - No stone]
61	BOWES,	Charles 1889 - 1900 Son
61	BOWES,	Edward 1850 - 1899 Father

CHELATCHIE   CEMETERY

Lot No.

61	BOWES, Thomas A.	1896 – 1909	Son

53   CAHILL,   Kenneth   Born 13 Mar. 1891 – Died 3 Nov. 1892
           [Two stone, one says simply "Kenneth"]

      CAHILL,   William   Born 4 Nov. 1837 – Died 9 Aug. 1900
                 Amiable and beloved husband of Rebecca
                 Father and brother: farewell.
                 Not on this perishable stone
                 but in the book of life and in
                 the hearts and minds of men
                 is thy true worth recorded.
           [Two stones,one says simply "Father"]

72   CAMPBELL, Lloyd M.   1906 – 1979

72   CAMPBELL, Mary L.   (Farwell)   1910 – ____

49   CARLSON,   [Baby – no stone – no date]

49   CARLSON, Pearl Mae   [Daughter of Art – no stone   1930]

98   COONS, Jacquelen   [Baby – no stone   1939]

98   COONS, Lawrence   [Baby – no stone   1935]

45   COX, Pauline   1918 – 1975   Loving Wife & Mother

59   CURTICE, Alva B.   Jan. 1906 – Oct. 1975   Til We Meet Again

59   CURTICE, Benjamin A.   1866 – 1950

59   CURTICE, Charles   [Baby   no stone   1904]

59   CURTICE, Emma L.   1884 – 1924

59   CURTICE, Lina Ulery   Born in Multnomah Co. Or. 22 June 1868
                   Died 28 Sept. 1898   Wife of B. A. Curtice
                   In Memory of

99   DAGUE, Webster   [No stone – 1937

57   DEHAVEN,   Baby Boy   1922

93   DOWNING,   [Twin boys   no stone   1926]

26   DRAKE, Kathleen B.   (Ham)   1924 – 1974

26   DRAKE, Willard E.   1923 – _____

16   EATON, Anna   1910   Daughter

16   EATON, Edna L.   1892 – 1978

16   EATON, Gene   1915 – 1918   Son

CHELATCHIE   CEMETERY

Lot No.

16   EATON, Joseph   1886 – 1936

72   FARWELL, Charles B.   1882 – 1946   Father

71   FARWELL, Debra M.   5 Nov. 1956 – 24 Aug. 1964
          Gone But Not Forgotten   Daughter

72   FARWELL, Frances M. [known as Ada – (Bradley)
                    1888 – 1959   Mother

71   FARWELL, Marion B.   1937 – 1942   Son

71   FARWELL, Marvin J.   25 July 1936 – 24 Aug. 1964
          Gone But Not Forgotten   Father

17   FIEGE, Robert [no stone, wooden marker was burned in
          fire – no dates]

Between
97 &
102   FRACH, Regal R.   [1954 – 1969   no stone]

95   FRASIER, Dollie J.   Born 17 Jan. 1925 – Died 26 Jan. 1925
                    [10 days old]

95   FRASIER, Earl L.   1889 – 1943

95   FRASIER, Ervin E.   June 1942

95   FRASIER, Ida E. (Hendrickson)   1898 – 1939

95   FRASIER, Leonard E.   26 June 1928

62   GALLWAY, Jennie Blair   [no stone]

6   GERBER, Wm. F.   Born 5 Feb. 1851 – Died 4 July 1917
               In Memory Of

80   GREGORY, Charles L.   1858 – 1939

77   GREGORY, Daniel   1892 – 1940

80   GREGORY, Daniel W.   Born 6 May 1827 – Died April 1897

73   GREGORY, Ella R.   1877 – 1940

80   GREGORY, Elvina   Born 7 March 1829 – Died 29 Dec. 1899

79   GREGORY, Hiram I.   1860 – 1949

73   GREGORY, John W.   1864 – 1944

80   GREGORY, Martha E.   1868 – 1942

79   GREGORY, Phoebe E.   1864 – 1939

CHELATCHIE   CEMETERY

Lot No.
Alley
btwn.

41	HAM, Francis H.	1887 - 1974	Father
&			
26	HAM, Ruth Eva	1898 - 1974	Mother
59	HANBY, Leona (Hunter)	1917 - 1975	[no stone]
39	HANLEY, Beckie E.	1900 - 1920	
39	HANLEY, Cora	1869 - 1957	
39	HANLEY, Etta L. (Raisey)	1897 - 1977	
39	HANLEY, Grover J.	1890 - 1967	
39	HANLEY, John	1862 - 1937	
39	HANLEY, John C.	1888 - 1961	
41	HANLEY, Linda Ruth	2 Oct. 1946 - 7 Apr. 1947	
96	HENDRICKSON, Frederick D.	1871 - 1950	
96	HENDRICKSON, Inez M.	1912 - 1937	[Daughter of Fred]
96	HENDRICKSON, Irene V.	1915 - 1925	[Daughter of Fred]
96	HENDRICKSON, John	1909 - 1968	[no stone ?]

96   HENDRICKSON,   Mary   28 Sept. 1838 - 14 Jan. 1915
                         His   Wife   At   Rest

96	HENDRICKSON, Mattie B. (Walrig)	1873 - 1934	
96	HENDRICKSON, Peter	25 Mar. 1837 - 24 Apr. 1918	
96	HENDRICKSON, Peter F.	1900 - 1919	[Son of Fred]
7	HICKEY, Margaret J.	1872 - 1942	Mother
28	HUFFMAN, J. R.	1859 - 1905	Father
59	HUNTER, Florence R. (Curtis)	1891 - 1970	
59	HUNTER, George A.	1923 - 1928	
59	HUNTER, Judson W.	1887 - 1966	

97   HUTCHENS,   Eligah   C. [spelled with G]   1847 - 1914
          [Two stones, on hand carved, side-by-side for Eligah]

97   HUTCHENS,   Eliza   J.   1855 - 1939
          [Two stones, one hand carved, side-by-side for Eliza]

CHELATCHIE CEMETERY

Lot No.

105	HUTCHINSON, George	1874 - 1958	[No stone]
40	INDERGARD, Oscar H.	1888 - 1979	
40	INDERGARD, Selma R.	1889 - 1977	
40	KOPLIN, Artie H.	Born 16 Aug. 1899 - Died 4 June 1918	
94	KRUKRA, Charlotte	[No stone - No dates]	
94	KRUKRA, Robert	[No stone - No dates]	
104	LAMB, James Roy	1881 - 1949	[No stone]
17	Mc ADAMS, John	1923	[No stone]
41	Mc CARTY, Nettie M.	1873 - 1960	Mother

[There are two stones with her name, one joint with her husband and a separate one beside it.]

41	Mc CARTY, Clark S.	1860 - 1942	Father
6	Mc KEE, Archie G.	1869 - 1938	
97	Mc KEE, Della (Hutchins)	1978	[No stone ?]
6	Mc KEE, Elvira	Born 26 April 1836 - Died 7 July 1914	

Mother

6	Mc KEE, Martha H. E.	Born 1 Feb. 1868 - Died 22 Apr.1894

She Rest In Heaven

75	MANWELL, Benjamin	Born 11 Sept. 1843 - Died 26 May 1881	
160	MANWELL, Charles T.	1967 - 1974	
76	MANWELL, Edward	[No stone - No dates]	
160	MANWELL, Ferrn John	1965 - 1965	
74	MANWELL, Francis M.	1862 - 1944	
75	MANWELL, George	[No stone - No dates]	
74	MANWELL, Leha E.	1913 - 1963	[No stone]
74	MANWELL, Lena M.	1873 - 1942	
75	MANWELL, Mae C.	1905 - 1964	
74	MANWELL, Peter F.	1900 - 1962	
?	MANWELL, Sylvia Anna	1919 - 1980	
74	MANWELL, Thomas Ira	1898 - 1961	[No stone]

CHELATCHIE CEMETERY

Lot No.

| 73 | MANWELL, | Thomas L. | Born 18 June 1864 – died 10 July 1898 |

73   MANWELL, Thomas L.   Born 18 June 1864 – died 10 July 1898

76   MANWELL, William   1857 – 1923   [No stone]

75   MANWELL, William H.   Born 10 Sept.   – Died 1 Oct. 1872

116   MOON, Earl E.   1893 – 1954

116   MOON, Hulda M. (Hendrickson)   1896 – 1972

116   MOON, Kingsley F.   1869 – 1954

116   MOON, Maude C. (Withers)   1872 – 1954

18   MOORE, Charles E.   1881 – 1958   Father

18   MOORE, Infant   Oct. 1935

18   MOORE, Maria A.   Born 4 Nov. 1827   Aged 20 years
              Wife of S. E. Moore

18   MOORE, Rosa Alice (Windle)   1880 – 1945   Mother

18   MOORE, Samuel E.   Born 28 Dec. 1812   Aged 85 years

18   MOORE, Willis   1920 – 1920

7   OLSTAD, Charles E.   1903 –

29   OLSTAD, Della F.   Born Dec. 31, 1896 – Died Feb. 1, 1905

29   OLSTAD, Minnie A.   1863 – 1929   Mother

29   OLSTAD, Nels O.   1873 – 1912   Father

7   OLSTAD, Opal I. (Hieky)   1895 – 1963

29   OLSTAD, Violet   Born 15 Dec. 1898 – Died 19 Dec. 1898

29   OLSTEAD, Donald G.   1938 – 1980

61   PATTERSON, Charlie F.   26 April 1899 – 18 Feb. 1970
             Washington   TEC 5   U.S. Army   World War II

79   PAULSON, Mary (Gregory)   [Died 1963   No stone?]

127   ROYSE, Sylvia A.   1897 – 1972   Mother

127   ROYSE, Thomas P.   1885 – 1958   Father

48   SILVIS, Roy Z.   23 Dec. 1898 – 21 Oct. 1976
             In Thee Have I Put My Trust

STEPHENS, Nora L. [married 2nd Bennet]
             17 May 1880 – 10 May 1969   Mother

CHELATCHIE   CEMETERY

Lot No.

97   BENNETT, Nora L. (see Stephens) (maiden Hutchins)
        [No stone 1880 - 1969   This woman listed as Nora
        Bennett in cemetary records, but Nora Stephen on
        her gravestone.]

11   SWINGLE, Herman   Died 25 Nov. 1908

117   THOMAS, Helen M.   1878 - 1963

7   THOMAS, Jerry Lewis   1941 - 1976   Dearly Beloved

117   THOMAS, Phillip V.   1871 - 1954

60   ULERY, David   1831 - 1911

60   ULERY, John   [No stone -   no dates]

60   ULERY, Martha J.   1835 - 1910   His Wife

26   WAGGENER, Mark Ellis   1961 - 1979   Son
                      In God's Care

18   WHITE, Infant   Mar. 1934

57   WINDLE, Charles   Sept. 1904   Our Baby

60   WINDLE, Frank G.   8 Sept. 1881 - 21 Jan. 1962

57   WINDLE, John   1853 - 1934

60   WINDLE, Lottie M.   (Eaton)   4 Sept. 1885 - 16 July 1934

57   WINDLE, Mary   (Ulery)   1862 - 1944

126   WYERS, James F.   1888 - 1949

126   WYERS, Laura   (Russell)   1895 - 1979   [No stone]

Bethel Methodist Cemetery

Bethel Methodist Cemetery is located next to Bethel Methodist Church , 2309 N.W. Carty Road, Ridgefield, Wash.

BETHEL EVANGELICAL METHODIST CEMETERY

AKIN	Alva L. Akin, 1898 - 1972 (husband of Lydia H.)
AKIN	Lydia H. Akin, 1891 -1968 (wife of Alva L.)
ALISHIE	Eliza Tom Alishie, 1908 - 1973
AMACHER	Ernest Amacher, 1895 - 1974 (husband of Frieda)
AMACHER	Frieda Amacher, 1891 - 1970 (wife of Ernest)
ARNDT	Alma Arndt, 1893 - 1965 (wife of Gottlieb)
ARNDT	Barbara Arndt, 1863 - 1942 (wife of William)
ARNDT	Gottlieb Arndt, 1882 - 1970 (husband of Alma)
ARNDT	William Arndt, 1861 - 1948 (husband of Barbara
BAUER	Augusta Bauer, Aug. 10 1880 - April 28, 1912
BAUER	Charles Bauer, 1868 - 1940
BEEMAN	Viola H. Beeman, 1920 - 1975
BEESON	John Loren Beeson, 1890 - 1969 (husband of Nellie Jane)
BEESON	Nellie Jane Beeson, 1886 - 1973 (wife of John Loren)
BERGMAN	Carl E. Bergman, died Sept. 22, 1917
BERGMAN	Charles A. Bergman, 1873 - 1952
BERGMAN	Esther Bergman, 1906 - 1978 (In Otillia Bergman plot, Vancouver Funeral Home Marker)
BERGMAN	Hacel Bergman (no dates, in Otillia Bergman plot)
BERGMAN	Martha A. Bergman, 1884 - 1958, Mother
BERGMAN	Otillia R. Bergman, July 22, 1881 - June 3, 1917 aged 36 years
BERTSCHINGER	Albert E. Bertschinger, 1844 - 1918 (husband of Anna)
BERTSCHINGER	Anna Bertschinger, 1855 - 1941 (wife of Albert)
BINDER	Emilie A. Binder, May 6, 1886 - March 27, 1915

BETHEL EVANGELICAL METHODIST CEMETERY

BOTTEMILLER   Arthur A. Bottemiller, 1887 - 1967 (husband of
                   Geneva L.)

BOTTEMILLER   August H. Bottemiller, 1854 - 1944 (husband of
                   Willemina)

BOTTEMILLER   Geneva L. Bottemiller, 1896 - 1974 (wife of
                   Arthur A.)

BOTTEMILLER   Grace E. Bottemiller, May 21, 1926 - July 8, 1927

BOTTEMILLER   Lydia E. Bottemiller, June 20, 1878 - Dec. 1918

BOTTEMILLER   Vernon and Vincent Bottemiller, 1928 (twins)
                   (sons of Albert W.)

BOTTEMILLER   Willemina Bottemiller, 1857 - 1925, Mother
                   (wife of August H.)

BOWLES   Mary J. Bowles, 1859 - 1935 (wife of Thomas J.)

BOWLES   Miriam P. Bowles, 1884 - 1950 (wife of Frank L.)

BOWLES   Thomas J. Bowles, 1857 - 1938 (husband of Mary
                   J.)

BRAACK   George Edward Braack, 1897 - 1967 (husband of
                   Thelma Ransford Braack)

BRAACK   Thelma (Ransford) Braack, 1903 - 19__ (wife of
                   George Edward)

BROCKIE   Lucas F. Brockie, Died Oct. 28, 1917, age 65 yrs

DIETRICH   August A. Dietrich, 1881 - 1956, husband of
                   Millie M.)

DIETRICH   David Dietrich, 1851 - 1942, Father

DIETRICH   David Dietrich, 1894 - 1954

DIETRICH   George Dietrich, 1879 - 1951 (husband of Marie
                   A.)

DIETRICH   Marie A. Dietrich, 1891 - 1953 (wife of George -
                   buried in Germany)

DIETRICH   Millie M. Dietrich, 1895 - 1978 (wife of August
                   A.)

DUNLAP   Harold Dunlap, 1908 - 1929, Brother

BETHEL EVANGELICAL METHODIST CEMETERY

DUNLAP	Lena Dunlap, 1855 - 1915, Mother
ECKLUND	Maria C. Ecklund, 1861 - 1923
GEHRKE	Albert J. Gehrke, 1866 - 1958 (husband of Albertina)
GEHRKE	Albertina Gehrke, 1875 - 1953 (wife of Albert J.)
GEHRKE	Edward W. Gehrke, April 10, 1868 - May 5, 1931
GEHRKE	Henrietta Gehrke, Nov. 2, 1883 - Aug. 13, 1951
GLUTH	Goldie Gluth, 1924 - 1925
GLUTH	Henry A. Gluth, Mar. 16, 1888 - Jan. 26, 1948
GLUTH	Reake W. Gluth, 1865 - 1940 (wife of Stephen C.)
GLUTH	Stephen C. Gluth, Nov. 17, 1848 - Jan. 29, 1926 (husband of Reake)
GLUTH	William H. Gluth, 1882 - 1952
GOODWIN	Alfonzo Theodore Goodwin, Dec. 9, 1900 - Dec. 2, 1977
GOODWIN	Alfred Goodwin, (Rev.), Jan. 15, 1863 - Dec. 8, 1958 (husband of Grace M.)
GOODWIN	Grace M. Goodwin, June 4, 1870 - Feb. 20, 1955 (wife of Rev. Alfred)
GROSS	Ernestine Gross, 1880 - 1948 (wife of George P.)
GROSS	George P. Gross, 1873 - 1958 (husband of Ernestine)
GUSTAFSON	Clarence A. Gustafson, 1910 - 1960, Husband Father
HARTMAN	William P. Hartman, Dec. 15, 1922 - Oct. 23, 1974 S 1 - U.S. Navy
HASTINGS	Clarence L. Hastings, 29 May 1904 - 22 March 1972
HASTINGS	F. Orval Hastings, Feb. 9, 1882 - Oct. 2, 1963 (husband of Margueriette M.)
HASTINGS	Margueriette M. Hastings, 1881 - 1955 (husband of F. Orval)

BETHEL EVANGELICAL METHODIST CEMETERY

HASTINGS	Robert Keith Hastings, 1937 - 1968
HENDERSON	Alta M. Henderson (no dates, wife of Verne L.)
HENDERSON	Lucinda A. Henderson, Nov. 6, 1879 - Feb 10, 1968
HENDERSON	Verne L. Henderson, 1900 - 1968 (husband of Alta)
HERMAN	Adolph T. Herman, April 7, 1894 - 28 Jan. 1975, Pvt., U.S. Army
HERMAN	Daniel M. Herman, 1862 - 1936
HUNNICUTT	Anna M. Hunnicutt, 1898 - 1953
HUGH	Earl Rollie Hugh, 1883 - 1951
HUTCHISON	John Hutchison, 1868 - 1941 (husband of Tillie)
HUTCHISON	Tillie Hutchison, 1887 - 1978 (wife of John)
IVERSON	Ted Iverson, Dec. 25, 1948 - Jan. 8, 1965
KERN	Christofer Kern, 1855 - 1942 (husband of Barbara)
KERN	Barbara Kern, 1861 - 1925 (wife of Christofer)
KOETHE	Adolph Koethe, 1885 - 1941 (husband of Bertha M.)
KOETHE	Bertha M. Koethe, 1890 - 1927 (wife of Adolph)
KOETHE	Charles D. Koethe, 1883 - 1955 (husband of Elsie A.)
KOETHE	Caroline L. Koethe, 1878 - 1969 (wife of Wiliam J.)
KOETHE	Elsie A. Koethe, 1887 - 1941 (wife of Charles D.)
KOETHE	Samuel J. Koethe, 1878 - 1948, Brother
KOETHE	William J. Koethe, 1869 - 1938 (husband of Caroline L.)
KOETHE	William Peter Koethe, Oct. 31, 1912 - Jan. 28, 1964, Washington, Pvt., M.P. Plat. 89 Inf. Div., World War 2)
KOCK	Ann M. Kock, 1851 - 1895
KRIEGER	Marie E. Krieger, 1871 - 1950 (wife of Max O.)

BETHEL EVANGELICAL METHODIST CEMETERY

KRIEGER	Max O. Krieger, 1863 - 1944 (husband of Marie E.)
LEOPOLD	Agatha K. Leopold, 1895 - 1976 (wife of Emil F.)
LEOPOLD	Emil F. Leopold, 1896 - 1974 (husband of Agatha)
LUDKE	Albert J. Ludke, 1900 - 1958
LUDKE	Fred Ludke, 1901 - 1922
LUDKE	Herman J. Ludke (no dates-Vancouver Funeral Home marker)
LUDKE	Otto Ludke, ____ - 1914
LYND	Viola F. Lynd, 1919 - 1944
MANN	Albert G. MANN, 1889 - 1956
MANN	H. B. Mann, Rev., 1878 - 1940
MANN	Marie A. Mann, 1876 - 1964
MANN	Pauline F. Mann, 1894 - 1975 (wife of Albert G.)
MAUL	Patricia Jane Maul, 1943 - 1945, Daughter
MEIRER	Edward F. Meirer, March 15, 1849 - Nov. 25, 1906 (husband of Maria K.)
MEIRER	Ernest Meirer, 1892 - 1914
MEIRER	Maria K. Meirer, Dec. 14, 1857 - Dec. 13, 1907 (wife of Edward F.)
MITZNER	Dorothea Mitzner, 1832 - 1923, Sicher in Jesu Armen (in German - means; Rest in Jesus Arms)
MUELER	Albert Mueler, April 11, 1890 - Feb. 23, 1963 Washington - Batry. C. 38 Field Arty. WW I
MUELER	Amelia Mueler, 1850 - 1930 (wife of Erdman)
MUELER	Carl Mueler, 1876 - 1899
MUELER	Carl E. Mueler, 1854 - 1921 (husband of Emilie)
MUELER	Edward A. Mueler, 1883 - 1969 (husband of Jessie E.)

BETHEL EVANGELICAL METHODIST CEMETERY

MUELER	Edward C. Mueler, May 21, 1882 - May 11, 1907, Son of Charles and Emilie
MUELER	Emilie C. Mueler, 1859 - 1888 (wife of Carl E.)
MUELER	Erdman Mueler, 1845 - 1925 (husband of Amelia)
MUELER	Frederick W. Mueler, 1888 - 1972 (Vancouver Funeral Home marker)
MUELER	Jessie E. Mueler, 1897 - 1972 (wife of Edward A.)
MUELER	Martha Mueler, Feb. 3, 1892 - May 20, 1892
MUELER	Mary Mueler, 1878 - 1958
MUELER	Ottila Mueler, 1880 - 1973
MOSER	Alfred Moser, 1852 - 1932 (husband of Lena H.)
MOSER	Dina Moser, 1856 - 1900, Mother
MOSER	Lena H. Moser, 1862 - 1937 (wife of Alfred)
OLSON	Clarence M. Olson, 1899 - 1942
OLSON	Melvin O. Olson, Aug. 14, 1903 - Feb. 12, 1954
PEARSON	Bernice Pearson, 1910 - 1968
PEARSON	Partricia Lynn Pearson, June 30, 1953 - Aug. 29 1954, Our Baby
PETERSON	Alvin E. Peterson, 1940 - 1972, Father
PETERSON	Fred E. Peterson, Oct. 7, 1893 - May 2, 1955, Husband & Father
PIERCE	Paul J. Pierce, 1892 - 1966, Father (husband of Ruby S.)
PIERCE	Ruby S. Pierce, 1901 - 19__, Mother (wife of Paul J.)
POEPPELMEIER	Gustav A. Poeppelmeier, 1866 - 1930
POEPPELMEIER	Henry L. Poeppelmeier, 1856 - 1921
PUGH	Martha C. Pugh, 1889 - 1957 (wife of William L.)

172

BETHEL EVANGELICAL METHODIST CEMETERY

PUGH   William L. Pugh, 1887 - 1956 (husband of Martha)

RADER   Barney M. Rader, 1876 - 1967

RADER   Charles Rader, 1838 - 1923 (husband of Eureka)

RADER   Eureka Rader, 1840 - 1898 (wife of Charles)

RANSFORD   Albert H. 'Al' Ransford, 1901 - 19__ (husband of
                Writa V.)

RANSFORD   Writa V. 'Vi' Ransford, 1905 - 1977 (wife of
                Albert H.)

REAGER   Bertha M. Reager, 1889 - 1972

RICHARDSON   George E. Richardson, Dec. 16, 1928 - July 6,
                1950, Son

SANDMAN   Lydia D. Sandman, 1911 - 19__ (wife of Victor J.)

SANDMAN   Victor J. Sandman, 1903 - 1975 (husband of Lydia)

SCHLEICHER   Albert Schleicher, 1895 - 1900

SCHLEICHER   Esther A. Schleicher, 1892 - 1957

SCHLEICHER   Joseph Schleicher, 1862 - 1928 (husband of Rose)

SCHLEICHER   Lawrence Schleicher, 1915 - 1915 (infant)

SCHLEICHER   Rose Schleicher, 1865 - 1959 (wife of Joseph)

SCHIMELPFENIG   Clarence Schimelpfenig, 1911 - 19__ (husband of
                Ruth E.)

SCHIMELPFENIG   Ruth E. Schimelpfenig, 1913 - 1978 (wife of
                Clarence)

SCHMIDT   Carl Schmidt, May 4, 1853 - Aug. 21, 1917
                (husband of Matilda)

SCHMIDT   Elizabeth M. Schmidt, 1877 - 1921 (daughter of
                Carl & Matilda)

SCHMIDT   Matilda Schmidt, 1854 - 1924 (wife of Carl)

SCHNEIDER   Bertha M. Schneider, 1874 - 1927 (wife of John)

SCHNEIDER   Clarence G. Schneider, 1910 - 1967

BETHEL EVANGELICAL METHODIST CEMETERY

SCHNEIDER	John W. Schneider, 1885 - 1943 (husband of Bertha)
SCHULDT	Amelia Schuldt, 1870 - 1956 (wife of John C.)
SCHULDT	John C. Schuldt, 1867 - 1941 (husband of Amelia
SCHWANTES	Edward S. Schwantes, 1893 - 1975, Pvt. U.S. Army
SCHWANTES	Ernestine R. Schwantes, 1855 - 1936
SCHWANTES	John A. Schwantes, 1887 - 1959
SCHWANTES	Lydia M. Schwantes, 1879 - 1945
SCHWANTES	Margaret M. Schwantes, 1889 - 1964, Mother
SCHWANTES	Paul A. Schwantes, 1856 - 1937
SCHWANTES	Reuben G. Schwantes, 1895 - 1970 (husband of Sarah M.)
SCHWANTES	Sarah M. Schwantes, 1894 - 19__ (wife of Reuben)
SENTI	Amelia Senti, 24 April, _____ (Knapp Funeral Home marker)
SENTI	Ruth Senti, 24 April, ____, age 10 yrs. 8 mos. 23 days
SENTI	Tobias Senti, 24 April, ____, age 37 yrs. 10 mos. 8 days (Knapp's Funeral Home marker-bad shape)
SMITH	Harriette M. Smith, 1877 - 1965, Mother (wife of Lloyd)
SMITH	Lloyd F. Smith, 1871 - 1941, Father (husband of Harriet)
SMOCT	Muriet Smoct, Aug. 23, 1896 - Oct. 15, 1917, Born in Walla Walla, Washington
STARNS	Rose Julia (Moser) Starns, Dec. 25, 1880 - May 9, 1965
STOLBERG	William Stolberg (no dates-on cardboard)
TETZ	Alfred Tetz, 1896 - 1959 (husband of Emma V.)
TETZ	Emma V. Tetz, 1903 - 19__ (wife of Alfred)

174

BETHEL EVANGELICAL METHODIST CEMETERY

THEIL   Adolph W. Theil, April 21, 1888 - May 8, 1970,
                Brother

THEIL   Herman H. Theil, April 20, 1889 - Jan. 26, 1975,
                Brother

THEILSEIFJE   Alvina Theilseifje, 1859 - 1953 (wife of William)

THEILSEIFJE   William Theilseifje, 1835 - 1928 (husband of
                Alvina)

TRACY   Carolyn Faye Tracy, 1945 - 1963

VOLTZ   Eva Voltz, Died Jan. 4, 1901 aged 76 years.

WARNER   Patricia Kay Warner, Died 1976

WEBER   Benoni Weber, 1853 - 1931, Dad

WEBER   Rosina Weber, June 1, 1859 - Nov. 20, 1922

WILSON   Mildred M. Wilson, 1897 - 1975 (wife of Victor)

WILSON   Victor R. Wilson, 1891 - 1956 (husband of
                Mildred)

WOEHL   Earl Woehl, Jan. 22, 1920, Son of Mr. & Mrs. H.
                L. Woehl

WULF   Antje Wulf, May 2, 1831 - April 29, 1917, Der
                herr ist mein hirte mir wird nichts mangein
                (German inscription)

WULF   Helene M. Wulf, 1866 - 1927 (wife of John H.)

WULF   John H. Wulf, 1864 - 1937 (husband of Helen M.)

WULF   Peter F. Wulf, Oct. 29, 1890 - Nov. 10, 1921

WULF   William Wulf, 1895 - 1916, Co. G. 15th Inf. 1st
                Div. Killed in WWI

YANN   Leroy George Yann, Oct 25, 1941 - April 17, 1969
                Airman 1st Class, U.S. Air Force

YANN   Mildred M. Yann, 1917 - 1958

ZASKE   Ella Zaske, 1890 - 1965, Mother

ZASKE   Harold E. Zaske, 1903 - 1976

BETHEL EVANGELICAL METHODIST CEMETERY

ZASKE   Julius F. Zaske, 1877 - 1963

ZIMMERLY   Emma Zimmerly, 1844 - 1935 (wife of Samuel)

ZIMMERLY   Fred Zimmerly, Nov. 28, 1883 - Feb. 5, 1900

ZIMMERLY   Infant Son of Samuel and Ivy Zimmerly, Oct. 9,
                    1904

ZIMMERLY   Ivy M. Zimmerly, 1882 - 1972 (wife of Samuel E.)

ZIMMERLY   Nancy Jane Zimmerly, July 20, 1935, Infant
                    Daughter of Robert and Viola Zimmerly

ZIMMERLY   Samuel Zimmerly, 1838 - 1912 (husband of Emma)

ZIMMERLY   Samuel E. Zimmerly, 1875 - 1939 (husband of Ivy)

Mt. Zion (La Center) Cemetery

Mt. Zion I.O.O.F. Cemetery is located
on County Road #41, LaCenter, Wash.

177

MT. ZION I.O.O.F. CEMETERY

AMIDON, Henry S.   Sept. 23, 1971 - Feb. 12, 1949

AMIDON, Mattie S.   July 3, 1881 - Dec. 12, 1961

ANDERSON, Almon Coy   1882 - 1899

ANDERSON, Anna M.   1871 - 1952

ANDERSON, Anne Margaret   [Aug. 16, 1894 -   1973]
    Obit. Clipping [Written date-12-13-73]   Anne Margaret Ander-
    son, 79, a former LaCenter and Battle Ground school teacher,
    died Friday in Battle Ground.   She had lived in Clark County
    since 1916.   She was born Aug. 16, 1894 in Los Banos, Calif.
    ...Survived by her husband Clyde, a daughter, Mrs. Beth
    Reich of LaCenter and five grandch.; two brothers James and
    Norman Jensen of Los Banos, Calif. and a foster sister, Hilda
    Brown of San Francisco.
        Funeral services held at the Charter Oak Evangelical Free
    Church with the Rev. James L. Barton officiating. Vault In-
    terment in La Center Cemetery....

ANDERSON, Benjamin   1870 - 1931

ANDERSON, Marie E.   1902 - 1929

ANDERSON, Merrill A.   1900 - 1923

ANDERSON, Ruth   1895 - 1919   and Infant Son

ANDERSON, Infant son   1901

ANDERSON, Curtis   1887 - 1964   Father

ANDERSON, Grace M.   1874 - 1939   Mother

ANDERSON, Glen Dorman   Dec. 29, 1902 - Sept. 16, 1908
        [son of Curtis and Grace Anderson]

ANDERSON, Ida B.   born Feb. 18, 1863 - died Dec. 22, 1890
              Wife of Jas. R. Anderson
    "Asleep in Jesus blessed sleep from which none ever wake to
        weep."

ANDERSON, John C.   1881 - 1900

ANDERSON, Marvin E.   1903 - 1923   Beloved Son

ANDERSON, Nils   1847 - 1924

ANDERSON, Thea O.   1851 - 1930

ASCH, Robert T.   1908 - 1949

ATWOOD, Lillie   [19 Nov. 1879 -   1976]
    Local Newspaper--[Written date LRN 2-26-76]   Services Monday
    for Lillie Atwood, 96, a LaCenter pioneer who died Feb. 16 at
    the Ridgefield Rest Home.   (next page

....Born Nov. 19, 1879, in Portland. She moved to the La Center area when she was two years old and lived there ever since.

At the turn of the century, she remembered to friends later, you could take a steamboat from Portland to LaCenter via the Columbia and Lewis rivers. She also told stories about the logging camps in which she cooked as youngster and of the Cedar Creek Grist Mill, a national Historical site, in which she took grain to be ground into flour.

....was charter member of the LaCenter Methodist Church. She is survived by two nieces. Services at LaCenter Cemetery.

BAKER, Katherin   Dec. 18, 1859 - Feb. 12, 1926

BARNHART, Clarence R.   1888 - 1967

BARNHART, Bertha M.   1898 - 1978
Local Newspaper--[Written date 3-2-78] Services for Bertha M. Barnhart, 80, of LaCenter were held Monday.

Mrs. Barnhart died in an auto accident last Thursday.

A lifelong resideent of LaCenter, Mrs. Barnhart was born Feb. 12, 1898. She was active in farming and was a member of a LaCenter senior citizens' group.

Survived by a brother, Oscar Nelson of LaCenter; a sister Emma Spencer of LaCenter; two sons, Donald Barnhart of Foster City, Calif. and William Barnhart of LaCenter; one daughter, Mrs. Phyllis Keys of West Linn, Ore; and six grandchildren,

Services were held at Vancouver Funeral Chapel with Rev. L. Warren Hansen officiating. Vault interment at LaCenter Cem.

BANZER, Christina Margarite   [1816 - 1882]
Born in the city of Offstein on the Rhine, Germany July 4, 1816 - died at Portland, Oregon - March 20, 1882 - Aged 65 years 8 months and 10 days.   wife of John U. Banzer

BANZER, Edward A.   1864 - 1953   [IOOF Emblem]

BANZER, Minnie L.   1870 - 1930   [IOOF Emblem]

BARR, George   1842 - 1931

BARR, Catherine   1854 - 1923

BARR, George F.   1884 - 1919

BARR, Laura Sarah   1875 - 1904

BARTLETT, Clinton W.   Born Jan. 27, 1897 - Died Dec. 2, 1902
Son of W. E. & Esther Bartlett [a small lamb atop this marker]
"Lie still little Clinty, take thy rest,
God took thee first, he loved you best"

BASTLICK, Ethel D.   1891 - 1951

BECKMAN, Alice E.   1903 - 1947

MT. ZION   I.O.O.F.   CEMETERY

BECKMAN, August   1857 - 1933

BECKMAN, Betsy C.   1867 - 1948

BECKMAN, Paul E.   Born Jan 22, 1899 - Died Nov. 27, 1963
    Washington   Cpl.   2460 Service Comd. Unit   W.W. II

BECKMAN, William Paul   Born March 4, 1950 - Died December 5, 1973

BENN, Charles   1867 - 1927   Father

BENN, Hanna M.   1872 - 1945   Mother

BESSEY, Hezikiah   1894 - 1915

BEVARD, Edward C.   1867 - 1937

BEVARD, Ida May   1866 - 1945

BEVARD, George A.   1891 - 1966

BEVARD, Mary S. Lone   Born Dec. 13, 1845 - Died July 23, 1931
              Beloved Wife and Mother
    "Rev. 14:13 Yea sayeth the spirit that they may rest from
      their labors and their works do follow them.

BEVARD, C. G.   born April 6, 1843 - died Sept. 10, 1906
    "8 Chapt St. John, 32 v. And ye shall know the truth and the
    truth shall make ye free."
                Beloved Husband and Father
    [small ground marker says Tooley Baby girl, which see]

BLOOM, Ellen I.   1905 - 1933

BOCKNER, Ewald A. P.   1881 - 1926

BOCKNER, Lorena G.   1885 - 1971

BOUCHER, Anna March
    Newspaper Clipping--A former LaCenter woman died Tues. at
    White Salmon. Funeral services Saturday in White Salmon
    and graveside services at LaCenter.
        Survived by daughter, Mrs. Harvey Fisher and a grand-
    daughter, Mrs. Donna Bryant, both of Woodland; and two
    sons, Tom March of Longview, and George March, Oakland.

BOUCHER, Edward N.   Died February 7, 1978   Aged 79 yrs 7mos.
        21 days   -   [grave marker -Anderson Funeral Home -
            Hood River, Oregon.]

BRADWAY, Ida M.   1896 - 1968

BRADWAY, Mary D.   Born and Died 1907

BRADWAY, M. L.   1880 - 1968

MT. ZION I.O.O.F. CEMETERY

BRANNFORS, Abraham   1889 – 1943

BRANNFORS, Greta L.   1894 – 19---
    [This monument has a metal plate mounted on the stone de-
    picting what appears to be a "pre-eruption" scene of Mt.
    St. Helens with pine trees on each side, a lake with
    pines in the background, looking up to the mounatin in
    center background. See Thornton monument for same scene,
    also Elisha Sheldon]

BRASHEAR, Charles H.   1900 – 1919

BRASHEARS, Charles W.   1871 – 1941

BRASHEARS, Lee   1874 – 1959

BRAZEE, Lurilla F.   1873 – 1898

BREITIGAN, Franklin D.   1901 – 1919

BREITIGAN, Roger   1907 – 1910

BRICKER, Oscar M.   1904 – 1975

BRIGGS, E. E. W.   [no dates
    Q.M. Sgt. E.E.W. Briggs   Xo. A 10th   U.S. G. H. A.

BROOKS, Nancy E.   1861 – 1976

BROTHERS, Ina M.   died Feb. 6, 1898   Aged 10
            Daughter of U. and W. Brothers

BROTHERS, Joseph   1859 – 1923

BROTHERS, Lucy E.   1898 – 19---   Mother

BROTHERS, William R.   1889 – 1976   Father

BROTHERS, Minnie A.   1856 – 1926   Mother

BROTHERS, Uriah S.   1856 – 1921   Father

BROTHERS, Pern   1891 – 1925   Brother –Father

BRUNDAGE, Frank D.   1870 – 1933   Father

BRYANT, Esther E.   1910 – 1964

BUCHANAN, Alcinous   born Sept. 13, 1842 – died April 26, 1907

BUCHANAN, Ivy Irene   born Sept. 15, 1876 – died Feb. 2, 1878

BUCHANAN, Essie   born June 16, 1878 – died March 16, 1899

BUCHANAN, David   Dec. 29, 1865 – Nov. 25, 1898

MT. ZION I.O.O.F. CEMETERY

BUCKBEE, Howard R.   [May 20, 1906 - March 22, 1983]
    Obit. Clipping--[Written date-3-30-83]....76, died March
    22, 1983 in Vancouver. Resident of LaCenter since 1930.
    Mr. Buckbee was born May 20, 1906 in Portland.
        ....retired dairyman and berry farmer. Attended LaCenter
    Evangelical Free Church.
        Survivors include his wife Lenore at home; three sons,
    David, Keith and William, all of LaCenter; one brother, Her-
    bert of Portland; 11 grandchildren; and four great grand-
    children.
        Services at LaCenter Evangelical Free Church with the Rev.
    Palmer Hansen officiating. Burial followed at LaCenter
    Cemetery.

CARLSON, Alverta   1870 - 1891

CARLSON, Helen   1899 - 19___

CARLSON, Roy   1889 - 1975

CASKEY,   In Memory of Cathryne and Joseph Caskey

CHARLEY, Henry "Hank"   [March 13, 1916 - July 1, 1983]
    Obit. Clipping--[Written date of paper 7-6-83]...A lifetime
    resident of LaCenter, died in a Vancouver hospital July 1,
    1983. He was 67. Mr. Charley was born March 13, 1916, in
    Battle Ground, a retired truck driver.
        He is survived by two sons, Rocky Johnson of Junction City
    Kan., and Jim Charley of LaCenter; two daughters, Wilma Des-
    ieve of Ridgefield and Arlene Bowers of Seattle; and five
    grandchildren.
        Mr. Charley was a member of the Yakima Indian Nation and
    a World War II Army veteran.
        The Rev. Rick Sonerholm officiated at a service July 6,
    at the Evangelical Free Church in LaCenter. Burial followed
    at LaCenter Cemetery.

CHARLEY, James W.   Dec. 25, 1908 - Jan. 10, 1974
            Sgt.   Army Air Forces   W.W. II
    Obit. Clipping--[Written date of paper 1-17-74]   James
    William Charley, 65, of LaCenter died Jan. 10 at home. Born
    Dec. 25, in Woodland, he was a lifetime resident of this area.
        ....veteran of world War II, a member of Yakima Indian
    tribe and the LaCenter American Legion. He worked for LaCenter
    School District 36 years as a mechanic and bus driver.
        Survivors include a brother Henry Charley of LaCenter, and
    a half-sister, Mrs. Edna Decateaus of Toppenish; three nieces
    and one nephew.
        .....services were held Tuesday in the LaCenter Evangelical
    Free Church with the Rev. Palmer Hanson officiating. Inter-
    ment followed in the laCenter Cemetery.

CERVENY, James Paul   [born April 10, 1902 - June 25, 1980]
    Obit. Clipping--Age 78,....born in coeur d'Alene, Idaho....
    Resident of LaCenter Wash. the past 32 years. Former owner,
    manager of Lewis River Telephone Co....and died in Woodland
                              -next page-

MT. ZION I.O.O.F. CEMETERY

CERVENY, James Paul (Cont'd)
     Wash. Wife Constance Cerveny, LaCenter. Son, James P. Cer-
     veny Jr., LaCenter. Daughter, Susan C. King, Vancouver,
     Wash. and 5 grandchildren. Brothers, George R. of Spokane,
     Wash. and Ralph E. Daytona Beach, Fla.
       [He was a member of many organizations] Memorial services
     will be held at 7:30 p.m. Monday June 30th at First Congregat-
     ional United Church of Christ, 1220 NE 68th St., with the
     Rev. Louis taylor officiating. Interment at LaCenter Ceme-
     tery. Woodland Funeral Home in charge of arrangements.

CHICKS. Etta A.   1011 - _____

CHICKS, Guy G.   1905 - 1978

CHICKS, Gladys T.   1908 - 1957

CHICKS, Lawrence L.   Dec. 2, 1954   Pvt.   9 Inf.   2 Div.

CHICKS, Millie A.   1874 - 19_____

CHICKS, Andrew J.   1866 - 1949

CLARK, Gaston L.   1891 - 1915

CLARK, Charles   Dec. 26, 1925

CLARK, Harold N.   1889 - 1953

CLARK, James W.   1896 - 1979

CLARK, Susan B.   1891 - 19_____

CLARK, Lillie B.   1882 - 1918

CLAYTON, William   1867 - 1940

CLEASBY, John   1858 - 1917

CLUTTER, Florence M.   1858 - 1917

COATNEY, Annie Tice   1896 - 1934   Beloved Wife of
          Charles - Mother of Wesley, Loyal, Clifton, Charles Jr.

COLBURN, Oscar   1893 - 1906

COLBURN, James W.   1856 - 1916

COLBURN, Nancy S.   1862 - 1947

CONGDON, Esther M.   1904 - 1945

COOK, Charles T.   1876 - 1950

COOK, Edward J.   1879 - 1934   [Masonic Emblem]

COOK, Frances   1875 - 1928

MT. ZION I.O.O.F. CEMETERY

COOK, Eva G.   1882 – 1917

COOK, Edwin A.   1869 – 1949

COOK, Frances   1911 – 1916

COOK, Ernest   1890 – 1913

COOK, Nora M.   1884 – 1950

COOK, Asa J.   1874 – 1935

COOK, Susan A.   born March 20, 1842 – died March 8, 1903

COOK, John   born April 25, 1824 – died June 1, 1907
     "The Lord is my shepherd, I shall not want"

COX, Albert A.   1871 – 1927

CRAWFORD, Frances C.   born Dec. 29, 1839 – died Feb. 18, 1907
                    Wife of G. W. Crawford

CROW, Lulu   Nov. 8, 1951

CROOKS, Isaac   1877 – 1928

CROOKS, Hannah   1882 – 1948

CROOKS, Leslie R. Crooks   1912 – 1972

DALIN, Marsha M.   1913 – 1972

DALLIN, Matilda   1881 – 1964

DALLIN, Erik E.   1877 – 1953

DAVIS, Lillian Estelle   Born Sept. 1, 1879 passed away Dec.
     18, 1900   –   Beloved daughter of Capt. & Mrs. W.A. Davis
  "She faltered by the wayside and the angels took her home."

DAVIS, William A.   1855 – 1946

DAVIS, Martha A.   1856 – 1918   His   Wife   Mother

DAVIS, Victor E.   1881 – 1910

DEIBELE, Marie   1914 – 1976

DILLARD, Doris M.   1903 – 1960
          "The Lord is my shepherd"

DILLARD, Virginia Grace   [Oct. 21, 1901 – July 9, 1983]
     Obit. Clipping--[Written 7-20-83] Born at Bertha, Mo. and
  resided LaCenter the past 22 years.
        Survived by two daughters, Mary Bradburn and Beverly Hart,
  both of Longview; one son, Lloyd Medlock of Beatty, Nev.
  Five stepsons, Joe Ackerman of Kelso, Richard Ackerman of

MT. ZION I.O.O.F. CEMETERY

DILLARD, Virginia (Cont'd)
    Seattle, Thomas Dillard of Vancouver, Wenton Dillard of Blaine
    and Joseph Dillard of Kent; one sister Susie Smith of Harts-
    ville, Mo; 27 grandchildren and 17 great-grandchildren. She
    was preceded in death by her husband Emit Dillard in 1982.
        Services were held at the Woodland Funeral Home with the
    Rev. Robert Giles officiating. Interment was at LaCenter
    Cemetery.

DIMENT, Osla J.   1878 - 1963   Mother

DIMENT, Edwin P.   1874 - 1944   Father

DIVISH, George S.   1917

DIVISH, Mildred   1920 - 1979

DOOLITTLE, Edwin W.   1911 - 1917

DOOLITTLE, Josephine L.   1919 - _____

DUNN, Audie A.   1890 - 1923

DUNN, Lyle Vernie   Feb. 12, 1913 - April 16, 1976
        Pfc   U.S. Army   W. W. II

ELSENER, John Joe   1886 - 1975 [American Legion Marker]

EVERSAUL, William E.   1875 - 1950   Father

EVERSAUL, Clara A.   1882 - 1944   Mother

FANNING, Maggie M.   born Sept. 9, 1850 - died July 9, 1899
                Wife of L. J. Fanning
        "Shed not for her the bitter tear nor give the hear to
            to vain regret.
        Tis but the casket that lies here, the gem that filled
            it sparkles yet"

FANNING, Levi   1851 - 1939

FANNING, Fannie   1861 - 1940

FEHR, Jenning W.   1878 - 1941   Father

FEHR, Lillie F.   1891 - 1974   Mother

FEHR, Robert E.   1924 - 1976   Brother

FITZGERALD, Hiram E.   1863 - 1906
        [a cement block marker, hand printed [

FLAGER, Barton L.   July 17, 1910 - Jan. 11, 1911
                Son of E. C. & R. E. Flager
        "A bud plucked from earth to bloom in Heaven"

FLEMING, Barney F.   1832 - 1910

MT. ZION I.O.O.F. CEMETERY

FLEMING, Achsah L.   1836 - 1899

FLEMING, Lucy A.   1865 - 1887

FLEMING, Charley   1865 - 1890

FLEMING, Viola   1892 - 1973

FLEMING, W. A. "Jack"   1898 - 19____
     Obit. Clipping--[Written date 12-22-82] William Arthur
     Fleming Sr., 94, died at a nursing home in Woodland Dec. 9,
     1982. He was born Aug. 29, 1888 in LaCenter. Mr. Fleming
     lived in Clark County most of his life. He was an outdoor
     enthusiast and enjoyed home remodeling. He was a former
     Clark County Road Department employee.
        Mr. Fleming is survived by one son, William of Vancouver,
     one sister, Chrystella "Ted" Tooley of Longiew; two grand-
     children and four great-grandchildren.
        A graveside service was held at LaCenter's Mount Zion
     Cemetery.

FLEMING, Jim   1876 - 1911

  ? MING, ?Ary E.   1886 - 1919   [broken marker]

  ? Ming, John   1858 - 1944   [broken marker]

    , H. W,.   [broken marker]

FLENKER, Alice F.   1887 - 1977   Mother

FLETCHER, Robert E.   Feb. 28, 1942 - Oct. 31, 1978

FLUCKINGER, Rudy   1886 - 1961

FOORD, Peter   1903

FOORD, George   Sept. 28, 1833 - Sept. 26, 1895
     "Death of Mercy, oh how sweet; theirs to rest at Jesus feet,
        In your world of light--- illegible--

FOORD, Harriet   Nov. 19, 1886 - May 4, 1898
     "Home at last, thy labors done safe and blest---illegible--

FORBES, Anna C.   1879 - 1964

FORBES, William G.   1880 - 1942

FORBES, Charles E.   1876 - 1938

FORBES, Marlea A.   1877 - 1971   [IOOF symbol]

FORBES, Charles L.   1884 - 1928   Father

FORBES, Adelaide   1858 - 1933   Mother

FULLER, Richard L.   Nov. 29, 1972

186

MT. ZION I.O.O.F. CEMETERY

FRANK, Howard   1888 – 1961

FRANK, Ingrid   1892 – 1967

FRAZIER, Cathryn L.   Nov. 15, 1901 – Sept. 29, 1975

FRAZIER, Earl R.   Aug. 22, 1901 – Nov. 28, 1957

GAITHER, Jessie   1869 – 1940

GAITHER S. Presley   1864 – 1952   [Masonic symol]

GAITHER, John K.   1838 – 1918   [IOOF emblem]

GAITHER, Mary E.   1835 – 1916   [IOOF emblem]

GAITHER, Perry T.   June 8, 1863 – Feb. 6, 1893
        Born in Bloomington, Monroe Co. Ind.
            "Not lost, blest thought but gone before
            Where we shall meet to part no more."

GARVER, [no name]   1849 – 1931

GARVER, Susan M.   1860 – 1930

GARY, John L.   1893 – 1973
        Obit. Clipping [Written date 5-5-73] DEATH TAKES JOHN GARY
        ......prominent LaCenter resident for years, died Sunday
    in a Vancouver hospital.
        He was recently honored with a plaque for community ser-
    vice. He had served the town until recently as its municipal
    judge and earlier for 13 years as its school superintendent.
        Born at Morrison, Ill., Gary was educated at Willamette
    University of Oregon. [clipping tells of many accomplishments]
    ....He also wrote a book, "History of Educational Legis-
    lation in Oregon".
        Survivors include his widow, Marie; two daughters, Margaret
    Watson, West Linn, and Audrey Allen, Portland, and six grand-
    children.
        Memorial services...at Vancouver First United Methodist
    Church. Burial....follow at the LaCenter Cemetery.

GARY, Marie A.   1896 – 19____

GEE, Earl   1904 – 1973

GEE, Ella   1905 – ____

GOEBEL, Meda   1884 – 1933   Mother

GOFF, Laura E.   1915 – 1979

GORDON, Kenneth D.   1956 – 1971

GORDON, Levi D.   1902 – 1962

GORDON, Pauline B.   1904 – 1974

MT. ZION I.O.O.F. CEMETERY

GORDON, Lynwood B.   Sept. 6, 1924 - Sept. 22, 1944
    Washington   Pvt.   327 Glider Inf.   1010 Abn Div.   W.W. II

GORDON, Sarah   July 9, 1807 - Dec. 29, 1881
    "My dear children, do not mourn, for I am going to Jesus"

GORDON, Mary M.   July 19, 1827 - Feb. 28, 1888 [Inscr. above]

GORDON,   Dec. 3, 1900   Infant son of F.F. & A.R. Gordon

GORDON, Fidello   Died May 23, 1901   Age 22yrs 4mos 11days
    "Death our dearest ties can sever take our loved ones from
        our side,
    Bear them from our homes forever o'er the dark cold
        rivers' tide."

GRABER, Elsie M.   1918 - 1965

GRAHAM, Samuel G.   Feb. 1, 1813 - June 20, 1885
    "We shall meet Again"   [Masonic symbol]

GRANLUND, Gust   1874 - 1964   Beloved Father

GRANLUND, Maria L.   1871 - 1934   Beloved Mother

GREEL, J. A.   [no dates]

GREEL, L. J.   1898 - 1917

GREEL, M. A.   [no dates]

GREEN, Arabelle   1865 - 1924

GREEN, Wells   1860 - 1935

GREEN, Viner Jay   1912 - 1916 [Vancouver Funeral Chapel Mark.]

GREEN, Addie Crumley   July 29, 1883 - April 19, 1923
    Erected by Husband and Son - Wife of Frank Crumley

GREEN, Henry Chester   1858 - 1944   Father

GREEN, Sarah Melissa   1861 - 1926   Mother

GREEN, Henry Fremont   May 23, 1887 - Oct. 9, 1948

GREEN, Lucy Anna   April 5, 1867 - March 4, 1898

GREEN, Helena   June 14, 1869 - died Oct. 9, 1882

GREEN, Virginia T.   Apr. 2, 1868 - died Jan. 30, 1891

GREEN, May Vivian   Oct. 2, 1871 - July 30, 1890

GREEN, Melvina   Feb. 10, 1859 - Sept. 28, 1893

GREEN, Michael F.   April 25, 1828 - July 3, 1884

MT. ZION I.O.O.F. CEMETERY

GROVES, John T.   [no dates]   Grandpa

GROVES, Catherine   [no dates]   Grandma

GUTORMONSON [?]   Auntie   1834 - 1928

HAMLIN, Kenneth   1900 - 1921

HAMLIN, Steven L.   1863 - 1925

HANKS, Oren Able   1837 - 1929   Grandfather

HANKS, Dora   1905 - 1919   Cousin

HANSEN, Anna   1857 - 1950   Mother

HANSEN, Lars   1858 - 1923   Father

HANSEN, Christian   1858 - 1935   Father

HANSEN, Christine   1851 - 1930   Mohter

HANSON, Thomas   1855 - 1918

HANSON, Margaret   1855 - 1925   His Wife

HANSON, Leroy   1879 - 1912   Their Son

HANSON, Thomas F.   1877 - 1933   Brother

HARNEY, Harry H.   1901 - 1956
            [Woodland Funeral Home marker]

HEADLEY, Ethel M.   1887 - 1925

HEADLEY, Rebecca   1855 - 1932

HEADLEY, Tom   1858 - 1932

HEADLEY, Tom B.   1886 - 1946

HOBERT, Frank D.   1860 - 1926   [Masonic emblem]

HOBERT, Florence M.   1868 - 1963

HOLM, Gust   1859 - 1937

HOLM, Tina   1865 - 1930

HORN, Robert F.   1884 - 1965

HORN, Sarah L.   1859 - 19____

HORN, Charles W.   1857 - 1933

HORN, Edna   [no date - small stone]

MT. ZION I.O.O.F. CEMETERY

HORN, Charles E.   [no date - small stone]

HUTLEY, Esther   1872 - 1902   Mother

HUTLEY, John S.   1859 - 1901   Father

HUTLEY, Hugh   1899 - 19____   Brother
       [the name HUTLEY is also on the FOORD monument]

IRETON, William   1844 - 1925   Father

JANHUNEN, Peter   1884 - 1962

JANHUNEN, Anna   1887 - 1962

JASKARI, August   1878 - 1951

JASKARI, Anna L.   1877 - 1966

JASKARI, Louise T.   1920 - ____

JASKARI, Wayne W.   1905 - 1968

JESSEN, Jacob Neilsen   Died Aug. 16, 1913
                    Native of Denmark   Aged 73 yrs.

JOHANSON, John H.   1888 - 1962

JOHANSON, Kristina   1866 - 1934

JOHNSON, Abe A.   1872 - 1925   . At Rest

JOHNSON, Alvin Jentoft   May 22, 1911 - June 11, 1969

JOHNSON, Dee Dee - Delia Ann   1940 - 1942

JOHNSON, Howard E.   1913 - 1979   [Masonic symbol]

JOHNSON, Mary   1861 - 1940   Beloved wife of Lee

JOHNSON, Lee   1886 - 1915

JOHNSON, Mathilda   died June 20, 1901
                  Aged   32 yrs   3 months   17 days

JOHNSON, Edward   died Nov. 16, 1897   Gone but not forgotten
          Aged 19 yreas   10 months   11 days

JOHNSON, Richard M.   1948 - 1975   Son and Brother

JOHNSON, Robert D.   May 10, 1898 - June 29, 1972
          Washington   Pvt   Army Air Force   W.W. II

JOHNSON, William A.   April 1, 1825 - Nov. 6, 1906
     "A light from our household is gone, a voice we loved is stilled,
      A place is empty in our hearts, that never can be filled."

MT. ZION I.O.O.F. CEMETERY

HEITMAN, Tillie O.   Sept. 8, 1871 - Sept. 13, 1895
        [this stone was on the William Johnson plot]

JOHNSON, Flora Sara   1867 - 1964
        [illegible lines of prose beneath name]

JOHNSON, Catherine O.   1832 - 1913

JOHNSON, W. Bert   1915 - 1929   Son

JOHNSON, Clyde W.   1889 - 1918   Father

JOHNSON, William G.   1893 - 1946

JOHNSON, William T.   1858 - 1935

JONES, Nora E.   April 7, 1877 - Feb. 9, 1950

JONES, Thomas Henry   July 4, 1870 - Oct. 26, 1947   Father

KANE, Patrick M.   1876 - 1949   Father

KANE, Eran   1885 - 1948   Mother

KATHZ, Valerie W.   1880 - 19_____
            Women's Relief Corps   G.A.R.

KATHZ, Alfred V. Captain   1888 - 1953   Born in Latvija

KETTWIG, Robert P.   1927 - 1970   Beloved Son
            Veteran W. W. II

KINDER, T. J.   Aug. 1837 - Feb. 28, 1906

KINDER, Galatin   Feb. 2, 1802 - July 27, 1875

KNIGHT, Elsie I.   1917 - 1964

LAMSDON, Fred   1867 - 1938

LAMSDON, Hattie   1876 - 1941

LANDERHOLM, Axel Emmanuel   1887 - 1978

LANDERHOLM, Charles M.   1860 - 1927   Father

LANDERHOLM, C. Wilhelmena   1850 - 1931   Mother

LANDERHOLM, Willie   May 20, 1890 - April 4, 1898
            Beloved son of G.M. and W. Landerholm
        "Budded on earth to bloom in Heaven"

LANPHEAR, Baby   Feb. 19, 1964   Infant Son

LAPPIN, Samuel   1831 - 1892   Father

LAPPIN, Amanda C.   1836 - 1907   Mother

MT. ZION I.O.O.F. CEMETERY

LAW, Eva T. (Davis)   1883 - 1915   Mother

LAWS, Alice P.   April 22, 1860 - April 1, 1880
          Beloved wife of Andrew T. Laws   "Gone but not forgotten"

LAWTON, David E.   1833 - 1903

LAWTON, Emily N.   1840 - 1908   His Wife

LAWTON, Francis G.   1832 - 1913

LAWTON, Maria   1835 - _____   His Wife

LEWIS, Delila G.   Oct. 10, 1848 - Jan. 29, 1886

LEWIS, James   Dec. 8, 1844 - Nov. 28, 1905
          "A precious one from us has gone, A voice we love is stilled,
          A place is vacant in our home which never can be filled."

LEWIS, John Paul   Dec. 7, 1953 - Dec. 8,   Baby

LOVE, Emmeline   Feb. 14, 1884 - Dec. 24. 1884

LOVE, Emorett   July 19, 1847 - March 5, 1912
          Age 65 yrs 7 mon   14 days -   Gone but not forgotten

LOVE, L. M.   Jan. 16, 1848 - Sept. 12, 1919   In Memory Of
          "He died as he lived, a pure upright man"

LOVE, Mary V.   Oct. 16, 1879 - Jan. 8, 1910

LUNN, Mabel C.   1891 - 1962   Wife and Mother

LYDA, Jeannette M.   1915 - 1973

LYDA, Harry T.   1911 - 1973

MANELY, Georgia A.   1863 - 1908

MARCH, William T.   1878 - 1933   Father

MARCH, Ann Boucher   1883 - 1965   Mother
                    Together Forever

MASON, Frank Albert   1859 - 1941

MATHER, Chester B.   1869 - 1929   Father

MATHER, Henry W.   1839 - 1912

MATHER, Myrtie A.   1881 - 1929

MATTSON, Anna   1876 - 1934   Mother

Mc CANN, William H.   1866 - 1935   Gramp

Mc CANN, Emeline   1865 - 1948   Gram

MT. ZION I.O.O.F. CEMETERY

Mc CALL, Mary T.   1904 - 1974   Beloved Mother

Mc COLLISTER, Lillie   1866 - 1945   Mother Dear

Mc CRACKEN, Beatrice (Johnson)   1894 - 1973

Mc CUTCHEON, Boone   1905 - 1960   Father

Mc CUTCHEON, John H.   1932 - 1967   Don

Mc DONALD, L. R.   1871 - 1914

Mc GROTTY, Thomas   1831 - 1929

Mc GROTTY, Ellen J.   1837 - 1910   His Wife

Mc ININCH, Robert   died Oct. 15, 1904   Aged 76 yrs 6 Mos.

Mc KEE, Alberta R.   [no stone]
      Obit. Clipping--[Written date 9-26-78] Alberta R. McKee,
   a 21-year resident of Ridgefield, died Monday in Vancouver.
   She was 83.
         .....lived most of her life in Clark County. She was
   born Aug. 18, 1896 in Holt County, Missouri.
        .Survived by two daughters, Esther Bailey of Battle
   Ground and Ruth Trout of Drain, Ore; Two brothers, Sam
   and Hugh Dawson, both of Salem, Ore.; Two sisters, Charlotte Kersey of Woodburn, Ore. and Lois Miller of Hood
   River, Ore: nine grandchildren and 12 great-granchildren.
      Graveside services were held at the Mount View Cemetery
   in LaCenter, Friday, Sept. 21.

Mc KEEN, Charles A.   died Sept. 12, 1902   Aged 46 yrs.

Mc KEEN, Leo Adelbert   died Sept. 12, 1902   Aged 1 yr.
            Son of C.A. and M.A. McKeen

Mc KEEN, Minerva Agnes   died Sept. 12, 1902   Aged 34 yrs.
      Wife of C.A. Mc Keen   "Dum Tacet Clamat" [Woodman Emblem]
            Here rest a Woodman of the World

MENDY, John G.   1843 - 1913   [I.O.O.F. Emblem]

MENTCH, John G.   1894 - 1969

MENTCH, Ellen Olivia   1903 - 1970

MEYER, George H.   Nov. 7, 1887 - Oct. 7, 1918
            Co. D.   961 Inf. - Died of wounds Fleury, France

MICKELSON, Matt   1885 - 1922

MICKELSON, Ida W.   1888 - 1968

MOE, Albert B. [no dates]   Co. F.   38 Iowa Inf.

MOE, W. H.   Feb. 17, 1881 - June 20, 1905   [I.O.O.F. symbol]

MT. ZION I.O.O.F. CEMETERY

MOE, Mc Kinley   1891 - 1918   Co. B   361 Inf.

MOE, Albert W.   March 6, 1884 - Jan. 9, 1914

MOLANDER, Ada Mellissa   died Oct. 7, 1905 Aged 23yrs 10ms 14ds
    "Just as the morning of her life was opening into day,
  "Her young and lovely spirit passed from out the land and died away."

MOORE, John C.   Oct. 25, 1835 - Oct. 18, 1907

MORGAN, Frank L.   1859 - 1940

MOORE, Bertha E.   Sept. 20, 1884 - June 24, 1901
    "Asleep in Jesus blessed sleep from which no one ever wakes
        to weep."

MOORE, Fannie Ferris   Dec. 19, 1865 - Feb. 13, 1933

MOORE, John A.   June 12, 1843 - Aug. 7, 1933
    Washington   LDS   U.S. Navy   Civil War

MOORE, Mary B.   1883 - 1932

MOORE, Lewis A.   1877 - 1936

MYERS, Elizabeth C.   1853 - 1931

MYERS, Frank F.   1853 - 1934

MYERS, Clark F.   1881 - 1951

MYERS, Ralph W.   June 21, 1874 - June 9, 1944

NEER, Martha E.   Mar. 11, 1871 - July 10, 1947   His Wife

NELSON,   Elizabeth   1857 - 1955   Mother

NELSON, F. Nels   1855 - 1935   Father

NEWMAN, Elizabeth E.   1884 - 1973

NEWMAN, James F.   1888 - 1947

NICHOLSON, Angus   1894 - 1918   Killed in Action
          Co. A   28 inf.   1 Div.

NICHOLSON, Frank   1866 - 1955   [I.O.O.F. Emblem]

NICHOLSON, Mary Mae   1870 - 1944   [I.O.O.F. Emblem]

OLSEN, Esther O.   1972

OLSEN, N. M. Carrie G.   Aug. 24, 1860 - Dec. 19, 1941   Mother

OLSEN, Carl N.   1890 - 1964

194

MT. ZION I.O.O.F. CEMETERY

OLSEN, Jens M.   1872 - 1900

OLSON, Axel   1856 - 1934

PARIS, Dennis R.   [no stone]
    Obit. Clipping--[Written date--6-4-82] ...a welder, died Thursday of an illness. He was 27.
    ...funeral held....Monday at the Highland Lutheran Church in La Center. The Rev. Rodney Ellertson will officiate.
    Born Aug. 4, 1954, in Longview, he had lived at 213 NW 68th St. He was a former employee of Schurman Machine Inc. Woodland. He was a 1972 graduate of Battle Ground H.S. and had lived in Vancouver since 1962.
    ...widow Judy. Other survivors include his parents, Mr. and Mrs. Ronald Paris of Ridgefield, a brother, Douglas Paris of Ridgefield; a sister Patricia Harris of McCall, Idaho; and two grandmothers, Daisy Risley of Woodland and Cecile Paris of Ocean Park, Wash.
    [Arrangements by Vancouver Funeral Chapel.] Burial will be in La Center Cemetery.

PECK, Mariel   1888 - 1953

PECK, Fred L.   1886 - 1962

PENCE, H. J.   [no dates]   Co. H.   10th W. Va. Inf.

PENCE, William W.   1875 - 1917

PENCE, Henry J.   1847 - 1900

PENCE, Martha E.   [no dates]   His Wife

PETERSON, Edward P.   1890 - 1976
    Obit. Clipping [Written date--8-12-76] Services were held last Saturday in Vancouver for Edward P. Peterson, who died last Wednesday. He was 86.
    Born July 11, 1890 in Portland, Mr. Peterson was a retired farmer and a resident of LaCenter for 80 years.
    Survivors include a daughter, Mrs. Joan Legg of Gresham, Ore.; two sisters, Hilma Peterson and Mrs. Selma Carr, both of Portland; and four grandchildren.
    Interment was at LaCenter Cemetery.

PETERSON, Edith H.   1896 - 1962

PETERSON, Erik   1857 - 1924

PETERSON, Mary   1861 - 1898   His Wife

PETERSON, Peter A.   Nov. 8, 1860 - Aug. 1, 1931
    [see Pollock, both on same monument]

PETTIT, Emma G.   1905 - _____

PETTIT, Ernest M.   1905 - 1978

Next page --

PETTIT, Ernest (cont'd0
    Obit. Clipping--[Written date--3-23-78]- Services for
Ernest Milan Pettit, 72, of LaCenter were held Monday. Born
Aug. 20, 1905, in Cheyenne County, Kansas, Mr. Pettit was a
LaCenter resident since 1945.
    Survivors include his widow, Emma G. of LaCenter; four
sons, Wesley M., Ernest D., Eugene W, and Richard H., all
of LaCenter; four daughters, Ethel DeLong and Gladys Sheldon
of Vancouver, and Hope Prouty and June Chipman of LaCenter;
five sisters, Mary Smith of LaCenter, Jody Pettit of Pierce,
Colo., Clarice Ashley of Warren, Ark., Maude Johnson of St.
Francis, Kan. and Maggie Engleman of Three Forks, Mont.;
38 grandchildren; five great-grandchildren and one fister
grandchild.
    ...Evangelical Free Church, with Rev. Rick Sonerholm
the Rev. Palmer Hanson officiating. Imtermemt... LaCenter
Cemetery. Layne's Funeral Home in charge of arrangements.

PETTIT, Kathryn Anne   Nov. 16, 1961

PETTIT, Kenneth Eugene   Jan. 21, - May 13, 1966

PETTIT, Leslie Marvin   Jan. 28, 1927 - May 27, 1963
        Cpl   U.S. Marine Corps Res.   WW II   Korea

PITCHFORD, Alice   died May 4, 1873

POLK, Emma L.   [no dates]
    Obit. Clipping [Written date--2-8-68] Funeral services were
held Friday, Feb. 2 at the Woodland Funeral Home for Mrs.
Emma L. Polk, 77, who died Jan. 30 at the Ridgefield Nurs-
ing Home.
    Mrs. Polk was born Jan. 17, 1891 in Minnesota.
    Her survivors include a son, James V. Polk of Oxnard,
Calif.; one grandson; three sisters Mrs. Mary Williams of
Woodland, Mrs. Clara Harris of Ukiah, Calif. and Mrs. Eva
Dixon of Portland; one brother C. O. Williams of Mentone,
Calif.
    Rev. Finis Johnson officiated and burial at LaCenter
Cemetery.

POOLE, Delia A.   1859 - 1940

POLLOCK, John T.   June 12, 1864 - July 21, 1924
        [on the P.A. Peterson lot.]

POOLE, J. D.   1856 - 1935

PORTIN, Andrew   1853 - 1921

PORTIN, Henry   1901 - 1908

POST, C. M.   1881 - 1915

POWELL, Mary O.   May 15, 1823 - Oct. 8, 1823

POWELL, Elizabeth B.   May 3, 1868 - April 28, 1882
        Children of Willis & Jane Powell

MT. ZION I.O.O.F. CEMETERY

PROCTOR, G. Alan   1907 - 1963   Dad

PROCTOR, Irene C.   1906 - 19____   Mom
                        Our Love is Forever

PRUITT, John T.   1829 - 1914

PYE, Ronald E.   Sept. 20, 1947 - Nov. 25, 1947   Our Beloved

RABB, Annette   died June 13, 1877   Wife of R. Rabb
            Aged 32 years   6 months 7 days   [this could be Rapp]

RATHBUN, Susan   1886 - 1891   [marker says] Sisters

RATHBUN, Mary   1896 - 1901   [Sisters]

REED, Addie   1849 - 1927   Mother

REED, Claude T.   1885 - 1949

REED, Eda N.   1894 - 1937

REED, Wm. E.   [no dates]   Co. H   5 Wisc. Inf.

REID, Orin E.   Aged 34 yrs

REID, Sarah Evaritta   Aged 31 years   Wife

REID, Minnie Irene   Aged 6 years   Daughter

REID, Mary Elsie   Aged 4 years   Daughter

REID, Robert Leslie   Aged 3 years   Son
        [This 5 member family perished in the forest fire on the
            Lewis River, Sept. 12, 1902]

REIGEL, Benjamin F.   1850 - 1931

REIGEL, Esther Mathilda   1854 - 1920

REIN, Carl   1870 - 1950

RELYEA, Arthur C.   1866 - 1951

RELEA, Rose M.   1884 - 1959

RHODES, Clara C.   1872 - 1960

RHODES, Charles Edwin   1864 - 1941

RHODES, Florence I.   1904 -

RHODES, Charles L.   1901 - 1978
        Obit. Clipping [Written date..11-2-89] ....died in Vancouver
        last Tuesday at age 77.
            Mr. Rhodes operated the old LaCenter Feed Store for five

next page--

RHODES, Charles I. (cont'd)
     years, and before that operated the old Rhodes Brothers
     Mercantile Store with his brother Ralph for 23 years.
          ...born Feb. 17, 1901, in Rapid City, S.D......past master
     of the Ridgefield Masonic Lodge 237. He also had worked for
     the forest service and the old state highways Department.
          Survivors include his widow, Florence, at home; two sons,
     Charles of San Jose, Calif., and Rodney of Seattle; two dau-
     ghters, Charlene Robinson of Edmonds, Wash., and Glennadyne
     Olson of Kent; three brothers, Ellis of LaCenter, Ralph of
     Gales Creek, Ore. and Ernest of The Dalles, Ore.; a sister,
     Jessie Sharkey of Kent; 12 grandchildren; and two great-
     grandchildren.
          Services held at LaCenter Cemetery with Rev. George
     schubert officiating. Layne's Funeral Home of Battle Ground
     was in charge of arrangements.

RISLEY, Arthur E.   1904 - 1946

RITCHEY,   Clara Tice   1893 - 1919

ROOT, Herbert L.   1885 - 1964

ROOT, Cynthia E.   1889 - 1956

ROOT, Thomas Leon   Dec. 15, 1946 - April 2, 1971
          Washington   QM   U.S.N.R.   Viet Nam

RUF, Freda   1876 - 1915   At Rest

RUSSELL, Jane   Nov. 10, 1818 - Nov. 10, 1893
          Born in Glasgow, Scotland, came to Philadelphia 1829
       Married to Jno. Russell Dec. 24, 1841 - Mother of 11 children

RUZICKA, Leland E.   Mar. 2, 1945 - Oct. 4, 1973
          Washington   SP 6   U.S. Army   Vietnam

SADLIER, Matthew J.   [no stone]
     Obit. Clipping--Matthew J. Sadlier, 23, died Oct. 22 in
     LaCenter. He was an eight-year resident of Clark County.
          Graveside service...LaCenter Cemetery with Rev. George
     Schubert officiating.   ...born Feb. 24, 1960, in Sacramento,
     Calif. He was a logger who last resided in Cougar.
          Survivors include his father, Philip Sadlier of Woodland;
     his mother Jewell Ellila, of Woodland; his stepfather, Paul
     Ellila of Woodland; three brothers, Lincoln, Michael and
     Creighton Sadlier, all of Woodland; and his grandparents,
     Philip and Madge Sadlier of Woodland and Sophia White of
     Vancouver.

SCOTT, Carrie T.   1856 - 1933   Mother

SCOTT, James H.   1852 - 1885   Father

SCOTT, Harry W.   1879 - 1947

SCHUBEL, August H.   1860 - 1945   Father

MT. ZION I.O.O.F. CEMETERY

SCHUBEL, M. Frances   1866 - 1944   Mother

SHAVER, John E.   Aug. 8, 1890 - Feb. 18, 1975
                Pvt.   U.S. Army   W.W. I

SHEARER, Olivia C.   1888 - 1946   Mother

SHELDON, Elisha   1864 - 1942

SHELDON, Frank S.   1885 - 1975   In Memory Of

SHELDON, F. S.   [no dates]   Co. H   74 Indiana Inf.

SHELDON, Kevin Michael   Mar. 9, 1962 - April 1, 1970
                "And the Angels will watch over him"

SHELDON, Minnie B.   1871 - 1923

SHELDON, Winnie M.   1908 - 1934

SHURTS, Sina E.   1869 - 1959

SIEBLER, Flora S.   [no stone]
    Obit. Clipping--[Written date 4-28-82] -Flora S. Siebler, 58,
    died April 9. She was born April 15, 1823, in New Berlin, N.Y.
    Mrs. Siebler was a trailer sales manager and trailer hitch
    specialist.
        She is survived by her husband Edward; one son Edward of La-
    Center; two sisters, Viola Funaro of Norwich, N.Y., and two
    grand-daughters.
        The funeral was last Monday at Memorial Gardens Funeral Chap-
    el with the Revs. H.W. Rydman and Rich Sonerholm officiating.
    Burial followed at the LaCenter Cemetery.

SMITH, Daniel   Dec. 28, 1823 - Sept. 11, 1903   [Masonic Emblem]

SMITH, Frank   Feb. 3, 1874 - Dec. 2, 1898
                    Son of J.A. & M.G. Smith

SMITH, George Wm.   [no dates]   Aged 37 years

SMITH, Henrietta Jackson [no dates]   Age 30 years   His Wife

SMITH, Catherine Matilda   Age 1 year   Daughter
        Perished in Lewis River Forest Fire   Sept. 12, 1902

SMITH, Henry S.   1855 - 1938   Father

SMITH, Martha E.   1858 - 1936   Mother

SMITH, Letha   1893 - 1916   Daughter

SMITH, James A.   1836 - 1916

SMITH, Mary C.   1843 - 1916   His Wife

SMITH, Jesse L.   Mar. 9, 1893 - Aug. 18, 1895
                Son of J.M. & S.A. Smith

MT. ZION I.O.O.F. CEMETERY

SMITH, John E.   died May 30, 1896   Aged 82 years

SMITH, Asenath Dillinger   died Aug. 23, 1891
          Aged   81 years   -   Wife of John E.

SOEHL,   -agda -ema   1875 - 1956

SOEHL, Beatrice M.   1906   Grandma

SOEHL, Henry W.   1897 - 1975   Grandpa

SOEHL, John P.   1864 - 1933

SOEHL, John Peter   Nov. 9, 1894 - Aug. 27, 1970
     Washington Cook   349 Baker Co   QMC   W.W. I
  Obit. Clipping--DEATH TAKES J.P. SOEHL, Funeral services were
  held Tuesday at the Vancouver Funeral Home for John Peter
  Soehl of LaCenter, who died last Thursday. Burial followed
  at the LaCenter Cemetery. Pastor A. F. Gerstmann officiated.
    .....retired farmer ...resident of LaCenter past 54 yrs.
  He lived at Rt. 2, Box 1-A. ..member of Lutheran Church and
  the American Legion. He was born November 9, 1894, at
  Scribner, Neb.
    Survivors include four brothers, Fred Soehl of Ocasta, Wash.,
  and Walter, Alfred and Henry Soehl, all of LaCenter, and
  three sisters, Mrs. Ellis Rhodes, LaCenter, Mrs. Edwin Kauf-
  mann of Portland and Mrs. Carl Green of Vancouver.

SOEHL, Peter A.   1835 - 1918

SOEHL, Walter E.   Feb. 12, 1914 - Oct. 19, 1976
          S. Sgt.   U.S. Army   W.W. II
  Obit. Clipping [Written date--10-28-76]....services for ....
  62, of LaCenter....resided in town since 1916...was retired
  postmaster from 1953 until his retirement.....member of
  American Legion post and the Wheel Club.
    Among survivors are his son, Jerry, at home; a stepson,
  David Morgan of LaCenter; a daughter, Mrs. Myrna Earl of
  Seattle; two stepdaughters, Mrs. Janice Ruland of Vancouver,
  and Mrs. Janie Rutledge in South Carolina; two brothers,
  Alfred Soehl of LaCenter and Fred Soehl of Montesano; and
  three sisters, Mrs. Margaret Rhodes of LaCenter, Mrs. Bertha
  Kaufman of Vancouver and Mrs. Wilma Green of Port Townsend.
    Vancouver Funeral Chapel in charge of Arrangements.

SOEHL, Winifred P.   Jan. 5, 1922 - Sept. 6, 1973
          Our Beloved Mother "Winnie"

SOMERS, Mary Ellen   May 6, 1934 - Oct. 9, 1937

SPENCER, G. Byron   1918 - 1968

SPENCER, George L.   1867 - 1931

SPENCER, Rhena M.   1867 - 1961

MT. ZION I.O.O.F. CEMETERY

SPENCER, Emma C.   1895 - 19_____

SPENCER, George P.   1895 - 1969

SPENCER, Florence E.   Nov. 12, 1884 - May 14, 1886
         Daughter of Thomas E. & Lurilla F. Spencer

SPENCER, Jesse Clyde   March 18, 1939
       Pvt S A T C   State College of Washington

SPENCER, Lewis   1817 - 1881

SPENCER, Elizabeth   1826 - 1903   His Wife

SPENCER, Charles W.   1869 - 1920

SPENCER, Thos. E.   1854 - 1916

SPENCER, Lurilla F.   1863 - 1960

SPENCER, William J.   May 8, 1844 - Dec. 18, 1902
     born in Kosciusko Co., Indiana - Husband of Sevilla C.
       Spencer -   Aged 58 years 7 months 10 days

SPENCER, William   1884 - 1933

SPENCER, Ruth   1892 - 1935

STEELE, Ira G.   Mar. 5, 1914 - Jan. 6, 1970
      Kansas   Pfc   Co. H   13 Inf.   W.W. I

STEIN, Elise J.   1880 - 1966

STEELE, Charles   1884 - 1942

STEINMETZ, Catheriena   Nov. 7, 1849 - May 26, 1890
       Beloved Wife of Peter Steinmetz

STEPH, Dan Henry   Mar. 19, 1937 - Jan. 9, 1966
         Our Beloved

STORM, John   1881 - 1968

STORM, Sophie   1890 - 19_____

STROM, Hannah   1863 - 1915   Wife of J. Strom

SUTTON, Sarah A.   1847 - 1890

SUTTON, Baby   1908 or possibly ? 1903

SWABES, Ernest L.   1889 - 1954

SWABES, Lulu M.   1893 - 1946

TANNER, A. H.   1845 - 1923

MT. ZION I.O.O.F. CEMETERY

TANNER, William B.   Feb. 19, 1896 – Mar. 26, 1949
      Washington Pfc   6 Field Artillers   1 Div   W.W. I

TANNER, W. Henry   1870 – 1950

TANNER, Ethel M.   1902 – 1915

TANNER, Eva R.   1874 – 1911

TAYLOR, Theodore R.   1885 – 1969

TAYLOR, Eva J.   1892 – 1979
      Obit. Clipping--[Written date- 10-3-79]...Eva J. Taylor, 87,
   a lifelong resident of LaCenter, died Tuesday in Woodland.
      She was born Aug. 25, 1882, in LaCenter, and last resided
   at Rt. 1, Box 294.
      Survivors include 3 sons, Angus A. and Ernest F., both of
   LaCenter, and Dennis R. of Portland; 10 grandchildren and 12
   great-grandchildren.
      ....Vancouver Funeral Chapel and burial in LaCenter Cemetery.

THATCHER, Travis Shawn   [no stone]
      Obit. Clipping--[Written date--3-9-67]   Travis Shawn Thatcher
   of LaCenter died saturday, Mar. 4 in Vancouver.
      Travis was born Aug. 9, 1965 in Vancouver and was less than
   18 months old at the time of his death.
      Survived by his parents Mr. and Mrs. Thomas W. Thatcher;
   a sister Dallas Thatcher and grandparent Mr. and Mrs. Miles
   Thatcher and Mr. and Mrs. Robert Hayden, all of LaCenter.
      Graveside services at LaCenter Cemetery,...Woodland Funeral
   Home in charge of arrangements.

THOMAS, Mae   April 2, 1889 – Feb. 26, 1948   Mother

THORNTON, Ella Teresa & Anna Thornton   June 1895

THORNTON, Florence J.   1918 – 1974

THORNTON, John W. Sr.   1911 – 1973

THORNTON, Hugh J.   April 12, 1909 – Oct. 13, 1954
      Washington   W.W. II

THORNTON, Jesse L.   1869 – 1912

THORNTON, William C.   1826 – 1905

THORNTON, Julia A.   1832 – 1918

THORNTON, John C.   1865 – 1940

THORNTON, Adelaide R.   1881 – 1971

THORNTON, Louis E.   1901 – 1964

THORNTON, Mary J.   1869 – 19____

MT. ZION I.O.O.F. CEMETERY

THORNTON, Frank A.   1862 - 1943

TICE, Charles Russell   Oct. 28, 1908 - Nov. 5, 1968
            Oregon   Tec 4   104 Inf. Div.   W.W. II

TICE, Kenneth E.   April 22, 1920 - Oct. 9, 1924

TICE, Lillian M.   1874 - 1911

TICE, James J.   1858 - 1932

TITUS, Eliza   Feb. 6, 1842 - Nov. 14, 1913   Mother

TOBEY, Edith M.   1884 - 19____

TOBEY, Charles W.   1872 - 1922

TOBEY, Lois   Sept. - Dec. 1912

TOENJES, Laurence B.   April 25, 1890 - Dec. 22, 1971
            Washington   Sgt. U.S. Army   W.W. I

TOLLYSON, Mary E.   1848 - 1918   Wife of A. Tollyson

TROXEL, Annie O.   1888 - 1977
        Obit. Clipping [Written date]--Services for Annie O. Troxel,
    a 70 year LaCenter resident, were Wednesday....87, died
    Sunday. She was born dec. 5, 1889 in Neillsville, Wis.,
    and last resided at Rt. 1, Box 409.
        ..... member of Highland Lutheran Church, the LaCenter
    Garden Club and LaCenter Grange.
        Survivors include her daughter, Beatrice M. Soehl of
    LaCenter, two grandchildren, 11 great-grandchildren.
        Graveside services at LaCenter Cemetery with pastor Rod-
    ney Ellertson officiating. Vault interment followed.

TROXEL, Leonard   1881 - 1952

TOOLEY, Baby girl   April 22, 1946
        [this grave is on the C.G. Bevard Lot. which see]

TRAVIS, Permelia   born June 5, 1818 - died Aug. 5, 1904
        [this grave is on the Susan A. Cook lot probably]

TROXEL, Leonard   1881 - 1952

TURNER, Julia J.   1900 - 1931

TUSS, Thomas   May 6, 1937
              Montana Corp Army Service Corps

UNGEMACH, Iva Bell   1881 - 1922   In peace we rest

UNGEMACH, John H.   1876 - 1934

UNGEMACH, Mildred   1913 - 1934

MT. ZION I.O.O.F. CEMETERY

VAN LOO, Delia L.   Nov. 26, 1896 – June 22, 1972

WAMPLER, Claude E.   Sept. 21, 1906 – Oct. 12, 1908

WAMPLER, Ida   July 16, 1908 – Aug. 22, 1910

WARD, Clara L.   Jan. 9, 1879 – Oct. 30, 1880
    Aged 1 yr.   9 mo   21 day   –   Daughter of J.P. & L. Ward

WARD, Laney   Jan. 3, 1836 – June 5, 1914   Mother

WASER, Anton "Tony"   1901 – 1980
    Loyal & Loving to Family, Friends & Country

    Obit. Clipping-[Written date--1-30-80]   Anton A. Waser, 78,
a long-time LaCenter resident, died Jan. 26 in Wolfenschlesen,
Switzerland. He lived most recently at 1104 NE 66th St.,
Vancouver, and had lived in Clark County since 1930. He was
a retired dairy farmer.
    Survivors include his widow, Elizabeth M., at home; sons,
Arthur A. Clarence A., Fred E. and Carl W., all of Vancouver,
and Allen E. of LaCenter; daughters, Emma Grindle and Shirley
M. Trimbo, both of Vancouver, and Mary Ann Becker of Brem-
erton; sisters, Anna Inderbitzen, Sweewen, Switzerland, and
Maria Odermati of Ennetmoos, Switzerland; 11 grandchildren
and numerous nieces and nephews.
    Interment was at La Center Cemetery.

WASER, Jennie M.   1909 – 1974   Wife   Mother

WASHBURN, Daniel M.   1879 – 1961   Father

WASHBURN, Lulu E.   1888 – 1966   Mother

WATSON, Warren K.   Feb. 20, 1821 – Dec. 21, 1888
    Born in Norway, Maine

WEAVER, Alta Ruth   Jan. 21, 1907 – Feb. 14, 1914

WEAVER, Charles C.   1875 – 1960   Father

WEAVER, Bessie   1878 – 1971   Mother

WEAVER, Margauritte   Born Feb. 22, 1901 – Died Feb. 24, 1905
    Daughter of Chas. & Bessie

  "Our Darling Margauritte is Gone from this World of Toil and care
  To Join the Angel Band that has Climbed the Golden Stair."

WEBER, Anne E.   Apr. 14, 1872 – Oct. 23, 1919   Mother

WEBER, Emil H.   April 12, 1863 – Mar. 7, 1939   Father

WEIR, Christella E.   1884 – 1963

WEIR, Durrell C.   1878 – 1949

MT. ZION   I.O.O.F.   Cemetery

WEIR, Hannah   born July 1, 1841 - died Jan. 9, 1893
                                Wife of Captain W. G. Weir
              "Sacred to the Memory of a Devoted Wife and Loving Mother"

WEIR, Captain L. C.   1875 - 1957   [Masonic Emblem]

WEIR, William G.   1834 - 1902
                        Pioneer Columbia River Captain

WENDLAND, Karolina N.   1883 - 1960

WENDLAND, Emmanuel M.   1881 - 1962

WHITE, Christina   1877 - 1968

WHITE, Neil L.   1886 - 1956   Father

WHITE, Evelyn L.   1922 - 1930   Daughter

WILSON, Charles A.   Oct. 27, 1893 - Oct. 2, 1961   Father

WILSON, Jettie M.   Apr. 29, 1894 - Oct. 2, 1961   Mother
                        [Masonic Emblem - OES Emblem]

WILSON, Charles R.   1941 - 1963

WILSON, Emma C.   1860 - 1948   At   Rest
                        Born at Hayes Wn.

WILSON, Hilma H.   1897 - 1922   Wife of Daniel H. Wilson
                        Wife of Daniel H. Wilson
WILSON, Irene F.   1896 - 1956

WILSON, Marguerite M.   1886 - 1976

WILSON, James G.   1883 - 1938

WILSON, Nina V.   1887 - 19___
            Obit. Clipping- Wed. Sept. 22, 1982   Nina V. Wilson a long
        time LaCenter resident, died in Woodland on Sept. 15, age 94.
            Graveside services at Mount Zion Cemetery with Rev. George
        Schubert officiating.
            Mrs. Wilson was born November 8, 1887, in Wisc. and was
        a homemaker.
            Survived by a son, Thomas Wilson of LaCenter; a daughter
        [the rest of this clipping is missing]

WILSON, John E.   1885 - 1972

WILSON, Thomas   Dec. 22, 1855 - Aug. 25, 1911
                        Born in Hoolinwood, England

WILSON, Infant D.   1924 - 1924

WILSON, Infant son of J.E. and N.V. Wilson   Jan. 13, 1911

MT. ZION   I.O.O.F.   CEMETERY

WOODWARD, Charles H.   1904 - 1977
     Obit. Clipping-[Written date--5-26-74]   Services for
     Charles H. "Chuck" Woodward, 72, of Wooldland were Monday
     in Vancouver Funeral Chapel.   Employed as an iron worker
     for 30 years and retired eight years ago.
        Survivors are his widow Evelyn, at home; four sons,
     Robert of Woodland, Brian of Vancouver, donald of Pioneer
     and Kelly of Bellingham; two daughters, Gloria Pinard of
     Olympia and Laurel Ewing of Kirkland; two sisters, Ardis
     Dye and Germaine Carey, both of Woodland; and 10 grandch.
        Dr. Bill Ritchie officiated at the service. Private
     burial in LaCenter Cemetery.

WOODWARD, Eddie   Born April 7, 1917 - Died Jan. 29, 1920

WOODWARD, Evelyn V.   1917 - 19___   Wife of Charles H.

WOODWARD, Matt E.   1873 - 1946

WOODWARD, Bertha F.   1884 - 1973

WREN, Lemuel C.   1875 - 1939

WREN, Lulu May   1884 - 1964

YEIGH, Elmer M.   Mar. 11, 1885 - May __, 1907

YEIGH, James M.   May 22, 1853 - Oct. 26, 1919   Father

YEIGH, Josephine J.   Nov. 26, 1866 - May 25, 1935   Mother
                    In Loving Memory

  ?   William W.   1861

  "   Maxine   1869

    [two metal markers placed by Laynes Funeral Home- last names
        missing]

Information given by Mrs. Clyde Schurman of Woodland, Washington:

SCHURMAN, Bertha   died about 1875
           [First wife of August Schurman]

SCHURMAN, Caroline   died 1903   [2nd wife]
           [buried in Highland Lutheran Cemetery]

MT. ZION I.O.O.F. CEMETERY

People known to be buried in Mt. Zion-LaCenter Cemetery with no tombstones

MASON,   Luther Thomas   born 1826 New York - died Feb. 27, 1914
Lewisville, Wash. Husband of Mary Ann

MASON,   Mary Ann   born 1834 New York - died about 1893
Lewisville, Wash.

MASON,   Levi Alfred   born 28 July 1853 Wisc. - died 1934
La Center, Wash.

MASON,   Mary Belle Harrell   born 9 April 1868   Indiana
died 12 Oct. 1903   Portland, Ore.

MASON, Clarence   born Feb. 23, 1903 Lewisville, Wash - died
Sept. 1903   Portland, Ore.   [Twin]

MASON,   Lawrence   born Feb. 23, 1903 Lewisville, Wash -
died April 1903   Lewisville, Wash.   [Twin]

MASON,   Nora   born 1864   Iowa - died 1877 in Lewisville, Wash.
of Whooping Cough   daughter of Luther

MASON,   Charles E.   born 1851   Wisconsin - died March 1, 1914
in La Center, Wash.

MASON,   Minnie Belle Walden   born 5 Feb. 1865   Kent -
died 20 Nov. 1893   LaCenter, Wash   Wife of Charles E. Mason

MASON,   Neva   born 1895   Infant daughter of Charles and
Lillie Belle Lewis Mason

MASON,   Leland   born 1941 LaCenter - died 1944   Son of Delbert

BAILEY,   Alma Virginia Mason   born 28 Sept. 1885
died 16 April 1982   born and died in Clark County, Wash.

ADAMS,   Stephen   born 1834 in Virginia - died Dec. 11, 1918
in Clark County, Wash.

WALDEN,   Sarah Melissa Greene   born 1843   Indiana
died 10 Feb. 1877   La Center, Wash.

[She was wife of William Henry Walden who was born in Orange
County, Indiana 10 Sept. 184_. In his old age he moved to
California and died in 1925 at the Soldiers home in Sawtel
8 June 1925]

HARRELL,   George Washington   born 1828 in Virginia-died 1904
[Cannot verify yet but he is buried in La Center or Lewisville
Cemetery]

Submitted by Margaret Colf Hepola.
Levi and Mary Belle Harrell Mason are my Grandparents.

Highland Lutheran Cemetery

Highland Lutheran Cemetery is located
north east of LaCenter on County Road
#39 and 41st, LaCenter, Wash.

HIGHLAND   LUTHERAN   CEMETERY

ANDERSON,   Christian   1825 - 1916

ANDERSON,   Ingeborg   1836 - 1913

ANDERSON,   Hjalmar B.   Sept. 18, 1907-June 3, 1977
                        U.S.   Army   W. W.   II

ANDERSON,   John   1876 - 1929

BAKER,   Lawrence Ivan   Mar. 6, 1924 - Sept. 14, 1979
              Korea   U. S. Army   W. W. II

BONG,   Helen R.   1918 - 1959

BONG,   Olof E.   1914 - 1959

BONG,   Peter O.   1875 - 1954   Father

BONG,   Edla   1889 - 1979   Mother

BOYCE,   Thomas E.   Oct. 2, 1948 - Sept. 9, 1969
              See you in the morning

BRAUN,   Kimberley   Feb. 4, 1973 - Aug. 10, 1978

BROWN,   Harold R.   Oct. 13, 1910 - April 30, 1978   Father

BROWN,   Magda H.   Aug. 9, 1910   Mother

CHRISTIANSEN,   Alma M.   Nov. 5, 1889 - March 30, 1923
                   In Loving Memory
CHRISTIANSEN,   Edwin C.   1889 - 1972   Father

CHRISTIANSEN,   Mollie E.   1892 - 1967   Mother

CHRISTIANSEN,   Ella M.   1882 - 1938   Beloved Mother

CHRISTIANSEN,   Sam H. H.   1881 - 1972   Beloved Father

CHRISTIANSEN,   Gerhard L.   1829 - 1899

CHRISTIANSEN,   Welhelmina F.   1829 - 1901

CHRISTENSEN,   Albert   1882 - 1966

CHRISTENSON,   Mary J.   1901

CHRISTENSEN,   Jennie M.   1880 - 1973   Mother

CHRISTENSEN,   Martin P.   1885 - 1972   Father

CHRISTENSEN,   Martin A.   1850 - 1924
               In Loving Memory Of

CHRISTENSEN,   Pauling M.   1861 - 1922

HIGHLAND LUTHERAN CEMETERY

DILLARD, Daniel R.   1952 - 1972

DOBLER, Charlotte   Mar. 23, 1845 - Nov. 11, 1911

EHLBECK, Charles   1866 - 1949   Brother

EHLBECK, Frederick   Oct. 13, 1837 - Jan. 8, 1910
           72 years   2 months   25 days

EHLBECK, John A.   Nov. 4, 1887 - December 29, 1946
        Washington   PFC   20 Engrs.   W.W. I

EHLBECK, May E.   March 25, 1888 - Jan. 30, 1928

EHLBECK, Otto   1870 - 1936   "At Rest"   Father

EHLBECK, May E.   1874 - 1952   "At Rest"   Mother

ELEPSEN, Serine   Jan. 19, 1884 - Died Sept. 2, 1912
     Wife of Ed Villa,   Born in Sandlia Norway,   Age 26 yrs.
     7 M's   13 days.

ELIASON, Hans   1866 - 1943   [This is another bronze
     on stone marker with pine trees on either side, a lake
     surrounded by pines, looking up to a mountain which
     appears to be St. Helens--pre eruption. At Mt. Zion IOOF,
     see also Thronton (John C.) Brannfors, Elish Sheldon]

ELIASON, Mary   1872 - 1932   This is the same marker as above.

ELIASON, James E.   Dec. 30, 1931 - Feb. 1, 1932   Our Baby

ELLIFSON, Ingaburg M.   Born Jan. 9, 1820 - Died Apr. 7, 1898

ELVRUM, John   March 1881 - March 1956

ELVRUM, Ida R.   1883 - 1973

ELVRUM, John G. L.   Sept. 17, 1922
              SI   U.S. Navy

ERICKSEN, Charles E.   1883 - 1944
     "The Lord is my shepherd"

ERICKSEN, Joakim E.   1856 - 1932   Father

ERICKSEN, Maria   1881 - 1956   "The Lord is my Shepherd"

ERICKSON, James C.   Born Aug. 18, 1884 - Died Nov. 19, 1909
     Age 25 Yrs.   3 mo's   1 day.   On front of marker   "In
     Loving Remembrance of James C. Erickson".   In back "Rock
     of ages, Cleft for me,   Let me hide myself in Thee"

ERICKSON, Karen E.   1863 - 1948   Mother

ERSTAD, Mabel G.   1888 - 1976   [small metal marker]

210

210

HIGHLAND   LUTHERAN   CEMETERY

ERSTAD,   Baby   Aug. 30, 1908   [small metal marker]

ERSTAD,   Ole   1860 - 1932   Father

ERSTAD,   Marie   1864 - 1929   Mother

GABRIELSEN,   Anna   1901 - 1970   [Mas. symb.]

GABRIELSEN,   Edward   1893 - 1976   [Mas. symb.]

GABRIELSEN,   Benedikte P.   1854 - 1922   Mother

GABRIELSEN,   Hans C.   1848 - 1927   Father

GABRIELSEN,   Geda K.   1883 - 1962

GABRIELSEN,   Gunda C.   b. March 7, 1882 - d. Aug. 8, 1912
                    "Rock of Ages - In Remembrance"

GABRIELSEN,   Mark Daniel   Aug. 25, 1946   Baby

GABRIELSEN,   Peter   1897 - 1979   [metal-in ground
          marker placed by Laynes Funeral Home]

GRAHAM,   Ingrid H.   1905 - 1975   In Memory of

HAMILTON,   Harry T.   1873 - 1972

HANTHO,   Harry S.   1882 - 1958   Father

HANTHO, Sigrid O.   1880 - 1949   Mother

HEISER,   Bertha R.   1879 - 1927   Mother

HEISER,   B. Helen   Mar. 16, 1910 - Oct. 19, 1930

HEISER,   Gordon W.   Mar. 17, 1906 - Apr. 26, 1973
               Cpl.   Army Air Forces

HEISER,   Otto D.   1872 - 1937

HEISER,   Robert C.   2nd Oregon Inf. Spanish American War

HOBART,   Henry   b. Aug. 6, 1836 - d. Apr. 15, 1889

HOBART,   Sarah Jane   b Nov. 17, 1841 - d. Sept. 16, 1903
               wife of Henry Hobert

HOPKINS,   Amanda   1894 - 1927   Mother

JABUSCH,   John P.   Jan. 19, 1894 - Mar. 21, 1952
            PFC   76 Inf.   13 Div.   W.W. I

JELLUM,   Clara Maria   May 17, 1890 - Feb. 8, 1939

JELLUM,   Helge O.   1876 - 1972   Father

HIGHLAND LUTHERAN CEMETERY

JELLUM, Nobel D.   1906 - 1977   Father

JELLUM, Rita F.   1913 - _____   Mother

JENSEN, Baby   Nov. 27, 1916

JENSEN, Olga P.   1898 - 1977   Mom

JOHNSEN, Henrikke P.   1872 - 1956   In Memory of

JOHNSON, A. Alfred   Sept. 25, 1871 - Sept. 25, 1919
        born in Finland   "Blessed are the dead who die in
            the Lord"

JOHNSON, Amelia H.   1867 - 1956

JOHNSON, Anna N.   1865 - 1904

JOHNSON, John A.   1864 - 1915

JOHNSON, Arthur   1897 - 1974

JOHNSON, Barnhart   1892 - 1971

JOHNSON, Caroline E.   1888 - 1968

JOHNSON, Catherine E.   1906

JOHNSON, Peter E.   1900 - 1962

JOHNSON, Clara S.   1890 - 1960

JOHNSON, Ole S.   1884 - 1970

JOHNSON, David   1886 - 1966   Father

JOHNSON, Edward S.   1854 - 1932   [Edward & Julia]

JOHNSON, Julia   1860 - 1925   Beloved Mother and Father

JOHNSON, Edwin J.   1888 - 1964

JOHNSON, Effie R.   1905 - 1975   Mother

JOHNSON, Ella M.   1886 - 1972   Mother

JOHNSON, Emil   1882 - 1952   Father

JOHNSON, Hanna   1826 - 1902   Beloved wife of C. C.
        Johnson, Native of Norway   "In my Fathers house are
            many mansions"

JOHNSON, Alfred   b. Oct 17, 1901 - d. Sept. 19, 1909   Aged
        2 yrs. 11 months,
        " A little time on earth he spent,
            'til God for him His Angel sent"

212

HIGHLAND   LUTHERAN   CEMETERY

JOHNSON,   F. Vea T.   1914 - 1977

JOHNSON,   Frans W.   1902 - 1911   "Rev. 14:13
            Blessed are the dead who die in the Lord"

JOHNSON,   Johanna H.   1874 - 1963   "Rev. 14:13
            Blessed are the dead who die in the Lord"

JOHNSON,   Grace M.   1907   Wife

JOHNSON,   Ray F.   1892 - 1979

JOHNSON,   Gust A.   1868 - 1944

JOHNSON,   Herbert E.   Nov. 18, 1916 - March 10, 1976
                PFC   U.S. Army   W.W. II

JOHNSON,   Ella M.   1886 - 1972   Mother

JOHNSON,   Helene   1903 - 1906

JOHNSON,   Helen   1906 - 1919

JOHNSON,   John O.   1877 - 1944

JOHNSON,   Marie   1851 - 1927   Marie

JOHNSON,   Otto   1880 - 1920   Father

JOHNSON,   Hilda C.   1882 - 1960   Mother

JOHNSON,   Peter L.   1857 - 1921

JOHNSON,   Ruth   1902 - 1924

JOHNSON,   Simon   Died April 14, 1938   Aged 77 yrs.   9mos.
            13 days   [Marker by Limber's Funeral Home -
                Vancouver, Wash.]

JOHNSON,   Tilda   1863 - 1958   Mother

JOHNSTON,   Clara H.   1890 - 1967

JOHNSTON,   William F.   1889 - 1972

JONES,   B. Jeff   July 9, 1955 - Oct. 26, 1971
            "Nothing can separate us from the love of God which is
            in Christ our Lord."

JONES,   Esther   1887 - 1922

KAFFERLIN,   Sandy Lynn   May 18, 1950 - Jan. 7, 1956

KNOWLER,   Callie   1865 - 1933   Mother

KNOWLER,   Frederick   1851 - 1946   Father

HIGHLAND   LUTHERAN   CEMETERY

KNOWLER,   Arthur   1899 - 1932   Brother

KNOWLER,   Fred   1910 - 1969

LINDBLOM,   Alfred   T.   1880 - 1955

LINDBLOM,   Hazel   C.   1870 - 1955   Aunt

LINDBLOM,   Helena   Feb. 17, 1838 - Dec. 9, 1895

LINDBLOM,   Ida   S.   [no dates]

LINDBLOM,   John   O.   Nov. 28, 1834 - July 1916
*   [American Legion Marker]

LUDKE,   Sophie   1875 - 1943

LUND,   Anna   M.   1885 - 1969

LUND,   Robert   1883 - 1964

LUND,   Baby   aged 5 days

LUND,   Annie   A.   1902 - 1922

LUND,   Christina   1888 - 1917   "Asleep in Jesus"

LUND,   Eric   H.   1857 - 1906   Father

LUND,   Joel   1889 - 1907

LUND,   Laura   1878 - 1917   "Gone but not forgotten"

LUND,   Lars   1840 - 1912   Father

LUND,   Christina   1847 - 1942   Mother

LUND,   Leonard   W.   1885 - 1911

LUND,   Oscar   Nov. 14, 1892 - Apr. 15, 1909

LUND,   Vander   H.   1884 - 1957

LUND,   Wendla   1862 - 1924   Mother

* LOBERG,   Rena   C.   Feb. 2, 1887 - Nov. 24, 1972

LYONS,   Cordelia   E.   1827 - 1909

LYONS,   Joshua   S.   1825 - 1915

LYONS,   Lettie   1856 - 1924

MARTIN,   Bernard   M.   April 13, 1897 - April 2, 1975
                    U.S.   Army   W.W. I

MATTSSON,   Anders   E.   1882 - 1914   "Asleep in Jesus"

HIGHLAND   LUTHERAN   CEMETERY

MATTSON,   Helja   M.   1897 - 1974

MATTSON,   John   E.   1891 - 1960

Mc MULLEN,   Benjamin F.   Aug. 25, 1825 - Feb. 9, 1892
                    " At   Rest "

MEYER,   Saima   J.   1900 - 1969   Mother

MILLIANO,   Gladys   A.   Mar. 17, 1906

MILLIANO,   Joseph   P.   Oct. 25, 1909

MICKELSON,   Uno   1894 - 1965

MILLS,   Anita Mae   Feb. 5, 1922 - Dec. 29, 1974   "Momma"
                God Grant Me Serenity

MOE,   Peter   N.   1848 - 1907   Father

MOE,   O. S.   1850 - 1949

MOE,   Bertha   1851 - 1938

MOE,   Olaf·Sigvard   Nov. 7, 1883 - Dec. 23, 1903
         " God gave, He took, He will restore, He does all things
            well."   In Loving remembrance

MOE,   Elen Anna   1854 - 1927   Mother

MOE,   Arthur   C.   1891 - 1939   Father

MOE,   Alfred Nikolai   June 12, 1877 - Oct. 31, 1896

NASTROM,   Marie   1882 - 1935

NEGSTAD,   Henry   J.   1833 - 1922

NEGSTAD,   Marie   1844 - 1925

NELSON,   Aina   1896 - 19__

NELSON,   Sigrud   1895 - 1975

NIXON,   Minnie   S.   1896 - 1952   Mother

NORGARD,   Herman   1859 - 1893

OFFICER,   Ebon   1865 - 1948   Father

OFFICER,   Nora   1873 - 1964   Mother

OFFICER,   Elsie   Louise   Mar. 21, 1931   Our Baby

OFFICER,   Glenn   1899 - 1976

OFFICER,   Elise   M.   1904 - 1977

HIGHLAND   LUTHERAN   CEMETERY

OFFICER,   Neely   1904 – 1967   Father

OLSEN,   John Arnt   1885 – 1967

OLSEN,   Margaret   1890 – 1972

OLSEN,   Jonas   1869 – 1939

OLSEN,   Mikal   1864 – 1950

OLSON,   Martin   1905 – 1952   Veteran   W.W. II

OLSTEDT,   Otto   1872 – 1950

OLSTEDT,   Sofia   1867 – 1938

OSTERHOLM,   Louise K.   1879 – 1958   Mother

OSTERHOLM,   M. J. E.   1886 – 1968   Father

PARKER,   George H.   1870 – 1915   [American Legion Marker]

PEARSON,   Mary   1886 – 1923
              [This is on a piece of wood, about 12-15 inches long--
              like a piece of 2 x 4. New wood, dates, and name
              burned into the wood.]

PEDERSON,   Christain   1868 – 1942
                    "Ones worthy of Remembrance"

PEDERSON,   Marie C.   1865 – 1944   [his wife]
                    "Ones worthy of Remembrance"

PEDERSON,   John E.   1871 – 1947   "Gone   Home"

PEDERSON,   Rachel   Mar. 2, 1881 – Aug. 10, 1937
                    "God Bless You"

PERLBERG,   Albert F.   Beb. 27, 1882 – Nov. 13, 1951

PERLBERG,   William S.   born Jan. 12, 1834 – died Aug. 5, 1917
                    "At Rest"

PERLBERG,   Amelia   born Sept. 12, 1845 – died Feb. 1, 1896
              [his wife]   " At   Rest "   [Cross with GAR]

PETERSON,   J. M.   born April 19, 1865 – died Aug. 5, 1924
                " Gone but not forgotten "

QUESSETH,   Olea G.   1850 – 1924   Mother

RICHARDS,   Norman   1903 – 1978   NORMAN

RICHARDS,   Neva B.   1910

RUDY,   John   1868 – 1943

HIGHLAND   LUTHERAN   CEMETERY

RUDY,   Johanna   1868 - 1944

SCHEERER,   Julia   1883 - 1933
          [this is on a piece of wood, about 12-15 inches long
            like a piece fo 2 x 4. New wood, dates and name
            burned into wood.]

SCHURMANN,   August H.   born Feb. 10, 1845 - died Aug. 18, 1925
          "While in this grave our father lies,
            his spirit rests above in realms of bliss
               and never dies,
            but knows a Savior's love."
     [this is on a book-type cement marker in front of tall
      "Schurmann" monument.]

SCHURMAN,   Baby Boy   July 18, 1928

SCHURMAN,   Baby Wilma Alice   Mar. 19 - Apr. 19, 1933

SCHURMANN,   Caroline Borchardt   born Feb. 23, 1851 - died July
          28, 1903.
          " O cease dear ones, from your weeping above this spot
               where I am sleeping-- [the rest of the words are
            illegible. No names on tall "Schurmann" monument, but
            on book type cement markers in front.]

SCHURMAN,   William E.   1887 - 1970

SCHURMAN,   Ella C.   1899 - - -

SCHURMANN,   Willie C.   born March 3, 1898 - died July 23, 1902

SIMPSON,   Ben   Aug. 26, 1863 - March 31, 1909
          " Dearest Father thou hast left us,
            Here thy loss we deeply feel.
            But tis God that have bereft us
            And all our sorrows heal."

SIMPSON,   Martin R.   1906 - 1967
          [A metal marker on stone from Hamilton Funeral Home]

SMITH,   Baby   June 30, 1902

SMITH,   C. Aster   1886 - 1955

SMITH,   Charles G.   1851 - 1941   Father

SMITH,   Christine S.   1859 - 1936   Mother
          " The Lord is my Shepherd"   [this phrase on the above
            two name stone]

SMITH,   Louis S.   1881 - 1903

SORENSON,   Axel E.   1883 - 1958   [Metal plate on stone
          from Vancouver Funeral Home]

HIGHLAND LUTHERAN CEMETERY

SORENSON, Hannah M.   1881 - 1956
        [cement stone with metal name from Vancouver Funeral Home]

SORENSON, Gladys   July 1, 1906 - Sept. 20, 1979

SORENSON, Wallace   Jan. 8, 1909 - Oct. 13, 1978
                    U. S. Navy   W.W. II

STRATTON, James Allison   July 31, 1861 - May 4, 1919

TEAL, Dorene M.   1935 - 1939

THORESON, Carrie   1867 - 1961

THORSEN, Baby   [no dates] THORESON, Sore   1859 - 1921

TRYON, Terry Lee   Dec. 20 - Dec. 23, 1950

WALSTAD, Christina   [no dates]

WALSTAD, Emma   [no dates]

WEATHERLEY, Alex A.   1910 - 1965

WEFER, Di'edrich   1849 - 1938

WEFER, Margaret   Oct. 12, 1852 - Jan. 25, 1930   Mother

WEFER, William J.   Apr. 27, 1892 - Sept. 24, 1921
                [American Legion Marker]

WEISE, Dorothy B.   1895 - 1960

WEISE, Otto Paul   Feb. 26, 1892 - Feb. 21, 1961
        1st Sgt.   Co. C.7   Infantry   W.W. I & W.W. II

WIARD, Dudley Todd   Oct. 23, 1912 - March 21, 1977
                CCM   U.S. Navy   W.W. II

WILEN, Leo A.   1934 - 1975   Father

WILEN, Tuure A.   1888 - 1972   Father

WOODY, Alvida   1889 - 1949   Mother

WOODY, James T.   June 23, 1877 - June 29, 1961
        Washington Pvt   Co D 6   Regt U.S. Vol. Inf.
                        Spanish American War

WOODY, Ted R.   1900 - 1979

YOUNGQUIST, John E.   died Nov. 28, 1918   aged 56 yrs.

ZORN, Alice Maud   1888 - 1957   "In memory of Mother"

ZORN, Otto J. H.   1888 - 1963   "In memory of Father"
                [Masonic Symbol]

HIGHLAND LUTHERAN CEMETERY

ZUHL, Bertha   1871 - 1942   Mother

ZUHL, Carl H.   1902 - 1936

ZUHL, Frederick   1859 - 1934   Father

ZUHL, Henrietta   Jan. 12, 1827 - Dec. 11, 1907
                    Mother and Grandmother

ZUHL, James   [infant]

ZUHL, Charlotte   [infant]

ZUHL, Anna   1873 - 1924

ZUHL, Carl   1861 - 1936

ZULAUF, Louisa M.   1874 - 1926

LA CENTER RESIDENT DIES SEPT. 24th

Matthew S. E. Osterholm

Funeral services were held Friday for Matthew S. E. Osterholm who died Sept 24 at Moorehaven Nursing Home in LaCenter.

Born Oct. 15, 1886 in Finland, he had been a resident of LaCenter the past 50 years and was a retired farmer.

He is survived by two sons, T. W. Osterholm of Portland, Elmer J. Osterholm of Beaverton. There are five grandchildren adn seven great grandchildren.

Services were held at the Hamilton Mylan Funeral Home in Vancouver with burial following at Highland Cemetery.
                    [Oct. 3, 1968]

MRS. ELIASON BURIED TODAY

WOODLAND - April 21 - Funeral services for Mrs. Hans Eliason, age 60, who passed away Monday evening at her home in the Highland district, were held this afternoon at 1 o'clock at the Limber chapel, Vancouver, with a concluding service at the Highland cemetry at 2:30. Mrs. Eliason had been a resident of this vicinity for 35 years.

The deceased is survived by her widower, four daughters, Mrs. Margaret Fitzgerald, La Center, Mrs. Lizzie Weaver of Independence, Ore., Mrs. Minnie Nixon and Mrs. Daisy Risley of Woodland, three sons, Carl of Vancouver and Howard and Edward at home and a brother, John Rudy of La Center.

HIGHLAND LUTHERAN CEMETERY

*****

...Obituaries From Local Newspapers...

ELMER OLSTEDT

Elmer W. Olstedt, age 68, died June 25 following a long illness at the Camalot Care Center in Forest Grove.

He was born Nov. 29, 1907 in La Center, the son of Otto F. and Sofhia West Olstedt. After attending Higland schools, he worked on his parents' farm and later on mint farms in the area. Mr. Olstedt then bought a grocery store at Fargher Lake which he operated until 1946. He moved to the Portland area and worked as a house painter.

He is survived by one sister, Elizabeth Paullin of La Center; and two nieces, Mrs. Dan (Louise) Benedict of Ridgefield and Opal McMillan of Aberdeen.

Services were held June 29 at the graveside in the Highland Cemetery near La Center. The Rev. Rodney Ellertson, pastor of the Highland Lutheran Church, officiated.

[July 1, 1976]

HELJA MATTSON

MATTSON -- Mrs. Helja, 76, of Hayes Star Rt., Box 96 -A, Woodland, died March 5 in Vancouver. Born April 7, 1897 in Finland, she had lived in the Woodland area the past 29 years.

Survivors include three sons, Elvin Mattson of Beaverton, Ore., Elmer Mattson of Deming , N. M., and Harley Mattson of Ellendale, N.D.; two daughters, Mrs. Helmi Larson of Siren, Wis., and Mrs. Helen Palmer of Forsyth, Mont.; 18 grandchildren and 10 great grandchildren.

Funeral services will be held Saturday at 2 p.m. at the Woodland Funeral Home with the Rev. E. Duane Tollefson officiating. Interment will be in the Highland Cemetery in LaCenter. Those wishing to pay their respects may call at the funeral home from 3 p.m. Friday until noon Saturday. Woodland Funeral Home is in charge of arrangements.

[Mar. 7, 1974]

PETER M. GABRIELSEN

GABRIELSEN, Peter M. -- Age 81, May 9, 1979, LaCenter, Wash. Born July 19, 1897, LaCenter, Wash. Retired farmer. Daughters, Mrs. Patricia Saum, Mrs. Elma Schram and Mrs. Kathryn McHargue, all of Vancouver, Wash. Six grandchildren and one great granddaughter. He has lived his entire life in the LaCenter-Highland district. Member of the Highland Lutheran Church. Graveside funeral services will be held Monday, May 14, 1979, 2:00 p.m. at the Highland Cemetery Vault interment will follow. Mr. Gabrielsen will lie in state from Friday evening until Monday noon. Layne's Funeral Home in charge of arrangements.

[The Columbian, May 11, 1979]

YOUTH DIES UNDER AUTO

Daniel Robert Dillard

***

Daniel Robert Dillard, 19, of Woodland was crushed to death beneath an auto Saturday when it slipped of a set of wooden blocks while he was working beneath it.

He was found dead by Sanford L. Reisbick at the Reisbick barn at Rt. 1 Box 474. Dillard had chosen not to use four safety stands found near the car. He had raised the front end of the car and supported it on wooden blocks, one of which reportedly was barely large enough to hold up a wheel.

Survivors include his mother, Mildred Dillard of Woodland; his father, Wenton Dillard of Ferndale; a brother, Mike, in the U.S. Navy at Adak, Alaska; a sister, Mrs. Kathleen Wilson, Ariel; an aunt, Bernice Lund of Woodland, and his grandparents, Mr. and Mrs. E. L. Dillard of LaCenter.

Funeral services were held Wednesday in Vancouver. Interment followed at Highland Cemetery.

[April 6, 1972]

HIGHLAND LUTHERAN CEMETERY

*****

...Obituaries From Local Newspapers...

TED WOODY

Graveside services for Ted R. Woody of Woodland were held Tuesday in LaCenter.

Mr. Woody died Sunday in Woodland at the age of 78. He had lived in Woodland the past two and a half years, having moved here from Vancouver. He resided at 312 Dunham St.

Mr. Woody was a retired carpenter and a member of the Masonic Lodge in Vancouver.

He is survived by Ivy Woody of Woodland; one daughter, Pat O. Harding of Vancouver; a step-daughter, Katherine Love of Portland; three grandchildren, Michael Harding and David Harding, both of Vancouver, and Cathy Moldenhauer of Ariel.

Services were held at the Highland Lutheran Cemetery, LaCenter, with the Rev. Robert Ziebarth officiating.

Woodland Funeral Home was in charge of the arrangements.

[Apr. 11, 1979]

HOWARD ELIASON DIES THURSDAY

CANYON ROAD - Funeral services were held Monday for Howard P. Eliason at the Highland Lutheran Church.

He was born Dec. 10, 1910 and died Oct. 27 in a Vancouver hospital. He had live his entire 55 years in Woodland at the home where he was born. A farmer, he was an active member of the Highland Lutheran Church and worked as a sexton for different cemetery districts in the Woodland area.

Survivors include one son Howard Paul Jr., and one duaghter, Sharon Patricia, both from Newport, Ore. One brother Eddie and one sister Mrs. Daisy Risley of Woodland survive him.

Burial was in the Highland Cemetery. The Rev. L. M. Redal conducted the services.

Woodland Funeral Home was in charge of arrangements.

[Nov. 3, 1966]

TUURE WILEN PASSES AWAY

Tuure A. Wilen, 83, a retired logger who lived at Rt. 1, Box 432D, died Saturday.

Born in Finland April 28, 1888, Wilen had lived in the Woodland and LaCenter area for many years. He was a member of the Lutheran Church.

Services were held Wednesday in Battle Ground. The Rev. A. F. Gerstmann of Highland Lutheran Church officiated. Burial followed in Highland cemetery.

Survivors include his wife, Helmi; five sons, David and Robert of Vancouver, Clifford (Jack) of LaCenter, Leo of Woodland, and Karl Wilen of Los Angeles; three daughters, Mrs. Norma Senter of Tacoma, Mrs. Elmer Mattson of Battle Ground and Mrs. Marshall Bauer of Auburn; a brother, Ralph Wilen of Lawler, Minn.; and six great grandchildren.

[Apr. 13, 1972]

OLE JOHNSON PASSES AWAY

Ole S. Johnson, 86, of Woodland, died Tuesday in Ridgefield. Mr. Johnson was a pioneer resident of Clark County. He retired several years ago as a farmer but had worked since for Clark County. He was a member of the Cedar Creek Seventh Day adventist Church.

Funeral services will be held at 1 p.m. Friday at the Presbyterian Church in Woodland. Interment will be at the Highland Cemetery in LaCenter.

Survivors include two sons, Robert C. and James O. Johnson, both of Longview; four daughters, Elsie Hablen of Carson, Mabel Andring of Naselle; Martha Mitchell of Burnt Woods, Ore. and Laura Johnson of Battle Ground; a sister, Margaret Olsen of Astoria; two brothers, Arthur Johnson of Seaside and James Johnson of Longview; 20 grandchildren, and 15 great grandchildren.

[Oct. 15, 1970]

HIGHLAND LUTHERAN CEMETERY

*****

...Obituaries From Local Newspapers...

GLADYS SORENSEN

Gladys Sorensen, 73, a La Center resident for the past 35 years, died in Vancouver Thursday, Sept. 20.

Born July 1, 1906, in Colgate, N.D., Mrs. Sorensen last resided at Rt. 2, Box 362 in La Center. She is survived by three brothers, O'Neil R. Elbrum of Pasco, Wash.; Raymond L. and Clifford M. Elbrum of Vancouver, Wash.; and five sisters, Mrs. Myrtle S. Muackay of Moose Jaw, Saskatchewan Canada; Mrs. Ethel I Bare of Victoria, British Columbia, Mrs. Viola G. Sorensen of LaCenter, Mrs. Margaret G. Wheat of Milwaukie, Ore., and Mrs. Ida m. Kindsey of Sacramento, Calif. Graveside services were held Monday at the Highland Cemetery in LaCenter with Pastor Rodney Ellertson officiating.

[Sept. 26, 1979]

WALLACE SORENSEN

Graveside services for Wallace E. Sorensen, a native of LaCenter, were held Tuesday.

Mr. Sorensen died last Friday in Vancouver at the age of 69. He was born Jan. 8, 1909 and last resided at Route 2, LaCenter.

Mr. Sorensen had been a retired route mail carrier for the LaCenter area. He was a veteran of World War II, having been in the Navy, and was a member of American Legion Post 189 of LaCenter.

Survivors include his widow, Gladys Sorensen, at home; two brothers, Ralph Sorensen and Harry Sorensen, both of LaCenter; and a sister Hazel Ward of Portland.

Services were held at the Highland Cemetery in LaCenter with the Rev. Rodney Ellertson officiating. The Vancouver Funeral Chapel was in charge of arrangements.

[Oct. 1978]

HAROLD BROWN

Services for Harold R. Brown, 67, of La Center were scheduled for 10 a.m. today (Thursday) at Woodland Seventh-day Adventist Church.

Mr. Brown, of Route 1, Box 371 AB., died April 30 in Portland. He was born Oct. 13, 1910 in Eureka, Mont. and had lived in LaCenter for the past four years, coming from Auburn, Wash.

He was a retired logger and farmer. He was a member of the Woodland Seventh-day Adventist Church.

Survivors include his wife, Magda H. of LaCenter; two sons, Harold Duane Brown of Oroville, Wash., and Laurence Dean Brown of West Linn, Ore.; a daughter, Shirley Diane Hoyt of Portland; one sister, Rachel Anderson of Tacoma; and nine grandchildren.

Pastor Max Torkelsen and Mel Rees were scheduled to officiate at the services. Interment was scheduled at Highland Lutheran Cemetery LaCenter. Woodland Funeral Home was in charge of arrangements.

[May 4, 1978]

LOUIS G. MEYER

Louis G. Meyer, 76, of 310 Fourth Street, Woodland, died June 23, 1978, in a Vancouver hospital. He was born March 14, 1902 in Caledonia, Minn., and had been a Woodland resident since 1945 when he moved here from Illinois. He was a retired logger.

Survivors include a step-son, Donald Kallio of Woodland; a sister, Ella Twite of Caledonia, Minn.

Services will be 2 p.m. Monday at the Highlands Cemetery in La Center with the Rev. Lee Andrews officiating.

Woodland Funeral Home is in charge of arrangements.

[June 24, 1978]

HIGHLAND LUTHERAN CEMETERY

*****

...Obituaries From Local Newspapers...

JENNIE CHRISTENSEN

Funeral services were held Saturday, April 14, for Jennie Marie Christensen of LaCenter. Mrs. Christensen died in Portland April 10 at the age of 92.

Born May 29, 1880 in Oslo, Norway, she lived in Portland at the time of her death. She had previously lived in LaCenter over 20 years.

Survivors included a son, Russell, Portland; two daughters, Mrs. Margaret Terry, Portland and Mrs. Maxine Lubbis, Fresno, Calif.; a sister, Mrs. Lillian Dolph; seven grandchildren and 10 great grandchildren.

The Rev. Larry Thomas officiated at services Saturday at the Evergreen Funeral Home. Committal rites with vault interment followed at the Highland Lutheran Cemetery.

[Apr. 19, 1973]

EDLA BONG

A 50-year resident of Woodland-La Center area, Edla Bong, 89, died June 14, 1979, in Woodland.

Mrs. Bong was born July 14, 1889, in Finland. She was a member of the Highland Lutheran Church in La Center.

Surviving her are four sons, Oscar of Woodland, Carl and Fred of Vancouver and Erik of Hoodsport, Wash.; four daughters, Sigrid Delgado of Kelso, Nanna Adams of Battle Ground, Marie Taylor of La Center and Mabel Robbins of Woodland; 21 grandchildren and 31 great-grandchildren.

Pastor Rodney Ellertson will officiate at the funeral service at 1 p.m. Monday in the Highland Lutheran Church. Interment will follow at Highland Cemetery.

Woodland Funeral Home is handling arrangements.

[June 15, 1979]

ELSIE OFFICER

Services for Elsie Marie Officer, a native of LaCenter, will be at 1 p.m. on Saturday at the Vancouver Funeral Chapel.

Mrs. Officer was born Oct. 29, 1904 in LaCenter and resided at 515 Washington St., Vancouver, at the time of her death. She was a member of the Grandmothers Club at Smith Tower and several church groups.

Survivors include three sons, Glenn Officer of Auburn, Wash., Charles Officer of Vancouver, and Ernest Officer of Seattle; two daughters, Elnora Kennedy of Hydesville, Calif., and Norma Jean Hendershot of Seattle; two brothers, Arthur Johnson of The Dalles, Ore., and Jim Erickson of Olympia; two sisters, Teckla Vehrs of Vancouver and Margie Haines of Seattle; 20 grandchildren and 10 great-grandchildren.

The Rev. Floyd S. Magsig will officiate at the funeral services. Interment will be at Highland Cemetery at LaCenter.

[Dec. 1, 1977]

BERTHA S. ZUHL

VANCOUVER, Wash., Jan. 10, (Special)-Funeral services will be held at 1:30 P.M. Tuesday in the Highland Lutheran church for Bertha S. Zuhl, 70, who died Friday at her home, star route, Woodland. Survivors include two daughters, Mrs. Fannie Hewett of Woodland, and Mrs. Minnie Lund; three brothers, Henry Sherman of Portland, and Frank and William Sherman of LaCenter, and six sisters. Interment will be in the Highland Cemetery.

HIGHLAND LUTHERAN CEMETERY

✳✳✳✳✳

...Obituaries From Local Newspapers...

FUNERAL HELD FOR JAKE GABRIELSEN

Funeral services were conducted Wednesday, Nov. 23 at 1 p.m. in the Highland Lutheran church for Jake Gabrielsen, 71, who died Nov. 20 in a Vancouver hospital.

Mr. Gabrielsen was born July 1, 1895 in LaCenter and had lived there most of his life, moving to Woodland three years ago. He was a retired log scaler and real estate salesman, and was a member of the Highland Lutheran Church, the Woodland Masonic Lodge and OES, and WWI Veterans.

He is survived by his widow Elma; two sons; Bernard L. Gabrielsen of San Jose, Calif., and Ralph Gabrielsen of Corvallis, Ore.; a step-son Charles Blum of Woodland; two grandchildren; two brothers Edward Gabrielsen of Scio, Ore., and Peter Gabrielsen of LaCenter; a sister Mrs. Rena Loberg of Echo, Ore.

The Rev. L. M. Redal officiated at the ceremonies. Burial followed at the Highland Cemetery. Woodland Funeral Home was in charge of arrangements.

[Nov. 24, 1966]

ANNA CHRISTENSEN

Services for Anna M. Christensen, 92, of LaCenter, were held Saturday at Highland Lutheran Church. Burial followed at Highland Cemetery.

Mrs. Christensen, a LaCenter resident all her life, was born Nov. 4, 1883. She lived at Rt. 1, Box 341-A.

She was a memeber of the Highland Lutheran Church.

Among her survivors are three sisters, Adeline M. Martin of LaCenter, Clara Stevenson of LaCenter and Irene Olson of Astoria, Ore.

[Nov. 11, 1976]

ROY F. JOHNSON

Roy F. Johnson of 630 CC St., Woodland, died June 6, 1879 in Longview. He was 86. Born Aug. 11, 1892, he moved to Woodland in 1940. He was a native of Lincoln, Nebraska.

Johnson was a retired logger. He was a member, and worked as custodian of the First Presbyterian Church in Woodland for many years.

Survivors include his wife, Grace M. at home; two sons, Loyle of Longview and Harold W. of Bolder Creek, Calif.; one daughter, Vivian Harris, McMinnville, Oregon; seven grandchildren and nine great-grandchildren.

Services were held at the First Presbyterian Church in Woodland with the Rev. Ray W. Moody officiating. Vault internment was at the Highland Cemetery in LaCenter.

Woodland Funeral Home was in charge of arrangements.

[June 13, 1979]

OLGA P. JENSEN

Olga P. Jensen, 78, of 127 Love Avenue, Woodland, died in Woodland Feb. 21.

She was born Aug. 4, 1898 in Erie, Penn. She had lived in LaCenter and Woodland areas most of her life. Mrs. Jensen was a member of the First Christian Church of Woodland.

Survivors include one son, Dwight Jensen of Longview; two daughters, Lucille Kafferlin and Maxine Jensen both of Woodland; on brother, Fred Pedersen of LaCenter; three grandchildren and three great grandchildren.

Funeral services were held Wednesday, Feb. 23, at 11 a.m. at the Woodland Funeral Home. The Rev. Finis Johnson officiated. Vault interment was at the Highland Cemetery in LaCenter. Woodland Funeral Home was in charge of arrangements.

[Feb. 24, 1977]

HIGHLAND LUTHERAN CEMETERY

✗✗✗✗✗

...Obituaries From Local Newspapers...

SERVICES HELD FOR CANYON RD PIONEER

Ole Erstad was resident of District for
Past Fourty Years. Was 72
years old at death

Funeral services were held a week ago
Tuesday for Ole Erstad, pioneer farmer
of the Canyon Road district, who died at
his home on July 11 at the age of 72
years. The services were at Limber's
Chapel in Vancouver. Rev. Paul Kingman
preached the sermon. Burial was at the
Hyland Cemetery.

Mr. Erstad, who was well and favor-
ably known throughout this entire district, was born February 29, 1860, in
Norway. He came to this country in 1884
and lived for a short time at Rock
county, Minnesota. In 1891 he came to
Vancouver, Wn., where he lived for two
years, then moving to his farm home
about two and a half miles from
Woodland.

Mr. Erstad was survived by five
daughters and three sons. The daughters
are Selma Erstad who was living at home,
Mrs. Anna Gapsch of Portland, Mrs.
William Freeman of Seaside, Mrs. Clara
Johnson of La Center, and Mabel Erstad
of Woodland. The sons are Oscar Erstad
who was at home, George Erstad of
Vancouver and Edwin Erstad of Woodland.

[1932]

RITES GIVEN IN AFTERNOON AT LA CENTER

Mary Elizabeth Ehlbeck

***

Funeral services will be held at the
Highland Lutheran Church at LaCenter,
this afternoon at 1:30 p.m. for Mrs.
Mary Elizabeth Ehlbeck who passed away
Saturday, Nov. 15 in Kelso.

Mrs. Ehlbeck was next to the youngest
of nine children of Ezra and Lucy Ann
Stratton, who crossed the Plains from
Iowa in 1866 and settled aobut four
miles up the Lewis River at what is now
known as Ross' Corner, where they lived
a number of years. It was at this
homestead that Mrs. Ehlbeck was born on
February 16, 1873. She was married to
Otto Ehlbeck who has preceded her in
death a number of years ago. They lived
all their married life in the Highland
District where Mrs. Ehlbeck continued to
make her home until recently when she
made her home with a daughter in Kelso.
She is survived by one son, Everett of
La Center; three daughters, Mrs. Violet
C. Green of Kelso, and Mrs. Edna Vetter
and Mrs. Nina Foster both of Montesano.

One brother, Charles Stratton of
Woodland, seven grandchildren and three
great-grandchildren and neices and
nephews.

[Nov. 20, 1952]

HIGHLAND LUTHERAN CEMETERY

✳✳✳✳✳

...Obituaries From Local Newspapers...

IVA M. WOODY

Former Woodland resident Iva M. Woody died May 7, 1983, at Battle Ground. She was 92. She was born May 17, 1891, at Springfield, Mo.

She is survived by two daughters, Katherine Love Medley of Portland and Pat Woody Harding of Vancouver; three grandchildren, Michael Harding, and David Harding of Vancouver and Cathy Moldenhauer of Brush Prairie; and three great-grandchildren.

Graveside services will be 3 p.m. Wednesday at Highland Cemetery, LaCenter with the Rev. Rodney Ellertson officiating.

Woodland Funeral Home is in charge of arrangements.

[May 1983]

MABEL ERSTAD

Services for Mabel G. Erstad, 88, of Woodland, were held Friday.

She was born in November, 1888 in South Dakota and lived in Woodland most of her life, traveling to Washington state when she was a child.

She was a member of the Woodland Chapter of Rebekahs.

Among her survivors are one sister, Selma Gapsch of Vancouver and several nieces and nephews.

Services were held in Highland Lutheran Church, LaCenter, with the Rev. Rodney Ellertson officiating. Vault internment was in Highland Cemetery. Vancouver Funeral Chapel was in charge of arrangements.

[Dec. 2, 1976]

NORMAN RICHARDS

Services for Norman J. "Dick" Richards, a former Woodland resident, were held Tuesday at Highland Lutheran Cemetery, LaCenter.

Mr. Richards died last Saturday in a Portland hospital at the age of 74.

He was born Aug. 29, 1903 in Natchez, Miss. From 1944 to 1972 he owned and operated Cascade Farms Preserving Co. in Woodland and resided at Route 1, Box 463-D.

Since retirement, Mr. Richards and his wife, Neva, had traveled extensively.

Mr. Richards served in the Navy for six years and attained the rank of first class ship repairman.

In addition to his widow, he leaves two brothers, Robert of Longview, Tex., and Charles of Nashville, Tenn.; and a sister, Florence Van Buskirk of Miami, Fla.

Sister Lucy from St. Vincent Hospital Portland, officiated at the services. Hamilton-Mylan Funeral Home was in charge of arrangements. Memorials may be made to the American Cancer Society.

[Jan. 1, 1978]

HANS ELIASON

VANCOUVER, Wash., March 30 (Special)- Hans Eliason, 77, LaCenter, Wash., died Monday at his home. He had lived in La Center for the past 48 years and is survived by three sons, Carl of Vancouver, Howard and Eddie, both of La Center; four daughters, Mrs. Daisy Risley of LaCenter, Mrs. Margaret Fitzgerald of Woodland, Mrs. Minnie Nixion of Kalama, Wash. and Mrs. Lizzie Weaver of Independence, Or. Funeral services will be held Thursday at 2 P.M. at the Highland church with interment in the Highland cemetery.

CORRECTIONS TO VOL. 1 and VOL. 2, CLARK COUNTY CEMETERIES

VOL. 2

SALMON CREEK METHODIST CEMETERY

Page 160   FRED BROOK (not BROOKS)
Page 160   LAURA [GODDARD] BROOK (not BROOKS)
Page 161   GEORGE W. (for Washington) GODDARD (not George
            A.)
Page 163   ADA M. MOLYNEUX (not MOLYNEAUX)
Page 163   ROSS M. McFADYEN (not McFADDEN)
Page 168   FANNIE BALDWIN - Buried in Salmon Creek
                Methodist Cemetery (not buried
                in St. John Lutheran Cemetery)

ST. JOHN LUTHERAN CEMETERY

Page 168   FANNIE BALDWIN 1877 - 1918 is buried in Salmon
                Creek Methodist Cemetery (not in St.
                John Lutheran Cemetery)
            Fannie Baldwin's grave, and some others, are
            near the West boundary of the Salmon Creek
            Methodist Cemetery, adjacent to the East
            boundary of the St. John Lutheran Cemetery;
            hence this mistake.

[C.C.G.S. thanks Ray H. Northcutt for the above corrections]

****

VOL. 1

OLD CITY CEMETERY

Page 37   VICTOR L. COITEUX (not Victor L. CORTEUX)

Index

228

232

PERNELA, John A.	81		PIETZ, Gettlieb	81
, Olaf John	81		, Matilda	81
, Laura K.	81		, Mickey	81
PETERSEN, Emilie E.	41		PIIRAINEN, Henry	81
, James	41		PINARD, Gloria	205
, Sophie	41		PIPPIT, Mary Edna	146
PETERSON, Alice M.	99		PITCHFORD, Alice	195
, Alvin E.	171		PLACE, Marian T.	62
, Chris	41		PLAMONDON, George L.	117
, Edith H.	194		, George R.	117
, Edward P.	194		, Isadore J.	117
, Erik	194		, Kathleen Ann	117
, Fred E.	171		, Leonard J.	117
, Hilma	194		, Mary G.	117
, J. M.	215		PLANKER, Jakob	41
, Mary	194		PLOTTS, Robert B.	99
, P. A.	195		PLUMMER, Rosella A.	100
, Perry B.	99		, Walter W.	99
, Peter A.	194		POE, Mabel E.	100
PETTERSON, Johan E.	41		POEPPELMEIER, Gustav A.	171
PETTIT, Emma G.	194, 195		, Henry L.	171
, Ernest	195		POLEY, Monte B.	41
, Ernest D.	195		POLK, Emma L.	195
, Ernest M.	194		, James V.	195
, Ernest Milan	195		POLLARD, Andrew Merrill	41
, Eugene W.	195		POLLOCK, John T.	195
, Jody	195		, LeRoy L.	42
, Kathryn Anne	195		POMERENE, J. D.	42
, Leslie Marvin	195		, Rose Bartlett	42
, Kenneth Eugene	195		POOLE, Delia A.	195
, Richard H.	195		, J. D.	195
, Wesley M.	195		PORTIN, Andrew	195
PFEIFER, ...	117, 120		, Henry	195
PFISTERER, Herman	41		POST, C. M.	195
PFUNDT, Franz	41		POTTER, Allen G.	22, 42
PHILLIPS, (Child)	41		, Baby	146
, Andrew	41		, Eliza	42
, Isaac	41		, Tilda	146
, Leota M.	99		, William	146
, Mary F.	41		POWELL, Elizabeth B.	195
PHINNEY, Dora E.	99		, Frank D.	42
, Jacob E.	99		, James Jr.	42
, Julia A.	99		, Jane	195
PIERCE, Paul J.	171		, Lela G.	147
, Ruby S.	171		, Mamie M.	100
PIERCY, James T.	41		, Mary O.	195
PIERSON, Daniel A.	41		, Samuel D.	147
, Maude	41		, Walter R.	147
PIETILA, Anna S.	81		, Willis	195
, Frederick A.	81		POWERS, ...	120
, John A.	81		, John T.	117
, Judith	81		, Robert William	42
, Waino	81		PRESTHUS, Gunnar	81
			, Selma A.	81

SMITH (cont.)
, George Wm.   198
, Harriet   173
, Harriette M.   173
, Henrietta Jackson   198
, Henry S.   198
, Ida   49
, Infant   49
, J. A.   198
, J. L.   150
, J. M.   198
, James A.   198
, Jesse L.   198
, John E.   198, 199
, Letha   198
, Lewis Clark   150
, Lloyd F.   173
, Louis S.   216
, M. G.   198
, Martha E.   198
, Mary   195
, Mary C.   198
, Mary Jemima   49
, Matilda   49
, Oliver J.   49
, S. A.   198
, Susie   184
, Thomas   49
, William J.   49
, William J. (Mrs.)   49
SMOCT, Muriet   173
SNEAD, Thomas B.   101
, Thomas E.   101
SNIDER, Jack R.   49
SNOW, Eugene   49
SOBOLEWSKI, Elizabeth   50
, F.   50
SODEN, Guy B.   50
SODERBERG, George   83
, Toini   83
SOEBY, Jens P.   50
SOEHL, _agda _ema   199
, Alfred   199
, Beatrice   202
, Beatrice M.   199
, Fred   199
, Henry   199
, Henry W.   199
, J. P.   199
, Jerry   199
, John P.   199
, John Peter   199
, Peter A.   199
, Walter   199

SOEHL (cont.)
, Walter E.   199
, Winifred D.   199
SOLBERG, Carl   83
, Mary J.   84
, Ole Oscar   84
SOLCANY, Thelma   50
, W. J.   50
SOLDOS, Annie L.   50
, George   50
SOMMERS, Mary Ellen   199
SOMMERVOLD, Hilma   84
, Peter Ludvig   84
SONERHOLM, Rich/Rick (Rev.)
                       181, 195, 198
SONNTAG, Otto C.   84
SORENSON, Axel E.   216
, Gladys   217, 221
, Hannah M.   217
, Harry   221
, Ralph   221
, Wallace   217
, Wallace E.   221
, Viola G.   221
SOUTHWICK, Harry C.   150
SPARREN, J. M. C.   50
, Margaret   50
SPAY, Joseph   50
, William   50
SPEAR, Herbert C.   50
, Minnie B.   50
SPENCER, Charles W.   200
, Elizabeth   200
, Emma   178
, Emma C.   200
, Florence E.   200
, Frederick   50
, G. Byron   199
, George L.   199
, George P.   200
, Jesse Clyde   200
, Lewis   200
, Lurilla F.   200
, Rhena M.   199
, Ruth   200
, Sevilla C.   200
, Thomas E.   200
, William   200
, William J.   200
SPINY, L.   50
SPIVEY, Carrie   50
, William   50
SPURLING, Beulah Dorothy   50
, George T.   50